Advance Praise for

Run the World

"In her incredible running journey, Becky Wade captures the beauty of the sport—chasing your goals, forming lifelong bonds, learning resilience, and, of course, eating delicious food."

—Shalane Flanagan, Olympic champion in
long-distance track running and author of
Run Fast, Eat Slow: Nourishing Recipes for Athletes

"I started reading Becky Wade's story and I simply could not stop. Her journey around the globe pulls you along like a great running trail with each turn promising something new and wonderful."

—Tom Foreman, author of *My Year of Running Dangerously:
A Dad, a Daughter, and a Ridiculous Plan*

"Becky Wade is one of America's best distance runners, yet more so an ultimate adventurer. In *Run the World,* Becky takes the reader along on her brave journey, providing an intimate glimpse into running cultures around the world."

—Deena Kastor, Olympic medalist and
American record holder in the marathon

"For anyone who loves running, loves to travel, or better yet, both, *Run the World* offers a chance to live vicariously through Becky Wade's incredible journey of training in the most hallowed grounds of distance running. Her adventures will teach you, inspire you, and probably light a fire inside of you to travel and embark on a running journey of your own."

—Ryan Hall, premier distance runner and author of
Running with Joy: My Daily Journey to the Marathon

"The beauty of running can always be found in the journey. Each and every mile holds something new, in the runner and in the world around her. Never has this been illustrated more beautifully than in Becky Wade's story. Her running journey, the people she shared it with, and what she learned along the way will inspire and inform runners and nonrunners alike."

—Dawn Dais, author of *The Nonrunner's Marathon Guide for Women: Get Off Your Butt and On with Your Training*

RUN THE WORLD

RUN THE WORLD

MY 3,500-MILE JOURNEY THROUGH
RUNNING CULTURES AROUND THE GLOBE

BECKY WADE

wm

WILLIAM MORROW
An Imprint of HarperCollins*Publishers*

Grateful acknowledgment is made to the following for the use of the photographs that appear throughout the text: photograph by Joel Rivera, Jr. (page iv); photograph courtesy of Rice Athletics Communications (page 5); courtesy of the author (pages 10, 11, 16, 35, 44, 51, 78, 94, 105, 107, 122, 127, 138, 143, 167, 176, 180, 204, 207, 211, 223, 242, 256, and 261); photograph by Kieran Carlin (pages 69 and 71); photograph by Mikael Grip (page 217); photograph by Joe McCladdie (page 252); photograph courtesy of the Dallas Marathon (page 257); and photograph by Edward Holmberg (page 260).

HarperCollins books may be purchased for educational, business, or sales promotional use. For information please e-mail the Special Markets Department at SPsales@harpercollins.com.

FIRST EDITION

Designed by Diahann Sturge

Library of Congress Cataloging-in-Publication Data has been applied for.

ISBN 978-0-06-241643-8

16 17 18 19 20   OV/RRD   10 9 8 7 6 5 4 3 2 1

For Mom, Dad, Matt, Rachel, and Luke: my world.
And for Jim Bevan: my pilot.

CONTENTS

RUN THE WORLD

INTRODUCTION

"The Devil is in Derartu. Today very, very not strong."

Stretching at the base of Mount Entoto, 8,500 feet above sea level, I caught my breath after lagging behind Banchi and Meseret in that morning's hill workout. I had an excuse ready: I'd arrived in Ethiopia only days before and would need several weeks to acclimate to the time zone and altitude. I longed to prove to these women that I was also a serious runner, having competed at the U.S. Olympic Trials and at the World Junior Track and Field Championship, but neither my language nor my lungs would let me. I'd have to gasp my way through the girls' "easy" runs, watch helplessly as they pulled away from me in workouts like this one, and grin with every shout of encouragement. "Aizosh, Becky!" "Berta!"

Derartu, though, was struggling. The twenty-two-year-old, born and raised in Srululta, a town ten kilometers outside Addis Ababa, could normally hold her own against the other two. Pound for pound, my five-foot friend was one of the stronger distance runners I'd encountered, with the quads of a soccer player and the spring of an antelope. But you'd never know it if you saw her that morning. As Banchi and Mesi bounded up the dirt road, Derartu lagged farther and farther behind. Glistening with sweat, a grimace on her face, she looked more like the local firewood carriers who piggybacked buffalo-size bundles up the mountain than she did her fleet-footed training partners.

In broken English and the same nonchalant tone she used to describe *doro wat* and *shiro* at dinner the night before, Banchi explained Derartu's dilemma: The Devil was inside her, sapping her strength.

I've never wished more than in that moment to understand a foreign tongue. But given the English-to-Amharic language gap—not to mention cultural chasm—I had to rely on a bare-bones explanation and my own limited experience to make sense of what I had seen and heard.

I thought back to the blue Rice University track in Houston, Texas, where I'd spent the past five years chasing faster times in the 10,000 meters, 5,000 meters, and 3,000-meter steeplechase, and tried to imagine the same conversation.

"Sorry, Coach Bevan, but I can't finish the last mile repeat [hard interval] today."

"What's going on? Are you getting that weird sensation in your lower legs again?" my coach of almost a decade, Jim Bevan, would ask, probably dreading the details about my latest injury.

"No, it's not that. I'm not hurt. It's just that the Devil is inside me, and he won't let me finish the workout."

There was a long list of excuses that my forgiving coach would accept from his runners—a stomachache, a sleepless night, poor recovery from the last workout, even a recent breakup—but inhabitation by the Devil had no place in it.

Worlds away in Ethiopia—the cradle of humanity, and of many of the world's best endurance athletes—Banchi's explanation wouldn't be given a second thought. In fact, it was one of the more acceptable reasons that Derartu, one of the most privileged runners in the area, would be too weak to complete a hill session.

Along with Banchi and Mesi, she had raced her way to a scholarship that entitled her to four months of comfortable housing, balanced meals, English and career-skills lessons, and her first structured running environment.

The Yaya Girls, named after the Yaya Village hotel and training camp where I lived and volunteered for two months, were the envy of Sululta, living like royalty compared to most of their family members and neighbors, whose homes were typically shacks lacking electricity and running water. The girls were still learning how to reconcile this new, temporary existence and its many resources with the familiar, simpler one that awaited them at the end of the program. They slept two to a twin bed for comfort when there were enough beds for all and declined the pre-run breakfasts offered each morning. Clearly the lifestyle preferred by first-world runners was not universally considered ideal.

Less apparent was if and how, by exposing Banchi, Mesi, and Derartu to new elements such as a varied, meat-inclusive diet, a strength program, and fresh shoes, the Yaya Girls Program was tinkering with their potential as runners. Would such added comforts keep my friends healthier and more focused, or make them softer athletes, more likely to fold during key decision points in a race? Conversely, I wondered how adopting some rural Ethiopian practices—the very ones which we were tweaking—might influence, even enhance, my own running. Would a huge leap in the distance I walked daily interfere with my training? Would treating every Sunday as a day of rest make me a more consistent runner, or less fit? And how would a nutrition plan that emphasized grains over fruits and vegetables, and little protein, affect my energy and ability to recover?

I had about eight weeks to find some answers. Then it would be time to pack up and start again in a new country. That morning, I accepted that I'd probably never fully grasp Banchi's reasoning about Derartu and the Devil—which I later learned was a blend of Ethiopian Orthodoxy and religious superstition, both foreign to my Catholic upbringing. But I was committed to trying, as I remained open-minded to other cultural beliefs and practices that inform how communities like the Yaya Girls approach long-distance running. I was searching for meaning in the universal phenomenon of running—the oldest, purest, and most global of all sports—and, just maybe, an edge on my competition down the road.

A YEAR EARLIER, I'd stood firmly on the opposite side of the world. I had lived in Texas all twenty-two years of my life, other than a few summers spent training in Colorado, and I was anxious to flee the coop, to see what the wider world could teach me about living, connecting, and, naturally, running. A scholarship athlete at Rice University and a runner since the age of nine, I had engaged in the sport as it was dictated to me: practice schedules, track repeats, travel itineraries, and rehab plans. My goal the past five years had become sunup-to-sundown productivity, punctuated by two runs most days and peppered with naps, ice baths, and ample time to cook and eat, even as I streamlined my nutritional and social needs. When my graduation from Rice approached, I faced an open-ended running future for the first time, and I wasn't sure what to make of it.

The prospect of copious free time and a more active social life was attractive. Would my body finally learn to sleep past 6 A.M.? What would it feel like to eat a hamburger and fries at lunch, not having to hold back for a looming afternoon workout? How many beers would I have to consume to catch up to my twin brother, Luke?

But I also didn't feel quite ready to find out. I was wrapping up a fruitful career at Rice that included four NCAA Division I All-American Honors and two Olympic Trials qualifiers, and I was miles away from wanting to hang up my spikes. I felt short-changed in my college career due to a string of injuries, and I was young and fresh by long-distance standards; I'd mainly focused on the 300-meter hurdles until college, and female marathoners typically don't peak until their mid-thirties—if they stick with it that long. Most important, I still had a deep, childlike love for running. Finding new routes, learning the nuances of my body, forming relationships on the move, and challenging myself at various distances still excited me, more than a decade after I first laced up a pair of Sambas and circled the block with my dad. I couldn't fathom a life without running as a huge part of it.

At Rice University, where I competed from 2007 to 2012, my passion for running soared.

Now, with my newfound independence, I wanted to be more deliberate with my running. To question the practices I had assumed were best, test how much of myself I would invest when the leash came off, and ultimately, find a balance between freedom and structure. Recalling Coach Bevan's philosophy that "a happy runner is a fast runner," I was on a mission to synchronize my heart and my feet.

THE MOST PIVOTAL EVENT in my running career up to that point was the 2008 World Junior Track and Field Championship, in Bydgoszcz, Poland. While debuting on an international stage in the 3,000-meter steeplechase, I first glimpsed the full spectrum of approaches to track and field. The Team USA distance squad emphasized short and easy runs in the days leading up to our races, while the Ethiopians continued running intense interval workouts. The Japanese team warmed up in silence, looking solemn and fierce, contrasted by the Italians chatting their way around the practice field. Differences emerged away from the track, too, as the athletes relaxed and supported one another. The Swedes runners always had a card game going in the hotel we shared, seemingly to help calm their nerves; the South African team performed infectious celebratory dances; and the Irish athletes and coaches were the clear extroverts of the bunch, requesting pictures and singlet swaps with everyone who passed by their training tent.

How all of those rituals influenced competitive performance, I couldn't tell. Though the usual suspects excelled in certain disciplines—the United States and Jamaica in the sprints, Kenya and Ethiopia in the distances, and Germany in the throws—there wasn't an obvious overlap in the approaches of the victors. More clear to me was the idea that having such rituals, and *believing* in them, went a long way in each competitor's experience of the event. In other words, the culture of a team, reflecting the place it comes from, seemed to matter. I left Poland not only with a suitcase full of new uniforms I'd traded for but also the desire to explore some of those cultures firsthand, and to apply my discoveries to my own running endeavors. Four years later, I'd get my chance.

THE THOMAS J. WATSON FELLOWSHIP sounds like one of Willy Wonka's Golden Tickets. Awarded annually to forty graduating college seniors "to enhance their capacity for resourcefulness, imagination, openness, and leadership and to foster their humane and effective participation in the world community," it basically funds the dream year of each recipient. Relying on a strict budget, each fellow spends twelve months traveling the world independently in pursuit of a personal passion—from beekeeping and meditation to unicycling and, in my case, long-distance running.

I proposed to spend my first year out of college diving into foreign running communities, searching for both unique and common ways that people around the world approach running and construct their lives around it. To find the pulse of each place's running climate, I wanted to tackle all angles: jogging with recreational enthusiasts, questioning coaches about training philosophies, emulating the routines of professionals, interviewing running historians, tracking down retired legends, watching and competing in races, and exploring the trails and courses that locals loved most. My original agenda, hatched through obsessive research and with the help of hundreds of contacts, included England, host of the 2012 Olympic Games and a strong club culture; Ethiopia, nest of countless endurance phenoms; New Zealand, birthplace of the jogging boom and one of the world's most influential running coaches; Japan, home to a famously disciplined running regime; and Finland, the tough and tiny nation that, having topped the long-distance world two separate times in the last century, epitomizes the ebb and flow of athletics. My curiosity was driven by the running culture I grew up in—a pressure cooker in which every result is scrutinized and Type A personalities are the norm. I loved it, but at times was left frustrated and drained.

Once I got on the road and started toying with the incredible flexibility of the fellowship, those plans evolved into a more organic strategy. The apartments and hostels I budgeted for? I only needed a few, in my very first destination and for the occasional rendezvous outside my base city. Eventually, I strung together seventy-two sleeping arrangements, most of my hosts in some way connected to their local running community and willing to open their doors to this small, curious American runner. The handful of countries I proposed to visit? I began using the money I saved on housing toward plane, train, and ferry tickets. Before I knew it, five countries had snowballed into twenty-two, some that I briefly explored in transit, and a dozen in which I lingered for at least a week and in some cases up to two months.

In exchange for my year abroad, all that I had to do was write quarterly reports to the Watson Fellowship headquarters, be financially accountable, and attend the Returning Fellows Conference when I returned home, where I would hear the tales of the remarkable journeys of the thirty-nine other fellows. I signed a loose list of guidelines that included traveling independently, avoiding countries I had already visited, using only the stipend from the fellowship to fund my travels, and remaining outside of the United States for a full year. The "independent" clause was the real kicker, as I had always known companionship: my twin brother, Luke; and our brother and sister, Matt and Rachel, also twins and one year older; my parents, never farther than a four-hour drive away; and the hundreds of teammates and coaches I had trained with, most recently the Rice University track and cross-country teams. Despite deciding to remain unattached on my trip, I was a few short weeks into a relationship with Will Firth, another Rice runner, whose charm trumped his timing. To appease my loving and protective mom—who had chaperoned every one of our field trips and dances growing up—I started a blog called BeckyRunsAway, where I kept her in the loop with my adventures (leaving out just a few details, such as getting lost deep in the Ethiopian forest).

The Watson Fellowship was my ticket out—away from my familiar routine, my cozy Texas environment, and the typical trajectory of an elite American runner.

SUDDENLY, IT ARRIVED: July 24, 2012, my final night in the United States for a year. My parents were treating me to a farewell dinner at a favorite Dallas restaurant, and my mom was doing a poor job hiding her unease. It wasn't totally unwarranted; I've always had a knack for getting lost, and a blind trust in strangers. I've also accumulated a number of "Bills" over the years—a streak that began with "Bill from Boulder," who, after a handful of interactions at my job the summer I lived there, had sent me a large package full of used running clothes, history books, and an eighteen-page handwritten note. How he got my freshman year dorm address, I wasn't sure. To alleviate my mom's anxiety, I reminded her, feeling mature and bold, "I am twenty-three, after all; I can handle this"—just as our waiter handed me the kids' menu for ages twelve and under. And twenty hours later, I waved goodbye to my family and boarded my first of two dozen international flights over the course of the next year.

A year's worth of packing, which I managed to cram into a large backpack and a small roller bag.

But truly, I was as prepared for the adventure as a five-foot, 92-pound, twenty-three-year-old girl could be. My packing list, whittled down through life-size Tetris games with my suitcase and belongings, included everything from the major stuff—my passport and the seven running outfits I would wear to rags— down to twelve Clif Bars, four Ziploc baggies, and two safety pins I expected to come in handy (Type A case in point). Like any thorough explorer, I had tested and retested my global adapter, gotten the laundry list of vaccinations that my destinations required, and devised a system with my dad for withdrawing and tracking an array of foreign currencies. I had compiled dozens of contacts, as well as personal bucket-list items—standing on the track that hosted the first sub-four-minute mile, running the historic 22-mile Waiatarua loop in Auckland, New Zealand, visiting a number of Olympic stadiums—in each of the five countries in my Watson proposal. I had also divided some valuables among my siblings, whose delight at acquiring a new laptop, cell phone, and iPod momentarily overshadowed their sadness about the year without me.

In front of my Dallas home, a few hours before my Watson Fellowship departure.

The real crux of my journey would defy research and planning. There would be discoveries about running and recovering; recipes gathered from hosts in each country; growth in adaptability and openness to new training methods; and relationships built with runners all over the world. My assumptions about the formula for athletic success, and the essence of distance running, would be both affirmed and shattered.

Banchi's explanation for Derartu's struggle—the Devil—was one of many obvious differences that I encountered in Ethiopia and elsewhere from the classical American approach to running. The disparities among cultures struck me earliest and hardest, but similarities were abundant as well. With few exceptions, Sundays are universal long-run days, and kilometer repeats (or mile repeats for U.S. runners) are a bread-and-butter workout. Oats—in the form of porridge in the United Kingdom, muesli in Switzerland, and pancakes in Scandinavia—are the breakfast of champions the world over. Runners across the globe never seem to get their fill of tea; the Finn Valley Athletics Club in Donegal, Ireland, ends each daily session with hot tea and scones in the clubhouse. And somehow, amid all of that caffeination, distance runners everywhere with the luxury to do so treat afternoon naps as seriously as business meetings.

DEVIATION FROM THE ALL-OR-NOTHING, gadget-driven, results-obsessed training style pervasive in the United States is neither comfortable nor secure. But stepping outside a conventional approach offers great potential to extend careers, foster unexpected connections, and find fulfillment in running's simplest form. Five months after returning from my trip and cherry-picking from each training style I encountered led me to the third-fastest marathon time in American history for a woman under age twenty-five and a contract with Asics, a shoe company with Japanese roots and a worldwide reach. More important, my experiences running with athletes in different cultures laid the foundation for a future of continued joy and friendship found through running. In these pages are many of the lessons, techniques, and rituals I encountered on my journey. Some I have incorporated into my own life, others I have included simply because they fascinate me. Together, they power the heartbeat of the global running community.

1

TRADING THE START LINE FOR THE SIDELINE

England
399 miles

If I couldn't *race* them, I'd just have to stalk them—from behind the barriers dividing spectators from the female Olympic marathoners snaking along the River Thames. The pavement separating me from the runners was no larger than the gap that, just weeks earlier in Eugene, Oregon, stood between me and Emma Coburn, the eventual Olympic Trials 3,000-meter steeplechase champion. Until the Big Spill, that is. In the middle of that race, every steepler's worst fear became reality as both my body and my 2012 Olympic dreams came crashing down, the former straight into the water pit, the latter into another arduous four-year wait.

Competing here in London had been a distant goal since my freshman year at Rice University, when my coach convinced me I had an unusually quick recovery rate and a huge upside; but it was only in my last track season that I climbed high enough in the ranks of the American distance fleet to actually envision myself as an Olympian without feeling like an impostor. Qualifying for the U.S. Olympic Track and Field Team is a little bit like nailing a mosquito with a slingshot on cue: a matter of skill, luck, and impeccable timing. Assuming you're healthy and supremely fit in the Olympic year (a tall order on its own), you first have to run the Olympic Trials standard to prove you're among the twenty-four fastest Americans in your event (with the exception of the marathon, which has a separate Trials and qualifying process); then you have to make it out of the preliminary round at the Trials and finish in the top three in the final; and finally, you must run the Olympic "A" standard at the Trials or in an earlier race. Sickness, off days, and misjudged water pits, although unfortunate, are not taken into consideration when it comes to determining Team USA—the "hardest team to make," as ads sprawled across Eugene reminded me. It would be a while until I got another chance, but it was too late; I was hooked on running, my fate as certain as the family of koi, a couple hundred dollars a head, that my siblings and I once relocated from the neighbors' fishpond to our bathtub. If not for the Watson Fellowship, I would be in a very different position, shaking off my disappointing performance with visits to a few of the dozen professional training groups scattered around the country, and—what else?—miles upon miles of running, both a punishment and a solace.

But my race's outcome had been written, and though these hundred whippetlike Olympians were a crushing reminder of my recent, nationally televised mishap, I was captivated. As the runners flew by in their colorful race singlets, some leading their packs and others settling behind, I made mental notes of it all: stride mechanics, arm carriage, body sizes, form flaws, signs of suffering, and visceral shows of strength. *Someday,* I thought, *if I do things right, this glimpse of the world's best marathoners might come in handy.* Though I was a steeplechase and 10K specialist in college, long tempo runs and high-volume workouts were my forte. I'd always felt a magnetic pull toward the marathon.

For now, though, I found myself in a stationary position behind the metal railing. And though I was watching comfortably from the sidelines—thankful to be there as a willing spectator rather than by force of injury—I was also more mobile than I had ever been, just days into a yearlong global adventure. For the first time in my life, I would be running without structure, and I intended to keep it that way for the year. Jim Bevan, my college coach, agreed to guide me from afar—monitoring my weekly mileage and e-mailing me flexible workout plans—but my exploration of new training styles would take precedence over my own running, and I wouldn't do any serious racing until I returned to the United States. To feel like I was still moving forward, still climbing the ranks, I framed the year ahead as an extended base-building block—a chance to develop my aerobic system and experiment with new elements before (hopefully) entering the world of professional running after my return.

London, England, my first destination, was shaping up to be the ideal place to kick off my tour. Not only was London hosting the 2012 Summer Olympic Games, it also had a sizable and growing recreational running community. I didn't know just how much this historic and international city would challenge my assumptions about running.

Though I'll always opt for a spot on the starting line, the sideline of the Olympic Marathon wasn't a bad alternative. As I jockeyed for position behind the barricade, waiting for the female leaders to fly by, I wasn't sure whether to be annoyed or impressed by the crowds. Despite a steady stream of rain all morning and the absence of an injured Paula Radcliffe, England's beloved world record holder in the marathon, it seemed that all of London had flooded the streets in order to catch a glimpse of these running superstars. I couldn't help but appreciate that so many people, standing four or five deep in some places, were fired up about a 26.2-mile race. As fascinating and dramatic as I found the marathon, I knew that watching one could be a logistical headache, and that a spectator's enthusiasm could easily wane over the hours of the race.

Undeterred spectators during the drizzly women's Olympic Marathon in London.

I found a spot at the 5K mark with a prime view of the runners, and was thrilled to see two Americans, Shalane Flanagan and Kara Goucher, sharing the lead. Shalane and Kara were training partners based in Portland, Oregon, and the dynamic duo of female American distance running, with an Olympic and a World Championship medal between them. Three miles into the race, they had settled into a comfortable pace, making it look as effortless as a typical training run (only with a hundred or so other runners in pursuit). They were just warming up, trying to keep their bodies relaxed in preparation for the brutal miles ahead.

A few strategies for racing a marathon seem universally practiced by the elites: minimizing energy output by running even, if not negative, splits for both halves (meaning the first half of the race is run at the same pace or slower than the second); spotting and grabbing staged fluid bottles every few miles to stay hydrated throughout the race; and being prepared to dig extraordinarily deep in the last 10 kilometers (6.2 miles), the point that many competitive marathoners consider to be the real start of the race, and where the dreaded "wall" lurks.

Beyond the basic strategies, the patterns of the lead pack were a mystery to me. A shoulder runner myself—most comfortable tucked right behind and slightly to the side of another runner—I was struck by the differences in the runners' preferred racing positions. Some, like Americans Shalane and Kara, chose to dictate the pace by running at the front of the pack; that also meant they would block the wind for their competitors, expend more mental energy, and be the first to navigate the course—this one with no fewer than 111 turns and four U-turns. Others, like the forty or so women bunched together behind them at the 5K mark, were happy to latch on and hunker down, riding the wave without having to think too much, but with little control over the pace and a narrow window of time to respond to unexpected surges. Still others disregarded their rivals entirely, running a predetermined pace or effort no matter who was around them, facing that demon of a distance all on their own. *Which of those types of marathoners will I be when I move up in distance?* I wondered, imagining myself in each position. *Which is the most efficient?* In about two hours, I hoped to have my answer to the second question, and some ideas about the first.

The next time I saw the field of runners, the leaders were approaching the Tower Bridge, the halfway mark. The true battle was still ahead. After rushing to find a new spot for watching—the marathon takes the term "spectator sport" to a new level—I found a small bridge overlooking the course. The fans around me cheered as wildly as if they each had a family member running; even the race marshals, who abandoned their duties in the heat of the moment, applauded as enthusiastically as the rest of the crowd when the lead pack sped beneath us.

The USA duo had relinquished the lead but were still in the action, looking comfortable and smooth inside the top fifteen runners or so, with plenty of time left to make a move. A safe spot to be for now. Valeria Straneo, the Italian record holder in the marathon, wearing bright blue, had taken over and was pulling along a group of about thirty runners, including two heavy favorites, Mary Keitany of Kenya and Tiki Gelana of Ethiopia. Though deep in the pack, I knew their positions were no indication of the final results; like many others around them, they were simply biding their time until *the move*—that abrupt moment when one runner takes control of the race, and tries to break her rivals through a sudden surge and psychological defeat.

I'm well-versed in the power of the surge, having experienced it countless times as an instigator and a victim. My most memorable surge, and a turning point in my running career, was in the 2009 Conference USA Championship 10K. I was up against an older and more accomplished runner whom I greatly respected. After I'd followed her around the track for fifteen laps, Coach Bevan gave me his signal and I put the hammer down with ten laps to go, running 200 meters almost all-out, and quickly gapped her en route to victory. I couldn't have maintained that speed for much longer, but the move gave me a mental edge long before either of us reached the finish line, the exact outcome my coach and I hoped for when we hatched that strategy the night before. In a race more than four times as long, I wondered what scheme each of the runners was brewing for herself.

I scanned every face for Desiree Davila (now Linden), the third American in the race. Ever since she'd "come out of nowhere" with a 2:22:38 marathon the previous year—though "nowhere" often means years of silent grinding, away from the public eye—Desiree was a competitor you couldn't help but admire. Five-foot-two and a pillar of strength, she ran a modest 16:17 in the 5,000 meters at Arizona State University. Desiree stuck with it, though, and by the time the 2011 Boston Marathon came around, she was able to run within thirty seconds of her college 5K personal record (PR), eight times in a row. Desiree Davila had arrived.

Now, a year and a half after her Boston breakthrough, I feared that Desiree's nightmare had arrived. Rumors had been flying about a possible injury sustained in the last month of her Olympic buildup, though I didn't put much stock in speculations before the race began. What world-class distance runner isn't harboring *something*, after all? I had spotted a few of the marathoners walking slowly, if not hobbling, beside the course, the devastation of having dropped out almost tangible—and I sincerely hoped that Desiree, one of our U.S. women and a personal inspiration, was healthy enough to avoid that heartbreak.

And then there were four. My last chance to see the runners before they crossed the finish line in a closed-off area was near the 25-mile mark, right down the road from St. Paul's Cathedral. With just over a mile to go, four women had separated themselves from the rest of the pack: Tatyana Petrova Arkhipova of Russia, Tiki Gelana of Ethiopia, and Kenyan teammates Mary Keitany and Priscah Jeptoo. The Kenyans had an advantage over the rest of the field, running together and feeding off each other's energy and confidence. Keitany and Jeptoo looked smooth and controlled, and I was ready to bet that one of them would run away with it all. But would they try to work together to break their rivals, or were they prepared for an all-out battle of nations *and* teammates? Behind them, the Americans had faded, Shalane sitting around eighth place, and Kara a few spots and forty seconds back. Still no Desiree. The next seven or so minutes would be the most action-packed of the morning (though the tight security near the end of the course necessitated a tape-delayed viewing of the fight to the finish).

Even for a noncontact sport, the word *fight* definitely applies to the marathon. As the final part of the race heated up, Keitany started to fade and Gelana, the diminutive Ethiopian with a high arm carriage and a green singlet meant for someone twice her size, made a decisive move that the two left in the lead pack were able to match—but only for a minute or two. Trying desperately to hang on, Arkhipova and Jeptoo eventually surrendered to Gelana, who tore down the homestretch, the finish line finally in sight. As she broke the tape in 2:23:07, Gelana recorded a new Olympic record and set into motion four years of official marathoning dominance—for herself as well as her homeland of Ethiopia. Knowing what I did about the Kenyan–Ethiopian running rivalry, I wondered how much of Gelana's final kick was inspired by national pride. I felt for Jeptoo, second place by a mere five seconds, and Keitany (fourth behind the Russian, Arkhipova), who would soon be returning home to Kenya having ceded the title to an Ethiopian.

Nearly three minutes back, the two Americans rolled in close together, Shalane taking tenth place with a time of 2:25:51 and Kara finishing eleventh in 2:26:07. Hugging and leaning on each other, they looked depleted, their faces revealing both relief and disappointment. Race reports confirmed that Desiree had started the race but pulled out just before the 5K mark, citing a nagging hip injury. With her second-place finish at the Olympic Trials the previous January, she had earned the right to run against the very best and had honored that privilege, injury be damned.

"I think every track athlete and distance runner should also be a fan of the sport," Kara Goucher wrote in a blog post in 2011. "Watching the world's best compete fires you up to achieve your own feats of greatness. When it comes to running, participation and spectating go hand in hand." The women's Olympic Marathon was among the most thrilling two and a half hours of my life. Not only did I get to witness, from a few feet away, the world's brightest running stars and some of my personal heroes, I also got in a full morning of sightseeing, with historical landmarks like Buckingham Palace, close enough to the start and finish line to be considered the race headquarters; the Tower of London, which marked the turnaround point; and Big Ben, the iconic tower with its enormous clock that signaled the end of the race was near.

Most important, as Kara had predicted, I came away from the race with valuable information for my own future in the event, and a burning desire to dive in before too long. The lesson that resonated most was of patience, which Gelana demonstrated beautifully with her dominant surge in the final mile of the race. Unsurprisingly, the victory went to a negative-split racer, who completed the second half of the race a full three minutes and nineteen seconds faster than the first. The discipline it took to keep her excitement in check during the first half—even the first twenty miles—must have been torturous when the effort still felt easy and her reserves were full.

I was full of questions about Gelana's Olympic training. Did she run with a group, have a coach, or use a pacer? What was her typical weekly volume? Did she ever take days off? What did she eat? And how did her training differ from her competition, especially that of her greatest rivals and next-door neighbors in Kenya? I scribbled them in my notebook for another day.

UNLIKE THE MARATHON, and a few other athletic events such as the triathlon and cycling, the Olympic track-and-field events were not free to the public, and tickets could be very expensive—especially for a girl traveling on a limited budget. Fortunately, London provided some nice alternatives to the Olympic Stadium. For a ten-day span, the city was ablaze, its thirty-two boroughs mosaics of colors and flags, the mood buoyant with patriotism, anticipation, and (mostly) good-natured rivalries. My viewing venues ranged from a big screen rigged up in Trafalgar Square to a couple of locals' homes, and often ended in a warm, dimly lit, and bustling pub. Even Edinburgh, Scotland—where I spent a long weekend with former Conference USA rival (and NCAA indoor mile champion) Chris O'Hare, his visiting teammate Brian Tabb, and the delightful O'Hare family—had a set of twenty-six-foot-tall Olympic rings on display in the middle of town. The buzz was everywhere, and it was infectious.

While it was easy to get caught up in the excitement, riling up more than a few locals with my U-S-A chants, one pub experience in particular brought out a whole new level of British pride. As the men's 10,000-meter field ran its final pre-race strides, I settled into a seat at the Teddington Arms, a local bar that was all-in for the Olympics and Team GB. It housed a wall-size projector screen that streamed the BBC's thorough Olympics coverage, as well as a group of regulars that could turn even the most mundane athletic competition into a life-or-death matchup. The

Teddington Arms, I figured, was almost as good as the stadium's nosebleed seats.

The runners began their 25-lap assault, and the pub's atmosphere began to change. Raucous and distracted at the start, the crowd grew quieter and more reverential with each tick of the lap counter, all eyes on hometown hero Mo Farah. A Somali-born Brit and the favorite in the 10K, Mo trained under Alberto Salazar, one of the United States' most successful coaches and once a feared distance runner himself. Mo's house was smack in the middle of Teddington, with Bushy Park virtually as his backyard; Sweatshop, the running store where he used to work, was right down the road from the Teddington Arms. Everyone was bursting with Mo Fever, and I couldn't help catching it myself: Mo was not only a running phenom but a twin like me and also an expectant father of twins.

The rest of the field strung out behind them, Mo and Galen Rupp—Mo's blond, youthful-looking training partner from Oregon—looked about as comfortable as two training partners could be, even on the biggest stage of them all. Though racing teammates has its advantages—working together and putting each other at ease, like Shalane and Kara at the beginning of the marathon, and the Kenyan duo at the end—it can also muddy the line between competitiveness and friendship with each person's awareness of the other's strengths and weaknesses. But I doubted friendship was relevant now. Mo and Galen were vying for the win not only against each other but, with a half mile to go, ten other exceptional runners. Within two minutes, the group had dwindled to five, and still in the mix were defending champion Kenenisa Bekele of Ethiopia, his brother Tariku Bekele, and Bedan Karoki Muchiri of Kenya. So many heated matchups in such a small space—training partners, siblings, and, as usual in the distance races, East African neighbors and foes.

Approaching the final curve, all five runners were in contention and the victory looked uncertain. Mo maintained his lead and seemed to be opening up his stride, but I'd seen enough unbelievable last-ditch kicks to know better than to discount anyone before the line has been crossed. Within a matter of moments, Mo extended the gap as he tore down the homestretch unchallenged, cinching gold with arms outstretched and an expression revealing both astonishment and ecstasy. Less than half a second later, Galen cemented his lead over Tariku Bekele as he followed his training partner across the line in second place. The race was a stunning show of both personal strength and teamwork; competitor Kenenisa Bekele (world record holder and double winner of the 5K and 10K in the 2008 Beijing Olympics) admitted later, "I knew they were dangerous. But I can't stop them."

Emotions and national pride were sky-high in the Teddington Arms. I momentarily forgot that I was only a visitor, the distinction melting with the high fives, back slaps, and chest bumps with Brits and other foreigners alike. Mo's victory felt like a personal achievement for Teddington, but his dramatic finish also concluded the winningest day in Great Britain's Olympic track-and-field history, as long jumper Greg Rutherford and heptathlete Jessica Ennis both won their events within hours of Mo's victory. Under immense scrutiny by the rest of the world as the host of the Olympics, London had those victories to relish and those heroes to celebrate as they set the tone for the rest of the 2012 Games.

And celebrate, they did. Nearly running the local pubs dry that night, Teddingtonians fulfilled the vow they made to Mo before the Olympics began. The town's most prominent postal box, painted in a fresh coat of shimmering gold and sitting right across the street from Sweatshop, suddenly became one of London's hottest landmarks. I made a point during the rest of my stay to pass it as often as I could, replaying scenes in my mind from that epic night and watching proud Brits strike the Mo-bot pose for pictures beside it.

MEANWHILE, I took my Olympic inspiration to the roads. While running in Greater London required a little forethought—on one city run, I was refused entry by a security guard outside of the Millennium Track because I didn't have the £3.75 entrance fee on me—Teddington, the quiet, green suburb of London that I chose as my first home base, was a runner's nirvana. Lacking the tourist attractions and skyscrapers of its booming parent, the town has a single Tesco, the grocery king in that part of the world; one main street with a handful of cafes, pubs, and shops; and zero two-lane streets. Plus, St. Mary's University, the temporary training headquarters for Olympic athletes from ten countries, was across the street from my flat. And Richmond Park and Bushy Park, the two largest of London's eight Royal Parks, were a convenient warm-up distance away, offering endless routes for soft-surfaced, pastoral runs.

Originally used by the United Kingdom's royal family to escape the limelight, the Royal Parks are now public and still vast, making Houston's Hermann Park, with a two-mile loop that I circled nearly every day for five years, feel like a hamster wheel by comparison. Technically, like Bushy and Richmond, Hermann is an urban park, featuring playgrounds, reflection pools, jogging paths, and picnic facilities, as well as a golf course, zoo, and outdoor theater. But despite my fondness for Hermann, standing in one of London's thousand-acre expanses, I could hardly lump it in the same category. Richmond and Bushy are natural habitats of their own that feel less like man-made attempts to reintroduce nature into the city than placid environments that have been tenderly cared for, undisturbed by the surrounding development. The 650 deer that roam Richmond Park, not to mention the multitude of horses, rabbits, and goats, make a mockery of Texas's beady-eyed possums and manicured poodles, and the possibility of getting lost in the woods seemed more like a reward than an obstacle. One local told me that King Henry VIII had ordered a herd of deer for the Hampton Court Palace grounds for hunting practice, and those that now inhabit the adjoining park are the offspring of the lucky survivors.

With such training grounds—on top of the town's mild summers, extensive transportation network, and proximity to London's Heathrow Airport—it's no wonder that so many English runners call Teddington home, and that even more foreign athletes use it as a base when racing around Europe. In one run alone, I passed runners wearing uniforms from Australia, Ireland, China, South Africa, and Great Britain. Also stationed in Teddington were a handful of U.S. athletes whom I occasionally recognized blazing around the St. Mary's track and through the wide-open parks. After the Olympics ended and athletes relocated to Teddington from the Olympic Village, I got to know two of the United States' middle-distance stars, Leo Manzano and Shannon Rowbury.

Leo—a Mexico-born, Texas-raised miler—was my track camp counselor in high school before he soared to five NCAA Championships and trademarked a vicious kick. Just days before, he'd ended the United States' forty-four-year dry spell in men's middle-distance races with his second-place finish in the Olympic 1,500-meter final. And Shannon, a Duke graduate who shared Leo's coach, John Cook, finished an impressive sixth in the recent women's Olympic 1,500-meter race. Her finish was the highest ever by an American woman in the event—even before some of the women who beat her tested positive for banned substances—and a huge step forward for female U.S. distance running.

One afternoon, I walked across the street to St. Mary's to watch Leo and Shannon behind the scenes in a track workout, the Olympics over but the summer season still ahead. It's fun to fantasize about celebrating a win by waving the U.S. flag and blowing kisses to fans, but the training that champions like them put in, day after day, is much less glamorous. The first thing I noticed was how seriously the duo treated their warm-up, spending about the same amount of time preparing to run hard as they did running. They jogged slowly around a grass field, performed a painstaking series of form drills on the track, and did some dynamic stretching before changing into spikes for a set of strides—a similar routine to many competitive runners, but executed slower and more purposefully.

Another takeaway was Leo and Shannon's controlled self-confidence and trust in their coach, who couldn't be with them during this particular stint. Though they easily could have blasted each repetition of their workouts (5×1-kilometer repeats for Leo and 6×400 meters for Shannon)—as "workout champions" notoriously do—they followed Coach John Cook's directions to keep their speed under control as they bounced back from the Olympics. Shannon ran without a watch, her boyfriend Pablo Solares timing her splits, and Leo slowly ramped up the speed with each repetition. Both finished their workouts looking energetic and satisfied, their self-discipline reminding me of the Olympic champion Tiki Gelana in the early stages of the marathon.

When the workout ended, Shannon had a short jog and some lifting on her schedule, so I joined Leo for his cool-down—only slightly shorter than the warm-up. He confirmed my observations from the workout, but surprised me with a few new revelations—

like his secret for staying focused and fit during the long racing season. After his last race, he indulges in fast food and takes a break from running completely, preferably on vacation at a beach. "By the end of that doing nothing," Leo said, "I come back and I'm hungry" . . . but less so for greasy burgers and salty fries. I know more than a few runners who would benefit immensely from true time off after a long season rather than a halfhearted pause, worried about getting out of shape and trying to maintain year-round race readiness. I'm not alone in feeling guilty and adrift in the off-season, struggling even during my annual two-week break from running to let go of the mindset that everything I do affects my performance down the road. And it might—but according to Leo, not always in the way I expect.

Leo's success on the track has been partially attributed to his five-foot-five, 122-pound body—with a heart determined through laboratory tests to be larger than that of the average six-foot-tall man, and an aerobic capacity higher than that of a *doped* Lance Armstrong. But his racing strategy, informed by his long-sighted, even-keeled attitude, also sets him apart. Comparing the mile to life, Leo said, "You can't go out too crazy, or else you're going to burn out." When an obstacle arises—be it a mid-race jostle, a stretch of doubt, or an early hint of fatigue—he focuses on moving forward without getting too discouraged. And when he reaches the homestretch with fuel left in the tank, his early patience is rewarded by the devastating kick that bred the "Lion" moniker.

Among Tiki Gelana, Shannon Rowbury, and Leo Manzano—all successful runners with different strengths and styles—I detected a trend. The best of the best don't hammer every rep of every workout or every mile of a race; they know when to push and when to dial it down, and in workouts they rarely seem to strain to the degree that they do in competition. Seeing that principle in action in the event I had my eyes set on, and then hearing it from two of the United States' best runners, made it a little easier for me—a chronic overextender—to see the wisdom in their strategy.

AFTER THREE WEEKS, I'd gotten used to living in a five-room flat by myself, other than the occasional friend of the owner who crashed in one of the other rooms for a night and then moseyed on out the next day. One afternoon, though, when I returned from a run, I was met with a flurry of activity in the tiny kitchen, which was packed with oddly familiar strangers. Their thin legs, defined calf muscles, and red, black, and green garb left no room for doubt: My new flatmates were Kenyan runners, and they were fast, Olympic-caliber fast—I recognized a few from the BBC's recent broadcast.

Duncan Gaskell, one of the directors of a large Teddington-based sports agency, was the integral thread in my string of luck; I had connected with him online before departing on my fellowship year and jumped on his offer to rent a spare room in the flat he reserved for athletes. So, a couple of weeks after I arrived, Winny Chebet, Gideon Gathimba, Maggie Masai, and Mark Kiptoo joined me in the humble bedsit for a month of post-Olympic summer training, while a few of their other teammates stayed down the road.

Over a steaming bowl of stovetop porridge—made of millet and meant for slurping, the first of many bowls I had with them—the Kenyans introduced themselves. As hard as I tried, I couldn't contain my awe at their accomplishments.

"*Two minutes,* Winny? For the eight hundred meters? Didn't you say you were a year younger than me?"

"And Mark, you're telling me that your best 5K time is faster than the *American record*?"

After a little more track yak, our conversation transitioned to another hot topic for runners: food.

Meat doesn't play as prominent a role in the Kenyan diet as it does in the land of marbled T-bones and plump holiday turkeys; though they do eat goat, chicken, and beef on occasion, such items are considered side dishes in Kenya. To combat the overwhelming amount of choices, unfamiliar products, and much more processed and nutritionless food in the West, the Kenyans always travel with some must-have staples, including their preferred type of porridge and a few heavy sacks of cornmeal flour used to make ugali. Comparable to tortillas in Mexico, naan in India, and pita in Greece, the spongy sand-colored dish is the heart of the Kenyan diet. Once it's mixed with boiling water and puffs up into a doughy dome, the ugali is flipped onto a plate and pieces are torn off, balled up, indented with a thumb, and used as a scoop for an accompanying stew, usually made of cabbage, onions, tomatoes, and, on special occasions, small bits of meat. As the husband of Vivian Cheruiyot, Moses Kiplagat, told me, the Kenyan reliance on ugali is one reason that they're generally healthier, leaner, and faster than Americans—and "the reason we're beating you at your own game." It struck me as ironic: Here were members of arguably the greatest running culture in the world and their diets were heavily—almost entirely—carbohydrate based; while the current trend in the United States, even among some serious athletes, was to focus on low-carb, high-protein foods. How incomprehensible our ever-changing diet fads, coupled with our rising obesity, must seem to foreigners like the Kenyans.

Before sunrise the next morning, our mingling moved from the kitchen—where pots of sugary pre-run tea were simmering—to the trails as I followed Winny, Gideon, Maggie, and Mark out the door and toward Bushy Park. They had arranged to meet Vivian Cheruiyot, their tiny yet enormously talented teammate who had just snagged Olympic silver and bronze medals in the 5K and 10K, for an easy shakeout run, and they kindly invited me along. Not concerned with my running credentials, all they knew was that I liked to run, and that I was acutely interested in their running and living habits.

As we started down the sidewalk in a slow stroll, I wondered if I'd misunderstood their offer. *Are we actually taking a walk? Or doing some special warm-up? Is this their way of including me without having to reveal their training secrets?*

About twenty minutes later, still walking and still fretting, I spotted Vivian, standing at five-foot-three and weighing only 86 pounds, stretching next to a tree. We introduced ourselves before the group finally broke off into a jog, although the pace wasn't much faster than our walk. *I can get used to this!* I thought, as we shuffled through the grass and began the Bushy loop at a leisurely pace. *If this is their secret, they've had the whole world fooled. Superhuman stamina? Insane work ethic?*

All of a sudden, we weren't strolling anymore. We weren't exactly moving fast, either, but we were at least running at a more reasonable clip, our breaths quickening and small talk subsiding. For the rest of our forty-five-minute run, we continued building momentum, but the increase was gradual, with no distinct breaks or surges. Every few minutes, I would become slightly more aware of my effort, and I'd know that our pace had dropped again. By the end of our run, we were moving at a good pace, quicker than my normal "easy" runs, but with a different feel as a result of our slow buildup. The "Kenyan Way," my friends would teach me, was not really a way at all; though most runs started in slothlike fashion and gradually accelerated, there was no cookie-cutter run. One morning we might plod around the park, getting passed by recreational runners until we came to a halt, and the next I'd find myself desperately trying to match their ever-quickening foot-steps. These East Africans were my first real examples of running by feel and warming up naturally.

I soon understood the reasons for our twenty-minute walk to Bushy Park. Not only did the walk prevent needless pounding on the pavement, an injury-inviting surface virtually nonexistent where they train in Kenya, it also gave their bodies more than enough time to wake up and warm up. Even though the Kenyans usually train in the early mornings, by the time they actually begin running, their bodies are likely more alive and responsive than most people's ever become during the day. To get even more out of their warm-ups and recovery runs, they run in long pants and long-sleeve shirts or wind jackets, no matter the temperature. September in London had extremely pleasant running weather, barring some occasional rain-fall, yet it didn't keep the Kenyans from wearing cold-weather gear for every run. Though my friends chalked it up to comfort, I won-dered if this was a cultural toughening-up exercise, like training in bulky shoes and then racing in slipperlike spikes. The only time they shed some layers, they told me, was during important, hard workouts—but only after first warming up in jackets and pants.

The day after we first met in Bushy Park, I took Vivian up on her offer to teach me the art of ugali-making in the house she, Moses, and a few Kenyan teammates were renting on the other side of Teddington. I showed up at 8 P.M. as instructed, and waited as Vivian and Moses, huddled close together on the living room couch, finished their Bible readings while their housemates sat entranced by *Walker, Texas Ranger*. I had read that Kenyan runners take relaxation very seriously during nonrunning hours, allowing their bodies to recover from demanding training regimes, and my friends confirmed it; if they weren't in the kitchen, they were guaranteed to be parked in front of the television, watching the news, recorded track races, cartoons, or *Walker*.

The television crowd chatted quietly in their native Swahili, laughed in unison, and eventually turned to me to ask about Texas and if it really is like what *Walker* portrays. I explained that anyone walking around Dallas in Walker's garb would be taken for one of three things: a hillbilly, a lunatic, or a frat bro on his way to a Wild West–themed party. They also wanted to know if I knew Joel Osteen, the televangelist from Houston with a piercing white smile and a mind-boggling following around the world. My answers to both questions seemed to disappoint them.

Once Bible study and the *Walker* episode ended, Vivian put me to work in the kitchen. Following her lead, I chopped vegetables and took notes while Moses helped us mix the dough. Though cooking is traditionally reserved for women in Kenya—my roommates explained that a man caught in the act can be fined a cow—circumstances like a sick wife or mother, an unmarried man, or a tough batch of ugali warranted the use of a little manpower. As we worked, Vivian and Moses gave me further insight into the deceivingly powerful woman beside me.

Like the majority of elite runners in Kenya, who hold positions at governmental organizations like Armed Forces and Kenya Prisons, Vivian is employed as an inspector by the Kenyan police force. While she's excused from work during her racing season, occasionally she's required to report to the Nairobi headquarters, which lack both water and electric lights. Every year there's a heated meet between police officers—the Nike-sponsored National Police Service Track and Field Championships—and the formidable inspector has won a handful of titles.

Moses explained that most Kenyans don't know exactly when they were born, so those who need passports often guess their birth dates; and it's common for runners to fudge their age a few years younger than they think they are, to compete for longer (and against younger opponents) in the junior category and at universities. Vivian, on the other hand, when applying for her first passport, said she was fifteen when she was really thirteen so she'd be old enough to compete at the World Junior Cross-Country Championship. She finished fifth that year and never turned back.

Around 9 P.M., a typical dinnertime for them, the rest of the Kenyan housemates came downstairs to dig in. Vivian ladled some stew into each bowl and then put the steaming puff of ugali in the middle of the table. They all knew that I had never tried ugali before, so as I chomped down on a piece from the wedge that Vivian served me, the first and largest slice, I noticed all five Kenyans staring intently at me.

"Do you like it?"

"Is it good?"

"Better than pizza?"

"You can use a spoon if you want. . . ."

Mouth stuffed—it took a few tries to perfect the ugali ball size—I flashed a thumbs-up, and they nodded their heads approvingly. The warmth, grainy texture, and especially the excuse to eat with my hands, was a welcome change from my ordinary meals; and my scribbled notes constituted the start of my global recipe collection. After finishing the ugali, we capped off the dinner Kenyan-style by stuffing one cheek with ugali, slurping a big sip of whole milk, and chewing it all into a soggy mass before swallowing and repeating.

I'd been asking the questions all evening, so during "dessert," they turned the questions on me. They wanted to know what I normally ate for dinner, so I promised to make them a Tex-Mex feast the following weekend (they were initially skeptical about the tortillas, but once they figured out they could treat them as ugali pieces and scoop up the taco fillings, they were sold). They also wanted to know all about my twin; Vivian, who is one of eight children, joked that she could be my Kenyan twin. "We can trick your family!"

It's no secret that optimal athletic performance goes hand in hand with a sound, balanced diet, and no coincidence that many runners are also fervent cooks. Deena Kastor—the American record holder in the marathon and half marathon, and the runner I admire most—has a reputation in the running community for her entertaining prowess, kitchen experimentation, and ravenous appetite; and Shalane Flanagan is working on a cookbook, *Run Fast Eat Slow*. Between Deena, Shalane, and the Kenyans, sustained running success seems tied to a healthy relationship with food—especially when it's shared with others.

Vivian Cheruiyot, Kenyan Olympian and World Champion, and me in Teddington.

Just when I thought my London stint had reached its pinnacle at the dinner party with Vivian Cheruiyot and her teammates, I found myself sitting directly in front of the fastest men in the world: Jamaican sprinters Usain Bolt and Yohan Blake. Daren O'Dea (not to be confused with Irish soccer player Darren O'Dea), a boisterous forty-year-old Irish bachelor with a connection to the athlete manager who owned my flat, had temporarily moved into one of the spare rooms and quickly assumed an older brother role to me. By a big stroke of luck, he also happened to be Bolt's personal assistant whenever he visited London, providing lifts to the practice track, watching training sessions, fending off fans, and dropping off groceries at his summer apartment. A former runner, current agent for professional soccer players, and equally quick-tempered and kindhearted, Daren was the kind of guy who made things happen. Within twenty-four hours of meeting him, I had plans to meet with Bolt, and the contact information for a few willing hosts in Daren's Irish hometown. As far as flatmates go, I had struck gold again.

In very few situations would a five-eleven, 168-pound man like Yohan Blake seem small, but seeing him in a backseat with Usain Bolt was one of them. Bolt's six-foot-five, 207-pound frame and equally large personality filled what was left of Daren's SUV after Blake and Bolt's best friend M.J. slid in. We were on our way to the Brunel University track that served as their training grounds as they, like the Kenyan and U.S. runners I'd met, put the finishing touches on their summer track season.

"Shorty!" Bolt exclaimed when we stepped out of the car at Brunel, laughing and bending down to nudge my shoulder with his.

These men were fresh off record-setting Olympic performances, in which the Jamaican sprinters single-handedly won more medals (12) than any Jamaican Olympic team before them. Bolt had lived up to the tremendous hype he had built before the Games, contributing to three of the four gold medals, breaking an Olympic and world record in two of them. His training partner Yohan Blake—who also ran for Coach Glen Mills's Racers Track Club, based in Kingston, Jamaica—took silver behind Bolt in both the 100 and 200 meters and handed Bolt the baton in the victorious 4×100-meter relay. The younger Warren Weir, also training with the Racers, completed the Jamaican sweep of the 200 meters and claimed the bronze. Unbelievably, four of those million-dollar legs had been resting mere feet from mine.

As I joined Daren for a day of carpooling and watching workouts, I was eager to learn more about the lifestyle of Jamaican sprinters, officially the best in the world. Sure, I'd heard the rumors that Bolt basically lived on Chicken McNuggets during the Beijing Olympics, but I was almost certain he didn't eat like that day in and day out. No McNuggets surfaced while I was around; instead, through the grocery lists Daren handled, I saw that the track titan thrives on milk, Gatorade (not to be confused with Lucozade, the English version of the sports drink), bananas, rice, apple juice, and the occasional muffin or box of Oreos. Daren told me that the Jamaican track team so frequently ate restaurants out of their entire rice and apple juice supplies that he had started calling them in advance to be sure they were sufficiently stocked.

I had also heard that Bolt was no stranger to late nights—confirmed when Daren had to wake him up for practice after a Call of Duty game that lasted until 2 A.M. (If only his online opponents could see the man they were up against.) Bolt's playfulness extends to the track, too, as those who have watched him race on television know well. In meets, as his competitors stride out and set up their blocks, stone-faced and focused, Bolt is known for dancing on the starting line (often in "Staying Alive" fashion), making up handshakes with the young volunteers, and hamming it up for the crowd. And after he dusts the field—which he does consistently, often pulling up long before the line—he resumes his horseplay as if he had never stopped, snapping selfies with photographers' cameras, busting out more dance moves, and striking the famous Lightning Bolt stance. That pose remained dormant during the workout I watched—maybe it's just a race day and photo op thing—but the laughs and practical jokes continued. More than once, I saw Bolt pull the age-old tap-on-the-shoulder gig in between strides. Judging from his teammates' reactions—or lack thereof—there was never any doubt about the source of the mischief.

And then there was the training. Anyone with a monopoly on the 100 and 200 meters is blessed with genetic advantages for sure. But there is an enormous amount of preparation that goes into Bolt's commanding stride and unmatched foot speed. His start, for one, requires more work than his teammates and rivals; it's arguably his biggest weakness, and no wonder, considering the sheer mass he needs to launch out of the blocks. The brute force that he puts into the ground with each step necessitates a new pair of spikes for each practice—which Daren collected to be auctioned off at charity fundraisers—and a massage therapist on hand, ready to treat whatever issues arise that day.

Ever since I first saw Usain Bolt light the track on fire a few years ago on ESPN, I'd wondered how his laid-back demeanor at races affected his performance. Is he good because he has a remarkable ability to relax in the face of immense pressure? Or is he so relaxed because he's in another league from his competitors, and thus has little fear of defeat? Viewed up close, it seems it's both. He might come off as a little goofy and a lot overconfident, but Bolt has made track and field relevant for the first time in a long time.

WITH LONDON STILL BASKING in the Olympic aftermath, my home base in the slower-paced suburbs was ideal for exploring the English running scene.

Aside from the deer and postseason Olympians, the Royal Park trails were getting use from another group of athletes I knew little about: racewalkers. Racewalking isn't included in U.S. high school or National Collegiate Athletic Association (NCAA) competitions, and American "elite" racewalkers often are unable to meet the international standards that competitions such as the Olympics require. I'd only come across racewalking once, when I accidentally caught the tail end of a race at the U.S. Trials—held during a morning session and sparsely attended—but in the Royal Parks, I ran by at least one racewalker during each of my outings. Intrigued by their funny waddle, I had to know more. One afternoon, I zeroed in on a young man walking swiftly around Richmond Park. His hips were in constant wiggle mode; all signs pointed to racewalker. I kept him in sight as I continued my run, and made a beeline toward him when he stopped to stretch. Fortunately, Devon—a recreational athlete who competed on behalf of his local club—hadn't noticed me stalking him (or was willing to talk to me anyway).

Racewalking is indeed a legitimate sport, featured at every

major international track-and-field meet (including the Olympics, the World Championships, and the Commonwealth Games) alongside running, throwing, and jumping. Some countries—such as China and Russia, who amazingly swept the top six spots in the women's Olympic 20K racewalk in 2012, and England, to a lesser extent—are heavily invested in the discipline. In the United States, by contrast, kids lack opportunities to try it or watch it, and talented endurance athletes are steered straight to running. One sports reporter captured the general sentiment in his coverage of the event at the Penn Relays: "And then there are racewalkers, and unless you're a relative or drew the short straw on the Franklin Field Saturday morning cleaning crew, you won't see the avant-garde foot patrol waddling with a purpose around the track."

"The main rule," Devon told me, "is to maintain constant contact with the ground so that no visible break occurs." Unlike running, which is essentially a continuous series of quick bounds, one foot must be touching land at all times. Furthermore, the leg that is extending out must be completely straight—no bending allowed—from the moment it makes contact with the ground until it becomes vertical. The form that results from these rules is the hip-shaking strut that raises eyebrows in the States. It also leads to severe hip injuries for the unlucky or the overtrained—another eyebrow raiser for a girl with hip surgery in her past. The rules go on. "Judges scrutinize us throughout the races," Devon said, which occur on the track as well as on roads for longer events, "and hand out red cards to walkers who break the rules." If a red card is validated by officials from three countries, the athlete is disqualified from the competition, though he or she won't know it until the race is over.

In about ten minutes—roughly the time it takes me to walk

an all-out mile, but three minutes slower than the world record pace per mile for a 31-mile (50K) racewalk—Devon had changed my perspective on racewalking. Despite my newfound respect, I had no urge to try it myself, other than a quick waddle so he could judge my form; but the next time I had the opportunity, I'd make the audience of a racewalking event one fan stronger. Far from wannabe runners, racewalkers are dedicated athletes whose sport is differently taxing—and come to think of it, I know *plenty* of runners with awkward gaits, and we're allowed to move exactly as we please!

If Devon had cleared up my racewalking misconceptions, perhaps the forty-something man in short shorts and a small, snug backpack skidding to a stop at a Richmond Park water fountain could do the same. I wanted an explanation for all the backpacked runners I'd seen darting through central London, occasionally slipping through one of the Royal Parks. They seemed to be fairly fit, clean-cut, middle-aged men and women, but they reminded me of parkour practitioners—daredevils who zip around urban spaces using curbs, railings, steps, and sidewalks as stunt props—only without the risky maneuvers. Hard as I tried not to stereotype, I couldn't help but suspect many of the running backpackers were gear nerds, dependent upon a CamelBak, Garmin, fanny pack, GU packs, and reflector vest.

"Excuse me, sir. I hate to interrupt—clearly you're on a mission—but do you have a second to chat?" I asked, as he swallowed his last gulp.

"If you don't mind chatting on the run, then sure!" he replied, his voice trailing off as he continued on his way.

I made a 180 and fell in line with his footsteps. "So, can you tell me what's up with the backpacks? I've noticed quite a few runners wearing them, especially in the downtown area, and I'm wondering if there's some sort of club or delivery system I haven't heard about."

His answer began with a long-winded description of each feature of his pack, down to the iPod case built into the strap, the ventilation mechanism in the back, and the insulated compartment for chilled snacks. Once we got through the gear talk, my latest park source revealed a small subculture of London runners who jog to and from work, Tube stations, grocery stores, restaurants, and even running meet-ups. Using their legs as their vehicles—built-in Oyster cards (prepaid cards used for public transport in London), you might call them—these runners avoid the hassles of limited parking spots and hefty congestion charges (imposed upon weekday drivers inside central London's busiest areas), all while getting fitter and reconnecting with nature. For this running enthusiast, Richmond Park was roughly on his way home from work and was his favorite place to clear his head and shake his legs out after a long, sedentary workday. With two young daughters and a wife at home, he had limited time for recreation, so his running commute killed two deer with one royal shot. And in his high-tech pack, this man stashed a spare set of clothes, wallet, phone, food, and keys.

Sure, the backpacks looked a little nerdy, and personally, I'm a gear minimalist—shoes, clothes, and a GPS watch are about the most I've suited up with. But if using exercise as transportation was the only way some people could squeeze in a run, I was all for it. Go on, backpacked runners. You too, racewalkers!

ONE SATURDAY MORNING late into my London stay, while stretching out my legs on an easy Bushy Park run, I sensed behind me the one thing that flips any runner I know into competitive mode: rear pursuit. One moment, I was circling the park, making tracks in the dew and daydreaming about my next destination on the globe. The next, I experienced what I imagine a lone zebra must feel when a pride of lions comes charging from behind, and I instinctively started hauling.

Legs churning and arms pumping, I swerved in a direction that I hoped was not on course with the predators. When the steady pounding behind me diminished, I finally turned and identified the source of all the commotion: a stream of runners of every imaginable form and fitness level—one wearing a singlet and compression shorts, another in overalls, a few pushing strollers, and a group sporting matching shirts. I'd seen plenty of road races around London, which attracted the young and the old, serious and recreational runners, and usually some race-walkers, too. A cross-country-style competition through a big grass field, however, with no referees, flags, or painted lines in sight, was a first. As the runners passed by me, I kept my eyes on the thinning line of moving bodies and took my turn pursuing *them*.

About fifteen minutes after the initial rush, a young man shot through a makeshift finish chute: a serious runner judging by his form, musculature, and enormous lead. The other runners behind him—most of them *way* behind—eventually finished, too, some looking surprisingly spent for a casual Saturday frolic. There were no uniformed race officials around, so I made my way over to some spectators milling around the finish to find out exactly what I had just witnessed.

"Is this your first ParkRun, love?" a curly-haired woman asked when I approached her. "Well, welcome! We're part of a move-

ParkRun participants charging through Bushy Park in Teddington.

ment started right here in London that's trying to make running popular again. You'll have to plan better next week so you can race, too!" She went on to describe the ParkRun logistics, which are blissfully simple and free of many typical race-related hassles (and price tags): You locate the ParkRun nearest to you or in the neighborhood of your choice, register online and print out your individual bar code (if you want to record an official time), and show up at your race's starting line the following Saturday a little before 9 A.M., with your bar code pinned to your shirt or tucked in a pocket for scanning at the finish line.

The woman explained that the Bushy ParkRun I'd just seen is one of the most popular, attracting nearly a thousand people on any given Saturday, but every single borough in London has its own ParkRun, too.

"Nine A.M. Saturday morning, rain or shine, Christmas or the queen's birthday," she said. They're free, timed, social, and inclusive of all ages and abilities. Powered by volunteers like her and sponsored by Adidas, Lucozade Sport, local shops like Sweatshop (Mo Farah's former employer), and the London Marathon, the races have become a successful, scalable model for cities throughout the United Kingdom and in other countries as well; at the time of my visit, a few United States locations were in the works. And maybe the best part of all? Anyone can start their own Park-Run. The directors want an event in every community that wants one, and offer help and guidance in getting them rolling.

Within just a few miles, I'd seen the many forms of London's fervent, no-excuse running culture—first demonstrated by the Olympic fans, later by the racewalkers and backpacked runners, and now by these free weekly ParkRuns. Drizzly race conditions, busy schedules, and lazy weekend mornings stood no chance against this city's active population. And you know who else was the real deal? The Bushy ParkRun champion that Saturday, Andy Baddeley, who I later learned was an Olympic miler.

BARON PIERRE DE COUBERTIN, founder of the modern Olympics, said, "The important thing in the Olympic Games is not winning but taking part."

Closing in on the next leg, I feared I'd hit the apex of my trip only one country in. Not only had I been a spectator at the 2012 Olympics and surveyed England's strong recreational running scene, as planned, but I'd also glimpsed the Kenyan and Jamaican running traditions, each world leaders in their respective disciplines—pure luck, since neither of those countries was on my travel itinerary. In one month, I'd witnessed a surprising spectrum of lifestyles, from running commuters to elite athletes, shaped by the culture from which they hailed as well as individual traits—like patience in warm-ups and in the early stages of a race—and a commitment to run no matter what.

While I hated to leave the community I had found, I knew it was a microscopic part of the wider running world, and I couldn't wait to get back on the road. First, I'd meander beyond London to explore a few more English running traditions, including an iconic team rivalry and the roots of cross-country racing; and in an impulsive alteration of my original itinerary, I'd also head to neighboring Ireland, where Daren had connected me with the historic running club that helped shape him.

As I packed my suitcase and backpack, one pair of worn-out shoes lighter, I felt a familiar sadness about the four-year gap until the next Summer Olympics. But this time, those feelings were driven not by a lost opportunity to compete but by the end of my stint as a spectator and a "local" in the celebrated host city. From the friendly volunteers manning every city corner to the fans who filled the pubs at night, my first Olympic experience was inspiring and less about USA pride than international solidarity. I hoped that the next time the Games rolled around, or the one after that, my participation would find me on the road instead of to the side of it.

Kenyan Chicken Stew with Ugali
(Vivian Cheruiyot, Kenya)

This stew, commonly made without chicken but always served with ugali, is a tasty and nourishing Kenyan dish introduced to me by Vivian Cheruiyot in Teddington.

4–5 small chicken thighs
Large head of cabbage, washed, cored and finely chopped (confetti-style)
½ red onion, diced
Vegetable oil
2 small tomatoes, chopped
Pinch of salt
1 heaping tablespoon of spicy beef mchuzi mix (available at ethnic grocery stores or on Amazon)
8 cups water
4 cups maize meal (or flour)

Stew

1. Cut off ends of chicken thighs, peel and remove skin, and chop thighs into bite-size pieces.
2. Heat a large ungreased pot over high heat. Add onion and cook for 2 minutes.
3. Cover in vegetable oil and cook for 2 more minutes, stirring with wooden spoon.
4. Add chicken to pot and cook for 2 more minutes, stirring constantly.
5. Add tomatoes and salt to pot. Cover and simmer for about 8 minutes.

6. Add cabbage to pot and flatten without mixing with chicken. Close lid and continue simmering, stirring regularly.

7. In a separate bowl, stir mchuzi mix into a cup of cold water. Pour into stew and continue cooking on low heat while you prepare ugali.

Ugali

1. Pour the rest of the water into a large pot on the stove and turn heat to high.

2. When water starts to boil, add maize meal to the pot. Lower heat to medium, and mix water and maize with a flat wooden utensil until smooth, about 15 minutes.

3. When fully incorporated and cooked, mold the ugali into a smooth mound with the flat utensil, and dump upside down onto a plate.

4. To serve, ladle stew into bowls and top with a big triangular hunk of ugali (sliced like pie). Using your right hand, tear off a small piece of ugali, roll into a ball, make an indentation with your thumb, and use it to scoop up the stew.

5. Optional: Finish the meal with whole milk and ugali. Put a chunk of ugali in your cheek, take a gulp of milk, and enjoy.

2

KITTING UP AND FORGING AHEAD

Greater England and Ireland
283 miles

"Ladies and gentlemen," Norris McWhirter began. Three thousand bodies sat motionless, holding their breath and hanging on the announcer's every word.

It was May 6, 1954, and the Iffley Road Track stadium in Oxford, England, was full of hopeful witnesses to an earth-shattering athletic feat, one that had been eluding runners across the world for years: the four-minute mile. A few had come very close—including Englishman Roger Bannister, Australian John Landy, American Wes Santee, and Swedes Arne Andersson and Gunder Hägg—but in that moment, the barrier remained intact, the ability of a human to break it still in question.

Moments before, the fans had watched their own Roger Bannister—an Oxford medical student—take to the track for his third concerted assault on the barrier. Running in the wake of two pacers, and ahead of five competitors, Bannister came through the first quarter in 58 seconds, passed the half mile in 1:58, and entered the bell lap with 3:01 on the clock—the same split he had run in his most recent personal best. He needed a final lap of 59 seconds, a full 2 seconds faster than he had been able to muster in his last race. With about a half lap to go, Bannister ripped past the remaining pacer and shot around the curve, both he and his fans aware that his margin of error was excruciatingly narrow.

"Here is the result of event nine, the one mile," McWhirter continued. "First, number forty-one, R. G. Bannister, Amateur Athletic Association and formerly of Exeter and Merton Colleges, Oxford, with a time which is a new meeting and track record, and which—subject to ratification—will be a new English Native, British National, All-Comers, European, British Empire and World Record. The time was three . . ."

That was all the crowd needed to hear, the 59.4-second part a mere accessory. The stadium erupted in cheers, the shot was heard round the world, and suddenly, the impossible was possible. Just forty-six days later, John Landy joined Bannister in the Sub-4 Club, and others soon followed. Though that accomplishment no longer makes international headlines—the world record has been trimmed to 3:43.13 (by Hicham El Guerrouj of Morocco), and more than four hundred runners in the United States alone have run below four minutes—it remains a sacred benchmark. *Running Times* magazine's Daniel P. Smith called it "one of the most lauded achievements in the running universe, a standard as recognized by laymen as by track-and-field aficionados, a mark etched in the American consciousness as a feat of athletic grandeur."

As I stepped onto the Roger Bannister Track in Oxford almost sixty years later, I felt like I was treading on hallowed ground.

Though I'd passed a few people on my way to the track—mostly diners in the Iffley Road Sports Complex's Sub-4 Café—and received permission to take a look around, the track itself was empty. It had been resurfaced since that groundbreaking feat, as cinder and clay gave way to faster surfaces like asphalt and then Mondo, but the allure remained, and I got chills as I envisioned Bannister's—and the crowd's—uproarious reaction to McWhirter's announcement. I don't imagine the number three had ever looked so beautiful.

Roger Bannister Track (formerly Iffley Road Track) in Oxford, site of the first sub-four-minute mile.

VISITING THE ROGER BANNISTER TRACK—one of running's most iconic landmarks, conveniently right down the road from my home for the week—was only part of the reason I'd come to Oxford.

Anyone who's played an organized sport knows what it's like to be part of a rivalry. Emotions run wild, the competition heats up, and the next thing you know, your sweet friend Leslie, as gentle as a lamb, is getting a technical foul for yanking the jersey of a competitor who just stole the basketball from her.

I don't recall ever getting physical—other than a thrown elbow here and there—but many of my best running memories involve fierce battles with individuals and teams I was determined to beat. Triumphing over teams from big public universities, with ten times the student population of Rice, always felt satisfying, and the competition was sometimes personal. It was only after the Mt. SAC 5K (one of the distance events held at Mt. San Antonio College in Walnut, California) that I learned why my coach was screaming from across the stadium at me, "DIVE! DIVE, Becky, DIVE!" when I wasn't even finishing in the top five: a friendly, long-standing rivalry with a competitor's coach, two similarly fit runners, and an In-N-Out burger on the line for the victorious coach.

Perhaps no rivalry in the world is as enduring and steeped in tradition as the one between the Oxford University and Cambridge University running clubs in England. The two cross-country teams lined up against each other for the first time nearly a century and a half ago and have raced annually since, interrupted only by war (and even then, they raced, but the results are asterisked as "unofficial"). There was one year (1952) that the race went on in the midst of a "pea souper" (black fog) that claimed twelve thousand lives in London. I'd heard friendly jabs from graduates of both schools while I was in London; many of them were still active in local running clubs, and nearly all fervently followed their alma mater's team. The rivalry was so impassioned and celebrated, I had to check it out.

In London, I learned more about the duel from Simon Molden, an Oxford graduate and the honorary secretary and club archivist of Thames Hare and Hounds ("Thames"), the oldest adult cross-country club in the world. Though no competition between the two universities is casual—the Cambridge University Hare and Hounds website taunts, "Hating Oxford is a full time occupation"—Simon told me that no event better conveys the rivalry than the Blues Cross-Country Race (between Oxford in light blue and Cambridge in dark blue). The inaugural event in 1880 was run on a 7.5-mile course that began outside an Oxford pub. Oxford bested Cambridge 22 points to 33, but the victory was later deemed unfair as records indicate that "malicious boys tampered with the trail," sending two Cambridge men on a frenzied midrace goose chase. The course and rules have evolved over time—currently, in the varsity match, eight men (six who score) and six women (four who score) compete on Wimbledon Common—but the pride on the line and ferocity on the course remain constant from year to year.

Though I would have loved to witness the Blues Race, I couldn't hang around England for another few months to wait for it. My best alternative, then, was to visit both campuses, to see each side of the historic rivalry and explore a different university athletic climate than the NCAA system I had just left.

First, I paid tribute to Roger Bannister and his alma mater: Oxford University. For such an academically renowned school, it also has a lengthy and impressive athletic resume. The Oxford University Rugby Football Club, founded in 1869, is considered by many to be the oldest athletic club in England, and Eddie Eagan, an Oxford graduate, was the first person to win gold medals in both the summer and winter Olympics (in boxing and bobsled, of all combinations). Oxford's cross-country and athletics (track-and-field) programs have been a major part of the university's legacy from the start; in addition to earning many Olympic medals, Oxford-graduated runners, jumpers, and throwers have set a handful of world records, beginning with M. J. Brooks's record-breaking high jump in 1876. Beyond Bannister, notable runners who have represented both Oxford and Great Britain include Richard Nerurkar (fifth place in the 1996 Olympic Marathon) and Chris Chataway (fifth place in the 1952 Olympic 5K).

I found my way to Marsten Street from the bus station, and a friendly face opened the door at the address I'd been given. The first few moments of an arrival are always unnerving—Am I at the right place? Have I fallen victim to a trap?—but Sean gave me a warm welcome. His roommate, Richard Franzese, one of the captains of the Oxford University Cross-Country Club and a two-time Blues Race champion, had generously offered me his bedroom during his vacation to Eugene, Oregon, "Tracktown, USA." Sean, also an Oxford runner, seemed as relieved to see me, a pretty unimposing five-foot-tall Texan, as I was to meet him (though I think some of my later hosts were disappointed at my lack of big hair, spurs, and Stetson; the old TV show *Dallas* is surprisingly well-known around the world).

After my visit to the Roger Bannister Track and a deep sleep, the Oxford singlets pinned up on Richard's bedroom walls reminded me whose territory I was in as I laced up my shoes for a run with Sean. His teammates would normally want to join us, he explained as he led me through South Park and Shotover Park, a hilly expanse where the Oxford team trains and hosts races—*especially* since I was interested in the Oxford–Cambridge rivalry—but they were on a break from school and most had left campus. Sean was heading out the next day, too, for a 10K race in another city, so he was only running a few miles in order to preserve his legs. "You'll have to come back when everyone's here," he said, apologizing before pointing me toward Oxford's home cross-country course and turning for home.

Following Sean's directions, I wove through the forest for the next hour, pushing the pace as if I were racing up and down the muddy hills, around the hairpin turns, and over nature's own water pits. *This is not the kind of cross-country I'm used to,* I thought, hurdling a tree trunk that seemed to be a permanent fixture on the route. Most of my experiences were limited to manicured intramural fields and pristine golf courses, and the only obstacles I consistently faced in races were the immovable barriers in the 3,000-meter steeplechase. Extreme weather and messy terrain are rare for most meets in the United States, as the quest for fast times in perfect conditions increasingly takes precedence over courageous racing in tough circumstances.

It wasn't always like that, I knew; Coach Bevan and *his* college coach, Dr. Joe Vigil (an international running authority and now one of my mentors) had plenty of counterexamples in Colorado's Adams State College (now University) runners during Coach Vigil's reign from 1965 to 1993. Mile repeats every Thursday, rain, blizzard, or sun, Saturday race or not, was one permanent fixture of the Vigil camp, as was embracing the simplicity of the Alamosa, Colorado, lifestyle, a small town in the San Luis Valley with few enough distractions to be considered a full-time altitude camp. "Eat like a poor man," Coach Vigil still says, in the words of post–World War II German doctor and distance coach Ernst van Aaken, half-jokingly steering his charges toward moderation and self-discipline. Coach Bevan, who was a triple jumper and graduate coach at Adams State before he relocated to Rice, often wore shorts and a short-sleeve shirt while his athletes trained in what feels polar for Houston—40 degrees and sunny—to show us that it wasn't *that* cold. He did the same during a NCAA Cross-

Country Championship held in Indiana in November—and it really *was* that cold.

I also knew about some runners of old who purposefully by-passed ordinary comforts to maintain a tunnel-vision focus. Pat Porter, two-time Olympian in the 10K, eight-time U.S. cross-country champion, and one of Coach Vigil's charges, permanently parked his car in his garage, preferring to build aerobic endur-ance the old-fashioned way. A more extreme case from across the world was Emil Zatopek, the "Czech locomotive." Rather than following convention, he logged miles in the snow with his wife on his back, wore heavy combat boots for trainers, ran in place in a bathtub full of pillows, and tested his limits with workouts like 50×400 meters, once in the morning and once in the evening, for two weeks straight. As if that weren't enough, he also pro-moted "hypoventilation training," which is about as dangerous as it sounds. I can't vouch for any of those methods myself, but they worked for him, to say the least: Zatopek won three gold medals in the 1952 Olympics in the 5K, 10K, and his first-ever marathon.

I felt like I belonged to a different generation of elite run-ners, more perfectionist than gritty, and more averse to chal-lenges than some of my predecessors and competitors. That sloppy run through the Oxford cross-country course drilled the point home. The experience in that forest was markedly dif-ferent from the fast, man-made courses I was used to, and I wondered if I should attempt to replicate that environment more often in my own training. I wasn't the only one with that idea; Warrior Dashes, Spartan Races, Tough Mudders, and other obstacle course races (OCR)—with elements such as walls, tunnels, barbed wire, and fire—are building an avid following in the United States and elsewhere. Major races attract over 20,000 participants and prize purses approach $300,000; hence the birth in 2013 of United States Obstacle Course Racing (USOCR), the alternative sport's own governing body. I can relate to the OCR participants' desire to test their mental and physical breaking points, and to extend them over time. But there's still something inherently human and staged in the OCR experience, as with the lawn-mowed fields I've raced on; the obstacles I found in Shotover Park felt authentic.

I finished that run, and the rest of my Oxford runs, inspired to embrace discomfort and to channel the Vigil spirit and Zatopek grit (barring the hypoventilation part). As I did with Mo Farah's golden postbox in London, I made a point to pass the Roger Bannister Track in the final minutes of each run as a physical reminder to find my own limits. As for simplifying my lifestyle, Pat Porter–style, I was already taking baby steps: paring my belongings down to what I could carry in a small suitcase and a backpack, and detaching from my cell phone (the GoPhone I traveled with was meant for emergencies, and generally turned off). For more radical lifestyle changes, I could wait until my visit to Ethiopia in a couple of months. What kind of guest would I be if I were to reject the cozy room I'd been offered in Oxford?

LIKE OXFORD, Cambridge University has educated an army of Olympic athletes, the count surpassing 300 by the end of the 2012 Games (including 123 medal earners, 80 of them gold). One of the most famous of them, Harold Abrahams, was immortalized in the 1981 movie *Chariots of Fire*. Fresh out of Cambridge, he became the 1928 Olympic champion in the 100 meters, also taking home the silver in the 4×100-meter relay. More recently, the announcers of the women's 2012 Olympic 5K and 10K races called attention to British runner Julia Bleasdale, a product of Cambridge's engineering program. Cheered on by a jubilant home crowd, Bleasdale posted eighth-place finishes and personal records in both races.

For the second time that week—a pattern was emerging for the rest of my trip—my e-mail seeking a place to stay landed in the right hands, and I received an offer for a spare room in Cambridge. James Gill, a former Cambridge runner and current triathlete, lived in a house near campus and, though swamped with medical school commitments, invited me to make myself at home. His landlord, Tim Johnston, was a former Cambridge runner and Blues Race champion who later placed eighth in the 1968 Olympic Marathon. When I arrived, I felt like I was entering a private running museum. The living room walls were covered from floor to ceiling with a colorful mosaic of running books, and mementos from Johnston's athletic career were scattered throughout the first floor. Unfortunately, he was out of town during my stay, but I discovered that my temporary landlord was on the front line of a current running trend: While preparing for the 1968 Mexico City Olympics in the host country, Johnston had befriended some members of the Tarahumara tribe—the mysterious endurance phenoms made famous by Christopher McDougall in *Born to Run*—and went on to win the 1967 International Cross-Country Championship barefoot.

My timing was better in Cambridge, because school was back in session, so I was able to meet a handful of cross-country runners. Three members of the team—James, Anthony, and Sam—met me outside of St. John's College to show me where they train, beginning with a running tour of campus. By the time we reached a soft dirt path half an hour later, we'd scratched the surface of famous Cambridge alumni (including a modest ten monarchs), and our discussion turned to running. Differences between their Cambridge running experience and mine at Rice University quickly arose. After either coaching themselves or being coached by a team captain for nearly a century, the Cambridge team had only recently hired a true coach and was still adjusting to the new schedule and sense of dependence. I could hardly imagine myself—much less an entire group of college students—training without a coach, and I also didn't know too many student-athletes with both the time and skills to manage an entire team. Perhaps I'd become too reliant on my coach, wanting specific instructions for every run and constant feedback during workouts, but much of my confidence came from Coach Bevan's thirty-plus years of coaching experience, deep understanding of the sport and the human body, and ultradiscerning eyes. Without him, I'd have a hard time trusting myself to do things right.

Like most university athletic clubs in England, the Cambridge team also lacks a training room and medical staff, so they're left to tackle injuries, strength programs, and recovery protocols on their own. As much as I dreaded ice baths and complained about rehab, I'm indebted to the Rice University athletic trainers for coming to my rescue after I dug myself into a number of holes. Though it may not be a good sign when you're friends with the whole training staff, every person who treated me in college—Candace, Joey, Jonathan, Dean, Dawn, and Adam—had a hand in my successes and an investment in my long-term goals. My conversation with the Cambridge guys reminded me that my access to those resources and individuals were luxuries that, though time-consuming and inconvenient at times, simplified the task of running fast and kept me on my feet.

On the other hand, the pressure one finds in the scholarship-driven NCAA system to perform, improve, and contribute is part of the price paid for those luxuries. In English running clubs, like Cambridge and Oxford, individuals still have to vie for the coveted varsity spots, but without contracts or scholarships, they aren't expected to prioritize running over a social life, other hobbies, or classwork, like at some (often large, state) schools in the United States. So for these Cambridge runners, that 6 A.M. practice might be avoidable after a rough night out, and the last mile repeat of a workout could always be scrapped. . . . But keeping tight reins on oneself is hard, achieving excellence alone even harder.

That's where the importance of team cohesion comes into play. One facet of the Cambridge running experience that I could relate to was the emphasis on traditions, none more cherished than the historic rivalry with Oxford. As we rounded the grass field at the end of the dirt path, a favorite spot for recovery runs, the guys reiterated what Simon Molden had suggested back in London and what I'd seen on the Cambridge Hare and Hounds website: Nothing mattered in the cross-country season as much as the Blues Race. The Cambridge team deliberately trains through every possible condition they might face on race day—mud, rain, hills, and obstacles—so that if they lose, it won't be for lack of preparation or toughness. Between that mindset and Oxford's rugged home course, I wasn't surprised to learn that the all-time record between the two teams was so balanced: a stunning 61 to 61, if you include the 2012 clash three months after my departure.

A more recent tradition of the Cambridge team is the Tea Run. A few years ago, the cross-country captains wanted members of all speeds to get together in a more relaxed atmosphere than practices and meets; the Tea Run was their solution. Each Friday, following an easy run, a different runner hosts the team at his or her place for warm drinks, appetizers, and desserts. My last full day in Cambridge fell on a Friday, so a group of about ten of us jogged a few miles around campus and then gathered in Abi's dorm room to refuel and relax.

Sitting with the other runners, I missed the easy access to my own teammates, and remembered how nice it felt to have earned a spot on the inside. Especially freshman year, the built-in companionship I found among the Rice cross-country girls was priceless; it became apparent I was part of something special when I spent several hours with them at daily practices, traveled with them most weekends, and still chose to spend most free moments with that same group. At Rice, our Tea Run equivalents were our annual Canadian Thanksgiving potluck dinner (celebrating the holiday tradition of our northernmost teammates), post-race meals at Ruggles or Hungry's, and themed dress-up practices on each runner's birthday. As badly as I missed the Rice girls, who by and large defined my college social life, that evening with the Cambridge team was a comforting reminder of one huge advantage of university athletic teams like Cambridge, Oxford, and Rice: Relationships are not only built during practice hours but in the classroom, in dining halls, and in the dorm rooms, too. Not surprisingly, performances on the cross-country course often reflect the bonds that have been forged in all of those settings.

SINCE BEING DAZZLED by the 2012 London Games, my daydreams were increasingly drifting to the Olympics. I could almost visualize how I'd fill the still pre-race hours, what songs I'd hear on my pump-up playlist, and how it would feel to pull on that shiny red, white, and blue singlet.

I didn't expect that the first Olympic uniform I'd wear would be Irish.

"Yes, Becky! Welcome! Daren told me about your trip, and I've got to hand it to ya. That's some good craic." Patsy McGonagle—

godfather of Irish track and field and chairman of a prominent running club—met me outside the Finn Valley Athletics Club (FVAC) Center the afternoon I arrived in Donegal. He swooped me up into a big hug and then showed me around the massive complex, featuring a track, jogging trail, two fields, multipurpose room, dining hall, and locker room, and an indoor pool in the works. The facilities were just as nice as those of a Division I school, yet there was no scholastic affiliation or membership requirement beyond yearly fees.

By temporarily joining FVAC, I'd be part of an inclusive, non–school affiliated running club for the first time. The running club scene in Ireland, as in England and many other European countries, is often more prominent and competitive than the school or university leagues. Each club can encompass a range of abilities, ages, and events (racewalking included), though it's not uncommon for the competition level to wane at the elite level. As a result, a significant number of talented Irish long- and middle-distance runners—including John Treacy (Olympic medalist in the marathon and world cross-country champion), Ray Flynn (national record holder in the mile and runner of eighty-nine sub–four minute miles), Sonia O'Sullivan (Olympic medalist and world champion in the 5K), and Alistair Cragg (national record holder in the 5K and 10K)—went to universities in the United States. For many foreign athletes like them, the competitive, resource-rich NCAA, and the fully funded college education that goes along with it, serves as a stepping-stone to future representation of their own countries.

Wasting no time, Patsy kicked off my visit with three offerings: a quick breakdown of the club's training schedule for the week; an Irish Olympic uniform, fresh from London, where he'd served as national team manager; and a blue and white singlet featuring the Finn Valley crest. He accompanied the last with a good-luck wish for the Donegal Championship 5K a few days later.

"What's that?" Patsy asked, noting the surprised look on my face. "You weren't planning on racing?" I thanked him for the offer but explained that the Trials had been two months ago, and since arriving in London, I'd been running a lot—70 to 80 miles per week—but without any intention of lining up soon, not at all like the three-hard-workouts-per-week structure of college. And if there's one thing I hate, it's lining up unprepared. (Just ask Coach Bevan how I handled his invitation to race in the NCAA Regional Cross-Country Championship a few months after hip surgery and only a handful of runs on land. My team ended up qualifying for nationals through a tiebreaker. But still.)

"Bollocks!" Patsy retorted. "All you have to do is run hard and get to the finish. I'm not asking you to set any records! Besides, you can meet the whole club at the post-race banquet."

If I've learned anything in almost two decades as an athlete, it's that food can be a pretty tantalizing incentive. And that it's best not to argue with a man of Patsy's credentials. In addition to founding FVAC more than forty years ago and building it into a national powerhouse, Patsy has coached a handful of world-class athletes, is Ireland's only three-time national Olympic team manager, and, soon after my visit, received the Freedom of Donegal, the highest possible honor in the county. I promised Patsy I'd see him at the race, kitted out in the Finn Valley uniform.

Just before 7 P.M., club members started trickling into the gym, such a grab bag of ages and body types it looked like a family reunion. FVAC boasts more than three hundred members and forty volunteer coaches, including a handful of multigenerational families. The center, open daily from about 9 A.M. until midnight, is the hub of socialization and activity—not dissimilar to a university locker room, but with a very different clientele.

Once all but a few stragglers had filed inside the gym, Patsy got down to business. After earning the crowd's attention—no small feat for an age range of about six to eighty-six—he analyzed the past week of training, recapped recent race results, and made a few announcements, including details for the upcoming 5K race. Patsy was animated, passionate, and articulate, and reminded me of both a preacher and another coaching giant: Coach Joe Vigil (just "Coach" to those who know him). In addition to masterminding the Adams State cross-country dynasty, Coach Vigil has guided Olympic medalists and about two dozen Team USA contingents, is widely recognized as a pioneer in altitude training and exercise physiology, and is a matchless motivational speaker. The man in front of me suddenly felt a lot less like a stranger.

When he finished, Patsy dismissed the members to their designated training pods, grouped by ability level and overseen by a volunteer coach. Like event groups within a track team, that division allowed the club to serve different strengths among such big numbers. A few groups headed out to the track, others took to the trails or roads, and the rest stayed inside the complex to practice drills and exercises.

As I approached the group Patsy placed me in, Coach Mark's senior group, I noticed the half-dozen runners around me putting on a peculiar accessory: a neon yellow vest.

One of my new training partners explained that the vests were lined with gleaming reflectors to show drivers on the winding, hilly, and eventually pitch-black roads "who the real bosses are." (I wished my mom were around to witness this ordinary Finn

Valley practice, so that maybe she wouldn't feel the need to offer to follow me in her car during my own dark and rainy runs, using her headlights as giant flashlights.)

With a group of five university-aged men and one other woman—the smallest group in the club—I hit the road for their midweek medium-long run. A few of the guys darted off, and I settled in beside Teresa McGloin, a petite brunette in her late twenties who was making a late entry into running. She told me she had limited racing experience, but within the first couple of miles she had demonstrated an easy stride and a natural sense of rhythm that hinted at some considerable potential. As we chatted our way through thirteen miles and the sun sank lower over the horizon, I was thankful for Teresa's company. Without her, I would have gotten either very lost on a dark, desolate road, or ditched my easy run to keep up with the guys; and I would have missed out on all the Finn Valley happenings, too.

About a mile away from the FVAC Center, I followed Teresa onto a narrow path in the woods. Darkness and the scent of pine trees enclosed us, and a cluster of reflectors bobbed faintly ahead. Without a word, Teresa and I kicked our pace up a notch, and then another, the neon getting brighter by the footfall. Just as we reached the final stretch, we caught the lead pack of guys and finished the run all together.

Back at the track, our group punctuated the run with a set of 100-meter strides, exactly as I did in Houston at least once a week—seemingly a staple for runners all over the world. As much as the neon vests we wore reminded me of my illustrious safety patrol career in elementary school, I had to admit that finishing a run in the chilly darkness filled me with a special sense of accomplishment, the kind that makes fanatics out of many runners. It was a different sensation, but no less satisfying, than trudging up my apartment stairs dehydrated and sopping wet after a run in the steamy Houston summer heat. I was learning that sometimes the most worthwhile and transformative runs are not the intense predawn workouts that leave me stiff and exhausted. They're also the slogs in tough weather and high altitude; the short shakeouts in a jet-lagged state; and the runs in the company of new and old friends, who bring to the roads a different perspective than mine.

"There's the American lass!"

"How'd ya go?"

"Did ya dust the lads? Course ya did!"

"Good thing you didn't work out on the track tonight—it was chockablock!"

The workout complete, I joined a slew of FVAC coaches inside the center's banquet hall. Thanks to interest in my project and Patsy's approval, I had an open invitation to their post-run ritual of tea, scones, and chatter. Before then, I had never thought of piping hot tea, heavy on the sugar, and a warm buttered scone as a recovery snack; nor was I inclined to socialize much right after a workout. I was so used to finishing a run, doing a quick stretch and maybe an ice bath, and hurrying home to shower, eat, and get on with my day, that the slow pace and fellowship that followed most Finn Valley sessions were a welcome shift in my routine. The guarantee of food didn't hurt, either.

Even before I first heard the Irish farewell—that long, chipper "byebyebyebyebye" that made me look forward to every parting—the evening was a resounding success. I traded stories with wise and witty coaches, enjoyed their good-natured jabs, and watched Patsy seamlessly transition from coach to grandpa when his grandkids—club members, of course—came around. The club was large but still personal, inclusive, and competitive.

The clear anchor was Patsy, whose "YES, lads!" reverberated long after he was out of earshot. He's assisted by dozens of volunteers and a culture rooted in sportsmanship, health, and cohesion. It's not equivalent to a system like the NCAA, which churns out enormous talent but is driven by scholarships, limited by age brackets, and filled with pressure to perform at the highest level. But that's not what FVAC is shooting for; rather than revolving around the elites, it's a development program and an extracurricular group, a social outlet, and one essential vertebra in the spine of the surrounding community.

KIERAN CARLIN, childhood friend of Daren O'Dea (my Teddington flatmate) and my host in Donegal, swore he worked a regular job. But from what I could tell, the redheaded bachelor spends about as much time acting as Finn Valley social media wiz, sports photographer, and clubhouse greeter as a normal person does at a nine-to-five. Somehow, he also squeezes in a healthy dose of running and hosts an average of four pop-in visitors a day, keeping his teakettle simmering and pantry stocked with biscuits, toffees, and Dairy Milk bars.

A few days into my stay, I began to realize why my host kept such a crazy schedule and was one of the most well-liked guys in town. Kieran's catchphrase seemed to be "No bother!" said with such sincerity that you felt as though you were actually doing him a favor by inconveniencing him. Driving me all sixteen miles of one of my runs in advance, for example. Or playing hooky from work to give me a "class" tour of Donegal. A native of Ballybofey (rhymes with "valley of hay"), a sleepy little town in the northwesternmost county of Ireland, with a population of five thousand and no schools or churches of its own, Kieran put together an itinerary fit for a traveling runner, beginning with a jog through the hilly, verdant, sheep-filled land surrounding his home.

After refueling with our weight in treacle bread—crumbly, dense, and chewy, sweetened by molasses—the first stop on our agenda was the River Finn, namesake of the Finn Valley Athletics Club, for a quick stroll and an ice bath. From the comfort of Kieran's car, the thought of dipping our legs in the chilly water sounded great. A common recovery method, ice baths are a post-workout habit I formed in college, made bearable only by my equally miserable teammates shivering in the cold tub beside me. Once Kieran and I arrived at the river's edge, shed our socks, and poked our toes into the frigid water, however, I suddenly remembered an article by Steve Magness, Houston-based coach and exercise scientist, suggesting that poorly timed ice baths can actually interfere with the body's natural healing mechanism. Surely this was one of those times, so I convinced Kieran that the ice bath could wait for another day. Still warm and dry, we loaded back up and carried on until we found ourselves in the first traffic jam I would call "charming"—I was more than happy to sit back and watch the flock of sheep cross in front of us, steered by their vigilant sheepdog and overalled herder.

A good while later—after a successful photo shoot with a drove of roadside donkeys—we rolled up to Slieve League, home of Europe's highest cliffs and one of Kieran's favorite nature spots. Looming over a turquoise sea and carpeted by grass that stretched about halfway up their craggy peaks, the cliffs could have inspired the magical tower in the Walt Disney logo. I wouldn't have been totally shocked had a family of fairies emerged from them—it's Ireland, after all—but instead, just as we were driving away, a brilliant rainbow stretched across the sky.

Roadside donkeys, one of many sights on Kieran Carlin's tour of Donegal, Ireland.

The rest of our stops, never any bother to the busiest man I had encountered in months, included a massive waterfall, turkey sandwiches in a quiet pub, a farmer's barn where we took refuge during an unexpected storm, and a seaside dinner sourced from the waves nearly lapping the restaurant walls. We were also treated to a quick spin around the Killybegs harbor on the ship where my host's friend, also a runner named Kieran, worked. During his tour of the ship, Kieran led us into a tiny bunkroom that he had converted into a gym, complete with an old-school set of free weights and a treadmill crammed in one corner. The room was about as large as my freshman year dorm room, a wall within arm's reach at all times, but as he explained, "The wall actually comes in handy on choppy days, when I need to steady myself so the waves don't send me flying."

"Don't you feel claustrophobic in here?" I asked. "Especially when you're on the water for months at a time?"

"Oh, sure," Kieran said. "That's why I also run circuits through the ship's hallways. I can do flat intervals if I stay on one level, or do charges up the staircases. The crew thinks I'm crazy, but I'd hate to know what they'd think of me if I didn't get in my runs somehow."

One tenet of Irish distance running had become clear. Like both Kierans, many of the runners I'd met so far in Donegal were what Americans would call hard-core, exuding a "no bother" attitude in matters ranging from favors and rides to weather and athletics. Kieran the sailor spent much of his time in a seemingly hostile running environment, but found enough physical and psychological rewards to make it happen; just as the Finn Valley runners didn't think twice about strapping on a reflector vest and putting in miles long after the sun had set and the air had chilled.

"YES, Becky! Good girl!"

It was strange at first, being spurred on during a race by a coach other than Coach Bevan. But at the same time, it felt oddly comfortable: a commanding voice, conveying excitement and conviction, that both relaxed and energized me. It did take the first few kilometers in the Donegal 5K Championship to stop cracking a smile each time I heard Patsy or one of the other Finn Valley coaches calling me "girl."

Sporting the FVAC blue-and-white-striped singlet, I found myself in a position that I'd tried to avoid during my entire running career so far: racing below peak fitness. Like many competitive runners I know, I'm reluctant to spike up and put myself on the line when I'm not in great—ideally, personal record—shape, sometimes forgetting about seasonal swings and the goal of consistent, long-term development. But this was an unusual circumstance, I had to admit, and as Patsy assured me, I had nothing to lose by lining up and running hard. The fact that I was a total unknown, and was racing for a team in the memory of Shane Bonner, a twenty-year-old Finn Valley runner who was killed in a car accident two years before, humbled me.

My first race since leaving the United States was the Donegal 5K Championship, which I ran on behalf of Finn Valley Athletics Club.

Though it's easy to forget in the heat of the moment, magic can happen when you race for reasons beyond yourself. Some of the greatest efforts I've seen and produced were prompted by self-less motives: my freshman year cross-country team at Rice, who strung together a dream season and rallied together to clinch the NCAA South Regional Championship without our number-one runner; my teammate Callie Thomas, who passed out in the final 400 meters of the NCAA Cross-Country National Championship, after inspiring teammates (and rivals, I'm sure) around her to press hard to the finish; and relay races in general, in which runners, wanting to do well for their teammates, often run faster with the baton than they do in open races of the same distance.

There was very little on the line for me during that Donegal road race, but committing to the effort and letting my competitive instincts take over brought me a whole lot closer to becoming the fearless runner I aspire to be than watching from the sidelines would have. I ran nearly two minutes slower than my personal best 5K time, but I felt surprisingly content when I finished. Besides gaining a little fitness and facing my fear of failure by racing when I wasn't in top form, I was also the second female finisher, behind my friend Teresa, and a scorer for the victorious Finn Valley team. The fifty euro I won officially elevated my status from amateur to professional, and would cover about half of the cost of my next pair of trainers. (Of the many perks I missed from my college running days, free shoes were high on the list.)

THE BANQUET FOLLOWING THE RACE was enjoyable, but the outing that evening was the social highlight of my week. I found out that all you need to ensure a good and rowdy time in Ireland is a warm pub, a bounty of Guinness, and a group of people ready to celebrate. I'm still not entirely sure what we were celebrating that night, but once the drinks started flowing, it was easy to justify more. The successful race . . . that round was on Patsy. A clear forecast for the next few days . . . Dermott was on it. The memories of Shane that these guys so clearly treasured . . . Kieran's turn. My first hitchhiking experience, which I'd tried the day before . . . Well, I offered to pay but the men stepped in (on the condition that I promised not to repeat that adventure).

I had a hard time keeping the lingo straight (Did "plain" mean water and "mineral" mean Guinness? Or was it the other way around?), and I couldn't hold a candle to their alcohol consumption, but I did leave the pub with a few key takeaways. First, a squeeze of black currant juice (tip courtesy of a sympathetic bartender) is a lifesaver in the land of Guinness. Second, I must never let the FVAC gang catch me in an embarrassing act; it will be brought up at every possible occasion, and exaggerated tenfold. But if I want a loyal, steadfast, and entertaining group in my corner, this is the one. And last, if my United States Olympic dreams don't pan out, I have an open offer from Patsy, the ringleader himself, to tap into my Irish roots and put that emerald-green, shamrock-emblazoned uniform to use.

WITHOUT THE MOORING of my own team, yet with my bags stuffed full of new singlets from the clubs I'd visited, I was reminded of the value of a team, and the many possible forms of one beyond what I had experienced at home.

A team player and runner for almost fifteen years, I was surprised to find such a different structure of athletic clubs throughout England and Ireland. Since my very first organized team—the Rams, a coed tee-ball team that Luke and I played on together—I've always represented my school, only joining an outside club when a particular sport wasn't offered. With the exception of the cream of the young athletes crop, who joined expensive private clubs hoping to guarantee college scholarships, school teams were by far the most common, and often competitive, way to go in the United States. And in my family of four active kids—with a record of seventeen practices, games, and recitals in a single Saturday—the private club route wasn't an option.

In England and Ireland, by contrast, nonscholastic clubs are often more organized, popular, and prestigious than the school teams that do exist. In Ireland's Finn Valley Athletics Club, I found a tight-knit group spanning generations and abilities that has managed to preserve the individual experience found in smaller, more exclusive clubs. Under Patsy McGonagle's leadership, FVAC has given the rest of the athletic world a blueprint for doing the same.

The running experiences at Oxford and Cambridge, while tied to academics, represent a more informal system of university athletics than the United States' NCAA. Runners at those schools lack some of the structure of their American counterparts, but have time-worn traditions to look to and iconic role models to follow—like Roger Bannister and the 130-year rivalry between Oxford and Cambridge, exhibited each year in the Blues Race.

England and Ireland were the perfect starting blocks for my journey, providing me with footing and momentum for the next ten months. In those countries, I joined my first team since leaving Rice University—the first of many foreign teams of the year—and reimagined my living situations for the rest of my trip, thanks to my first few hosts who put such a positive personal spin on my experience of their hometowns. But by late September, after two full months in that part of the world, I felt like I'd found my stride, and was ready to settle into a new rhythm in the next leg of my journey. No team will ever compare to those I'd been a part of since childhood—which is, of course, the point of team loyalties—but for now, my impartiality was proving to be as enriching as it was solitary.

BEFORE I MADE MY WAY to my next destination, I had one bit of business to attend to. Like so many in the United States, my family has ties to Ireland: We knew that we were related to a Haugh family in a small village called Kilmihil—my great-grandmother, mom, and aunt had visited them on separate trips about sixty and forty years ago—but we had lost touch, as well as, inconveniently, the Haughs' address. So along with my mom, the ultimate detective, I did a little online sleuthing and found reference to a clan of Haugh boys—in road race results, of course. Though tracking down distant Irish relatives wasn't exactly within the realm of my "global long-distance exploration," I couldn't pass up an opportunity to run the roads my ancestors might have traveled.

We pinned down an e-mail address for the youngest of the group, Padraig, a carpenter in his early thirties. From my first e-mail exchange with Padraig, technically my great-grandmother's cousin's great-grandson, I knew I was in for another Irish treat. He told me bluntly to "get yourself to Kilmihil and stay with my girlfriend Lisa and I until you get tired of us (or the other way around)."

After I settled in, and Padraig and I spent so long trying to trace our joint lineage that we agreed to just be "cousins" from then on, he and Lisa drove me a mile down the road to his parents' house, where Bernadette and Thomas welcomed me like a long-lost daughter, Bernie wrapping me in a warm hug and Thomas showing his affection with a broad smile and deep chuckle. After I borrowed a pair of knee-high boots and a rain jacket, we set off on a tour of the property, maintained over the last century by the hands of our relatives. We explored the rickety old barn and Padraig's greenhouse, greeted the cows, walked through the old hare coursing field (for greyhound racing), and stood on top of Knockmore Hill, the highest in Kilmihil, with an unobstructed view of the village and the land so rich in our family's history.

So close to my family yet so very, very far from my parents and siblings, I felt a pit in my stomach as I looked down over Kilmihil. Knowing that my mom had this same view decades ago brought both solace and sadness, and I could almost hear my dad checking to be sure we'd all noticed every last buzzard and rain cloud, a habit formed on the Texas farm that's been in his family for many years.

Our trek ended in a warm kitchen, and my homesickness lifted with the aromas filling the room. While we were out, Bernie had created a feast fit for Thanksgiving: baked potatoes (a requirement at every meal, as Thomas considered any potatoless plate a snack), roasted chicken, steamed broccoli, carrot and parsley salad, bread stuffing, sautéed mushrooms, and a vat of gravy. Everything was delicious, and before I polished off my plate completely, Bernie piled a second, possibly larger, serving of each dish before me. I kept eating out of politeness, but midway through the second round I had to take a time-out.

Moments later, Bernie reemerged from the kitchen, balancing three dessert plates on her arms, and asked, "Now, which dessert should you start with? I've got—"

"There are options?! Really, Bernie, it's all so good, but I can't possibly stuff one more bite into my mouth."

It turned out, I could. Without the energy to resist further, I found a way to swallow not only a warm currant scone but also a bowl of fresh strawberries, cream, and ice cream. If one of my competitors had paid Bernie off, they'd gotten their money's worth.

FORTUNATELY, I recovered overnight from that marathon of a meal and spent the next few days bouncing from Padraig's house to his parents', receiving royal treatment each time I entered a door. I gradually learned the lay of the land on my runs—not too difficult considering Kilmihil had a single pharmacy and post office, three grocery stores, and five pubs—and Padraig joined me for a handful of them, always sandbagging for a few miles before finishing in a frenzy, followed by multiple reminders of who "won." He helped me perfect the local salute for pedestrians and drivers we passed, refusing to let me embarrass him by looking like a tourist, and gave me the dirt on each of his neighbors—secrets didn't last long around there, I gathered.

On one run, just before he turned for home, Padraig challenged me to run to a massive wind farm that rose from the hills in the distance. I did, and during a seventeen-mile out-and-back run, saw a whopping two cars and one tractor the entire time. The freedom to run in the middle of the road, without worrying about distracted drivers, road-hogging bikers, or even intersections or traffic lights, was a luxury I could get used to. The twisting roads, cozy farmhouses, and rolling hills, which I imagined my relatives had passed numerous times over the last century on foot or by tractor or carriage, made each mile even more meaningful.

Between all the Irish fare I was consuming and my increasing familiarity with the land, I was starting to feel like an authentic Irish "bird" when Thomas sprang something on me that almost completed my transformation: an invitation to the Lisdoonvarna Matchmaking Festival. My first reaction was shock—here was a man who, due to shyness, difficulty hearing, and my unfamiliar accent, had smiled plenty, but had spoken only a handful of words in my presence. Now he, a devoted husband, wanted me, a young unmarried girl, to go single-mingling with him? One hundred percent, yes. Though no one told me what to expect, I could tell from the stifled laughs and groans of Bernie, Padraig, and Lisa that something amusing awaited me—though not amusing enough for any of them to come along.

The first thing I saw when I stepped out of Thomas's car, an hour after leaving his home, was a street lined with colorful banners and a bus unloading what seemed to be the entire population of a retirement home. We tucked into the line, covering ground inch by inch, and finally entered a yellow building called the Matchmaker Bar. Thomas explained that we were participating in a 150-year-old Lisdoonvarna tradition, complete with a full-time matchmaker, that results in countless engagements each year. (Although weekend flings aren't unheard-of, either.)

Thomas Haugh shows off the Matchmaker Bar in Lisdoonverna.

Inside we found a bevy of senior citizens hot-footing it around the checkered dance floor, waiting for drinks at the bar, and flirting in the maroon booths that lined the room. A geriatric prom, I surmised, as I sat down next to Thomas at a table facing the action. Though the average age in the room was probably seventy-five, you'd never know it by the way they danced; I have no doubt that some of them could rival my cousin Jeff and his krumping, if only they knew how, and that's quite a statement. Not only were their feet flying and skirts spinning, but the vocal chords of these old-timers were getting a good workout too. "YOOHOO!" they shouted at the end of each song and after especially impressive dance moves.

I wonder if I can count this as cross-training? I thought a few minutes later as I huffed and puffed around the floor, a little self-conscious that I could barely keep up with dancers five decades older than I. Thomas, it turns out, though otherwise reserved and quiet, found his groove on the dance floor and was determined to help me find mine, too. Along with a dozen other couples, we swung and waltzed and dipped our way through a few songs, following the rhythm the band gave us and switching partners whenever a stranger cut in.

At one point, a couple of bars down the road—dare I admit I was setting a bar-hopping personal record?—a man with two hearing aids approached me in my seat and asked me to dance. After two songs, he held me a little closer and gestured toward Thomas, still sitting, and asked, "Is that your fella?" with a wink for good measure.

"Nooo," I said, stifling a laugh at what my fella back home would say about me now.

ONE OF THE MOST CHALLENGING PARTS of my trip was deciding when my time in one place should end. With the freedom of my itinerary and the advice from Watson headquarters not to get too comfortable in one location, the best time to move on wasn't always clear. Leave too early and I might miss something important, but linger too long and I might wear out my welcome.

On my way home from Lisdoonvarna with Thomas, I knew in my gut that it was time to get moving. I had run, eaten, and wandered my way through a weeklong personal detour, and now felt nearly as comfortable around the Haughs as I did with my extended family in the United States. So in the spirit of my journey, I booked tickets to my next destination, with a full heart and a few extra pounds, thanks to Bernie's daily feasts.

Brown Soda Bread (Bernie Haugh, Ireland)

Served hot with a smear of butter and jam, this bread makes a perfect pre-run breakfast and an equally satisfying late-night snack.

3 cups all-purpose flour
1 cup wheat bran
1 tablespoon baking soda
2 cups buttermilk
Butter and jam, for serving

1. Heat oven to 400° F.
2. Mix dry ingredients.
3. Add buttermilk to dry ingredients, and mix again.
4. Pour batter into a loaf pan and bake for 30–35 minutes.
5. Serve warm with butter, jam, and tea (optional).

3

FLYING HIGH IN A MOUNTAIN RUNNING MECCA

Switzerland
342 miles

As I gazed up at the mountain, craning my neck to see the peak, a familiar sense of nervousness washed over me. From the bottom, it was hard to make out anything but trees, which covered the slope in layers that got darker the higher I looked, from yellowish green to army green and every shade in between. But I knew from our drive there that between the trees stood fields, farmhouses, cattle, wildflowers—and one very steep path to the top.

It had been a few years since my last mountain runs during a summer in Colorado, but my tense muscles and racing heart remembered the drill. Standing at the foot of the mountain, my instinct was to imagine myself struggling upward, breathing hard, suffering intensely, and losing momentum with each step forward. Worst-case scenario: I might not even finish, and I'd embarrass myself in front of my four new training partners.

As tempting as it was to continue down that mental path, I

knew better. A few summers before, Laura Haefeli—a top U.S. mountain and trail runner—had taken me under her wing while I trained for two months in Colorado, helping me transition from pavement to trails and exposing me to the unique challenges of mountain running. Following her lead (which always grew longer on the uphills), I gradually adjusted my perspective on the landscape and our workout. Rather than gazing, starstruck, at the mountain, and treating it as one enormous obstacle, I began turning my focus inward and immediately upward. On each run, I reminded myself of the strength I'd amassed over years of running, fed off Laura's excitement, and kept in mind that the gains I made on the mountain would pay dividends in future races.

Now, in Bern, Switzerland, capital of the mountain running mecca, those lessons were being put to the test.

SWITZERLAND'S NATURAL BEAUTY is a main attraction for any visitor—especially when that visitor spends a substantial part of each day surveying the land by foot. In my year designed around long-distance running, it only made sense to include one of the world's most scenic, idyllic, and running-friendly countries. In my poll of well-traveled runners, Switzerland came up repeatedly.

Beyond the gorgeous views and mountain trails, I had two other motives for including Switzerland in my itinerary. First, I'd heard about the country's punctual trains, orderly post office lines, and cooperative political system (seven collaborative presidents)—and the organized, perfection-seeking planner in me was curious to see if the Swiss athletic world followed suit. Second, I knew that Switzerland would offer a different kind of elite running scene than I'd experienced either at home or in my travels so far: much smaller and more intimate. I wondered how the opportunities for

Swiss Olympic hopefuls compared to those in the United States, and I was fortunate to connect with two girls my age who could fill me in.

Livia Burri was waiting for me when I arrived at the train station in Bern and peppered me with questions the moment I hopped in her car. "Do you have a boyfriend? Do you shop at Abercrombie? I can only go there when I'm in America, so I always buy too much. I have a hill session tomorrow—will you join me? Astrid will be there too!"

Livia, my host, was bubbly, brunette, and athletic-looking, two years older than I with a similar 5K personal record, which in Switzerland was sufficient for elite status and a gear sponsorship. Although Livia had her own small apartment near the marketing office where she worked in central Bern, she had packed her bags to stay with me at her parents' home that week. Her dad, a school principal, spoke great English, she told me, but her mom knew only a few words. I assured her that charades was my second language.

On the mend from an Achilles' injury, Livia had recently resumed serious training with a focus on the upcoming cross-country season, and was excited to have a resident running partner. Normally, she trained alone or with guys, her occasional meet-ups with Astrid Leutert—a talented steeplechaser and recent Florida State University graduate—a special treat. Livia told me about the long uphill tempo her coach had planned for the next day, one of the tougher workouts in her program, and had all but signed me up.

"I don't know, Livia," I said. "I'm used to training in a city that's as flat as a track. Lately I've been focusing on volume, not so much intensity, and it's been a *really* long time since I've run any major hills. . . ."

But Patsy McGonagle's voice was echoing in my ears: "Bollocks, girl!"

The next morning came quickly, and our workout partners met us in the parking lot at the foot of a mountain: Astrid and three men in their early thirties, Christoph, Valentin, and Stefan. During our three-mile warm-up, I tried to avoid looking too closely at the long road headed toward the peak.

The towering mountains, crisp air, and radiant sky reminded me of my summer in Del Norte, Colorado—elevation 7,800 feet and population 1,600—and the heart-pounding anxiety that preceded my first few uphill trail runs. But with every mile that I latched on to Laura, the professional mountain runner who happened to live down the road from the horse ranch I worked at, the more comfortable and confident I felt on her turf. She didn't give me much explicit advice, but she impressed me with her mountain goat agility and unflagging energy on the steep inclines. Once we got going, Laura's steps were nimble and light, even on the long uphill grinds, and she approached the downhills fearlessly. Naturally vivacious, the mornings we met for long mountain climbs—once or twice a week—she was positively buoyant. Most of all, she had a deep appreciation for nature that seemed to continually stoke her fire. She could identify the name and medicinal uses of nearly every plant we passed; she happily paused runs to point out animals in the distance; and once, she carried two huge deer antlers all the way down a mountain so her three kids could see what we'd found—and then insisted that I keep them as mementos from my Colorado summer. After two months, I still couldn't keep up with Laura's dashes up the mountain, but I was finally able to keep her in sight on the ups and match her pace on the flat. Remembering that summer, I felt ready to give the Alps a shot.

After our warm-up, I met Johnny—Livia and Astrid's young coach, who often recruited his friends to pace them. As he described the logistics of the workout, Livia translated for me. We'd be running two uphill charges, between 24 and 30 minutes each, Johnny estimated. He would tail us in his car and shuttle us down between reps so we could preserve our joints and recover on level ground. The road, he explained, using his hand to demonstrate, started kind of steep, soon became steeper, flattened out for a stretch, got steep again, and then rose to a 20 percent gradient for the last couple of minutes. There was no time to speculate or dig for more details; soon I was huddled with the others at the starting point, savoring my last deep gulp of air.

I started in the back of the group, trying my best to "get carried," as Coach Bevan reminded me to do in races at Rice, and narrowed my focus to the stretch of road immediately ahead. It made me a little nervous that Johnny had described the start as just "a little steep"; but as I often do during tough workouts, I pretended I would be finished after the first rep. Time was irrelevant in this unfamiliar workout, but I still had to resist the temptation to glance at my watch at each turn, a guaranteed way to make time seem like it's standing still.

At the halfway mark, I assessed my body and was surprised by how I felt. Tired, increasingly so, but not tortured. Christoph and Valentin indicated that they were going to pick up the pace, and acting on instinct, I moved around the others to stick on them. The three of us got rolling on the next flat section, and I visualized filling my body up with electricity, recharging for the climb ahead. A few minutes later, we curved around a big bend and there was Johnny, leaning on his car. *We must be close,* I thought, finally letting myself glimpse the time and seeing a glorious two at the beginning. All three of us were breathing hard now, and my legs felt like they were turning into stumps, but the tip of the mountain was in sight, and the prospect of finishing propelled me forward.

My watch indicated it had been 25:45 of mostly uphill running, the second-longest incline I'd ever attempted—after one hour-long climb in the nearly abandoned mining town of Creede, Colorado. In the next couple of minutes, the whole group finished, and we caught our breaths, high-fived each other, and loaded up in Johnny's car. Shortly afterward, as we jogged around the starting area in silence, trying to shake the stiffness from our legs, I felt more confident than a half hour earlier. I'd found my Colorado mountain mindset, and I was ready to push harder.

We lined up again, and Johnny assigned a two-minute handicap to Christoph, Valentin, and me. The first group took off, and eager to catch them, we went out aggressively and closed the gap around the five-minute mark. All six of us ran together for a few minutes before splitting up again halfway, the point I'd decided to start tightening the screws. Christoph and Valentin committed to my move. Channeling Laura Haefeli, I focused on taking quick footsteps, keeping my eyes on the path ahead aside from the occasional glimpse of the purple flowers and curious cows beside us.

Soon our trio was down to a duo when Valentin began to fade. As we closed in on the second steep incline, I could tell that Christoph was working; his breathing had become rapid and choppy, and his stride had begun unraveling. I read his effort as an invitation to dig deeper myself, so I found another gear, and again, felt him match it. When we got to Johnny, stationed at his post just before the final climb, I didn't need a translator for his excited shouts and gestures. Christoph and I put our heads down and continued pressing, and I tried not to use our earlier climb as justification for backing off. When the peak became visible, I found another gear, a faint taste of metal filling the back of my mouth. Breathless and spent, all we could muster once we'd finished was a weak handshake.

Our second effort took 24:50—nearly a minute faster than the first—and I felt an unusual sense of achievement. I had no idea how far we'd run or at what pace we ran; but in that rare moment, I didn't need concrete validation or a pat on the back to know I'd made gains. For the first time since my runs with Laura in Del Norte, I thought maybe, just *maybe,* I'd give mountain or trail racing a shot someday. The lack of precision, merciless terrain, and emphasis on effort over pace was a departure from the training I was used to, and the mountains offered a whole new arena for untapped potential.

LIVIA, ASTRID, AND I AGREED that we'd need a few recovery runs after the mountain workout. So the next evening, starting at the Burri home, we ran a big loop of the area, quickly leaving behind the residential backdrop for open farmlands. All three of us were much chattier and more relaxed than our last run together.

Astrid and Livia were longtime friends who had recently become training partners again after a four-year hiatus. Because school and sports were separate in Switzerland, they explained, they'd attended different schools growing up but ran for the same club through high school. Astrid then accepted a scholarship at Florida State University while Livia enrolled at the University of Bern, ultimately deciding to stay close to her family. Though intent on still competing, Livia said she'd been hesitant to enter the NCAA, where some coaches and schools have a reputation for over-racing and burning out their athletes.

The three-season NCAA structure is particularly tough on

distance runners—cross-country in the fall, indoor track in the winter, and outdoor track in the spring and early summer—but it's undeniable that the NCAA also churns out legions of the world's best athletes. In the 2012 Olympics, if University of Southern California athletes and alums were their own country, USC would have finished eleventh in the Olympic medal count with 25 total—more than Canada, Spain, and the 2016 Olympic host country of Brazil. A few other NCAA participants (University of Florida; University of California, Berkeley; and Stanford) also made it into the hypothetical top twenty.

"I can't decide whether I miss Panera or fro-yo more," Astrid said about her college running days. She had moved back to Switzerland after graduating, at roughly the same time as I embarked on my Watson journey, and was still adapting to the running environment she had reentered. Accustomed to joining a dozen or more teammates for daily practice as well as for gym work and social events, Livia was now Astrid's only female training partner; because they lived forty minutes apart and both had full schedules—Livia in a nine-to-five job, Astrid in graduate school—they met up only a few times a week. Livia, coming from a strictly Swiss running background that involved more solo sessions than team practices, could only marvel at the university experiences that Astrid and I described—especially the notion of full-time female training partners and snack-stocked training rooms.

When I asked Astrid why she didn't join a professional running group in Switzerland, I expected to hear that her school schedule would pose a conflict or that she'd have to relocate to a different city. Instead, she laughed. "Switzerland doesn't *have* professional running groups; unless you count small ones like Livia and me, that share a coach and make plans to meet up for hard workouts." Livia elaborated: "Oh no, those don't exist here.

I mean, it's possible to run fast enough to earn free shoes and clothes"—(she was dressed head to toe in Adidas)—"but to be paid to run? You have to be one of the very best." The general rule in Switzerland for runners is that you earn a modest amount of national funding if you hit a standard time for an international championship like the Olympics, world championships, or European championships. Astrid estimated that about a dozen female distance runners received funding (she and Livia included), but that the monthly stipend was, for most, insufficient to live on; they worked, studied, or did a combination of the two, and ran on the side.

I couldn't help but feel grateful for the opportunities available to elite runners pursuing a professional career in the United States: at least a dozen professional running groups scattered around the country, a handful of shoe companies that sponsor athletes, countless sports stores that eagerly employ runners, and a supportive network of other runners. There's no question that running takes a backseat to other sports in the United States, big earners like football, basketball, baseball—heck, just about every other sport—and that the earning possibilities for runners aren't even in the same ballpark as those other athletes. But after talking with Livia and Astrid, the chance to run professionally when I returned seemed to offer even more than it had before.

MY NEXT HOST, Beat ("Be-Aught") Ammann, had also run in the NCAA; but Beat was Swiss to the core, and the perfectionist in me immediately felt at ease. I knew I would be in good hands when I was greeted at the airport by a small-framed, gray-haired man with a gentle voice, holding a REBECCA WADE sign in one hand and a stack of Zurich maps and tourist pamphlets in the other.

The condo that Beat shared with his partner Julia Stokar, also a coach, had such a clear view of Zurich that the city may well have been stretched out below for our personal viewing pleasure. The Limmat River, translucent and minty green, perfectly reflected the narrow clock towers, turquoise spires, gold-embellished buildings, and hilly expanse that hovered over it. But as sprawling as the capital city appeared in the distance, Beat and Julia's apartment was as tidy and minimalist as a museum: clean lines, neutral colors, and no clutter in sight.

Following Beat's itinerary, meticulously planned from the moment of my arrival, we dropped off my luggage at his home—located on the side of a mountain and accessible by tram—and headed to track practice. He coached a local club called LAC TV Unterstrass, mainly supervising the senior group (over twenty years old), while Julia oversaw the younger runners. Beat's group had about twenty people, almost all men, who represented every point on the running spectrum, from just-for-fun joggers to aspiring national team members. The team's only elite female was Mona Stockhecke, twenty-eight years old and simultaneously pursuing a Ph.D. in sedimentology and a marathon in the low 2:30's. Though I got to know her during a stormy eighteen-mile run the next weekend, Mona was out of town for my first couple of days, leaving me to experience a few sessions as the sole female, like she usually was.

When we arrived at the track, Beat's athletes looked ready to run. He shook each of their hands and then revealed the workout for that night: a progressive out-and-back run—twenty minutes away from the track at a comfortable pace, then increasingly faster on the way back—followed by a few longer repeats on the track and some gym work. I could tell that my constant travels had added a few bricks to my shoulders, but

I decided to jump in the training session anyway, hopeful the effort would energize me.

So away we went, eight men and I coasting along a concrete path that paralleled the Limmat River and skirted trendy shops, compact houses, artfully graffitied bridges, and eventually a verdant countryside. I darted around the pack so I could meet each runner, trying not to trip anyone in the process, and I quickly figured out who spoke English and whom I'd have to befriend later, without having to gesture on the move. (I also gained a newfound respect for "joggling"—the competitive sport that combines running with juggling.) When we reached the turnaround point, where our progressive run began, our neat pack splintered and I settled into the second group, led by two men. Like an accelerated version of the Kenyan windup in Bushy Park, we built momentum as we went, and I hung on, but felt my hips sinking and posture slackening with each increase in pace. Five long kilometers later, I followed the guys back onto the track, feeling bedraggled and spent.

Beat was waiting for us on the infield, stopwatch and clipboard in hand. Switching between Swiss German and English, he explained that next we'd be running 3×1,200 meters, jogging a slow lap in between each one. The purpose was to simulate the end of a race when we'd need to change gears with fatigued legs. I joined the guys on the starting line before I could give myself an out, but a few strides in I could sense that my body was not on board. I felt more leaden with each footfall, and by the end of the first interval was lagging behind most of the guys. I jogged straight over to Beat during the recovery lap, embarrassed that he had introduced me as "a star American runner." I started to apologize and explain how zapped I felt, but didn't get very far before he interrupted. "You look tired. Why don't you finish out the session with a nice, slow, barefoot jog on the grass?"

More than five thousand miles from home, here was a textbook Coach Bevan solution. Just as I had done after most hard workouts at Rice, I'd give my feet, among the most sensitive of body parts, the tried-and-true antidote of soft ground and uninhibited contact with the earth. I can't count how many times such a simple solution has brought my legs back to life, and I already felt a difference after just a few shoeless laps. I'd found a new ritual for post-travel runs.

BACK IN THE GYM, the running part of the workout complete, Beat presented his runners with a hand-sketched, laminated sheet of exercises, each one illustrated by a series of drawings. The oversize paper, reminiscent of an architect's blueprints, was filled with arrows, hurdles, cones, human figures, and corresponding descriptions in Swiss German.

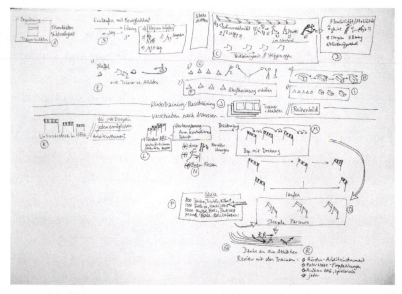

Coach Beat Ammann's diagram of exercises and drills for one of his club's practices.

"Wow! Do you draw one of these for every workout?" I asked Beat, marveling over his artistry.

"Not every single practice," he explained. "Sometimes I reuse the good ones. But the illustrations show proper form at every stage, and the pictures seem to help visual learners like me. . . . I also just really like to draw," he added, noting that he studied art while running at the University of California, Los Angeles.

Diagram in hand, I reviewed the beginning of the drill sequence, shed my shoes once more, and lined up with the other runners behind a long gray mat, about fifty meters of a wide, forgiving, one-lane track. One by one, we went through the exercises under Beat's watchful eye as he suggested small changes to our form along with specific cues to focus on for the next go-round. "Feel as light-footed and free as a kid skipping home from school!" he exclaimed at one point, before discarding his own shoes and demonstrating. His clean and quick movements hinted at his steeplechase skills, honed under legendary coach Bob Larsen at UCLA (still the coach of Meb Keflezighi, whom I cheered on to fourth place in the London Olympic Marathon).

We started out with some basic drills that I'd been doing for years—A skips, B skips, butt kicks, and high knees—and I imagined Coach Larry Jackson, one of my high school coaches, smiling from the sidelines, proud to see me putting his lessons to use and keeping up with my new Swiss teammates. It quickly dawned on me, however, that those early drills were only warm-ups for more complex ones to follow. The new ones required coordination of multiple body parts and reminded me why only one of about ten athletic pursuits had ever panned out for me. Instead of the standard "straight leg shuffle" I knew, I now had to windmill my arms in opposition to my legs; "outward bounds" now included a quick foot sequence in between each bound; and the mini-hurdles we leaped over turned out to be harder to clear gracefully than the thirty-inch ones I practiced on for the steeplechase. But Beat was relentless, and after enough repetitions, I had caught on to most of the drills.

Having primed our muscles to work fluidly and efficiently, Beat instructed us to break out into a twenty-meter stride at the end of the last few drills. The bursts were too short to reach maximum speed, but I could tell that my stride was smoother than when we started, and I almost felt like tackling the track workout again. My favorite drill of the night was a wide side-to-side skip, arms crossing over each other before opening wide (to form a T), that ended in a sprint. To this day, that sequence is part of my pre-workout and pre-race routine.

The group stretched in a circle for ten minutes, and then, a few hours after we'd begun, our work was complete. Beat called everyone into a huddle and complimented us on the workout, and the team broke out into applause and high fives. Finally, the coach ended the session exactly as he had started it: by shaking the hand of each one of his athletes. The professional and respectful atmosphere that Beat created struck me as more like a class than a training session, and it felt fitting; on this trip, I'd become an even more enthusiastic student of the sport.

WHEN I EMERGED for dinner the next evening, a pile of Swiss running magazines and laminated newspaper clippings was neatly fanned across the table like a peacock's tail: contents from Beat's color-coded, accordion-style "junk" folder. He apologized that the only English material he could find was a catalogue for athletic gear, but he'd gathered plenty of track stats and race results with times that required no translation.

Julia joined us at the table and, in her best English, described each dish she had prepared for dinner that night. Some words required extra effort, but with help from Beat and a Swiss-German-to-English dictionary, she eventually got through every ingredient. The main course was a stew made with pumpkin, potatoes, pasta, tomato sauce, and chickpeas, and on the side was a wooden cutting board artfully arranged with bread, cheese, plums, crackers, and jams. To drink, we each had a mug of fresh ginger steeped in hot water, one of Julia's favorite stomach soothers.

Julia made a heroic effort throughout dinner, and the whole week I stayed with them, to communicate with me in English. A few times, while she searched for a particular word, I asked her instead to teach me the Swiss-German translation. I meant to deflect the pressure, but what resulted was a list of vocabulary words, mostly food related, that I jotted below the Swahili words I'd learned from my Kenyan friends in England. *Spatzle* ("little bird") and *knopfli* ("little button"), two of my favorites, described the pasta shapes in our stew and gave new meaning to our dinner.

I learned later that Julia and Beat had agreed to speak only English during my visit. They wanted me to feel included while brushing up on their English, and refused to cave, even when a dictionary was necessary and conversations took twice as long. I placed myself back in the Spanish classes I'd taken for most of my life, and remembered how difficult it was to conjure foreign words, pronounce them correctly, and translate a native speaker's quick, accented sentences into English. My hosts had willingly done that all week long, and though they weren't the only ones, it was one of the kindest favors I'd receive all year.

"BECKY? HI! PLEASE COME IN!"

From our first interaction, Lisa Gubler struck me as my shiest host yet, and I wondered where she got the courage to bring a complete stranger into her home.

Lisa was a sub-elite distance runner in Uster, a city about thirty minutes outside of Zurich. We'd exchanged a few e-mails before I arrived and her passion for running was palpable. "I'm not the fastest, but I'm addicted to running and practice, and you're very welcome in my home," she'd written.

With a sea of freckles, a wavy mane of red hair, and an apron tied around her waist—a sign of good things to come—Lisa led me up the stairs to the spare bedroom next door to hers. At the end of the mattress were fresh towels, more Zurich maps, a Toblerone bar as big as my forearm, and a two-foot foam roller, based on the correct assumption that I'd be hungry and stiff from my accumulated travels. I had come during a down period in her running calendar, Lisa told me—she'd raced her last 10K of the season that morning—and she apologized for not being able to run with me much or take me to her club's practices. Despite her coach's suggestion to take a break, however, she was set on running just enough to show me the best trail nearby, a small act of rebellion that I completely understood. (The length of my break after each season is still a contentious subject for Coach Bevan and me even eight years into our relationship, and there might have been a time or two when my brisk walks progressed to brief jogs during my time off.)

But first, dinnertime. After settling into my bedroom, I met Lisa in the kitchen, an array of pans in front of her and a colorful mound of chopped vegetables to one side. "I hope you like ratatouille and pasta!" she exclaimed. As I watched her move from chopping board to pan, and pantry to pot, dicing and tasting and chatting as she went, it became obvious that running wasn't her only outlet.

Following a habit that began with Vivian Cheruiyot's ugali lesson in England, I recorded the ingredients and steps for Lisa's ratatouille, and many more dishes that week. My original intention for collecting recipes was to commit especially delicious meals to paper, so that I could replicate them later and share foods from my journey with friends and family. Once I explained to my hosts that I planned to assemble a global cookbook at the end of the year, all I had to do was pull out my pen and tiny Moleskine journal, and their favorite dishes or local specialties usually made their way to the table and into my notebook soon after. Though many of those meals, like ratatouille, had roots in other cultures, each recipe contained the chef's personal flourishes and tastes; to capture those, too, I recorded the stories that accompanied each recipe, and the circumstances of the meal.

From our brief e-mail exchange before I arrived, I knew that Lisa belonged to LC Uster, the local running club that wore red and black, and was a graduate student at the University of Zurich. As she cooked, I learned that, besides English, she spoke German, Swiss German, Spanish, French, and Catalan, and knew Latin; was a vegetarian (like many Swiss I met), but swore she could eat her weight in cheese and apples; and specialized in cross-country, the 10K on the track, and longer distances on the roads.

Lisa reiterated that, with a 38-minute personal best in the 10K at the time, she was not considered an elite runner in Switzerland, but was one of the faster local females and had elite aspirations. She traveled to races across Switzerland with LC Uster, and to a yearly altitude camp at St. Moritz. And though she spent the majority of her time at school, Lisa felt most connected to her running teammates; track practice was what kept her going during long, demanding workdays. "School can be really difficult sometimes—my main professor is impossible to please," she explained. "But when I go to practice, all of my negativity disappears. I'm just so happy to be outside and to be running; I already miss it and my downtime only started today!"

Many of my deepest friendships, both traveling and before, had been forged on the run, and I'd worried about getting to know my shy host without many shared miles. But that night, I was thankful that cooking had stepped in when running could not, and I had a hunch that the kitchen was where our friendship would bloom.

In two bowls, Lisa doled out a tangle of pasta ribbons and a scoop of ratatouille with a generous grating of parmesan on top. On the side, she tossed a romaine salad with thin apple slices and herb vinaigrette, sourced from the tree and garden visible from our seats at the table. The solid layer of parmesan on her pasta and salad confirmed her love for cheese, and I made a note in my journal to keep a block of it parked on my table at home, ready to be shaved and savored at a moment's notice.

THE NEXT MORNING, after a bowl of "Lisa's Muesli" (a small diced apple, about a quarter cup of rolled oats, a couple of spoonfuls of raisins, and a shake of crunchy wheat flakes, all doused in whole milk—still a regular in my breakfast lineup), Lisa and I took off down the road for my first run in Uster. About a mile later, we arrived at a small opening in the trees, hidden unless you were looking for it, where a trailhead began. Carpeted with wood chips and weaving through a shadowy evergreen forest, the "Mushroom Loop," as Lisa called it, was her favorite place to run from home and her go-to route for recovery jogs. The transition from concrete to wood chips felt like switching from a summer camp bunk bed to a Tempur-Pedic mattress, and I wondered how different I would feel—and how many injuries I would avoid—

if I moved just a few pavement runs a week to a springy surface like that one.

Lisa pointed out an important junction and repeated the turns that would take me home, then jogged back to get ready for a full day of school. It was odd to imagine that less than six months earlier, I was spending four or five hours a day in a classroom and at least that much time doing schoolwork, with track practice serving as my main and most enjoyable study break. So far on my trip, no two days had been remotely the same: The longer I traveled, the more I embraced an open-ended schedule and the freedom to roam aimlessly. *Progress,* I thought to myself, as I noticed two funny figures poking out of the ground next to the trail. When I got closer, I saw a couple of large fungi made of wood and painted red and blue, staring back at me with big, brown eyes. Lisa's Mushroom Loop.

My friendship with Lisa grew alongside my recipe collection. She did most of the cooking while I played sous chef and scribe, and together we filled eight pages of my journal. With each recipe came a slew of stories. Her apfelmus—a sugary, vanilla-spiked applesauce, made by simmering hand-picked apples—reminded Lisa of summer vacations at her family's lake house near Lucerne, and rösti—a Swiss classic made by shredding and pan-frying potatoes into crisp patties—brought her back to childhood holidays with warm meals shared in a full house. I told Lisa about my mom's lasagna, a layered tower of wide pasta noodles, ground beef, creamy cheese, and fragrant tomato sauce, and a track team favorite in high school. We agreed that it was only fair that Lisa visit me in Texas, so I could repay her kindness and introduce her to chile con queso, the spicy, Tex-Mex version of fondue, eaten with chips rather than bread chunks, and classified by my sister as its own food group. Toward the end of the week, while slicing zucchinis into coins before frying, Lisa spoke for the first time all week of her beloved father, who'd passed away four years earlier. "This recipe was one of my dad's," she said quietly. "He would be so happy that we're making it."

On my final night as her houseguest, Lisa turned her chef hat over to me. I decided to make quinoa- and vegetable-stuffed acorn squash, inspired by a lunch tradition with my sister Rachel and our aunt Debbie. As I diced the carrots, onions, and parsnips, and blanched them alongside peas and corn kernels, I talked about the two women I had shared the meal with last. A Wade family saga inevitably followed.

It felt good to bring family into our friendship, and with both a lump in my throat and a smile on my face, I eagerly described each member of mine in depth at her request. A few steps into the meal preparation, once Lisa could correctly identify the sets of twins in our old Christmas cards (a harder task than it seems), I noticed her behind me with a camera and a pen—the start of her own recipe collection.

WHILE YOU'D ALMOST have to go out of your way to find a bad running spot in Switzerland, there's one place that is "mandatory for a visitor," as my next host put it. Ueli Bieler is a science teacher, coach, marathoner, and triathlete, with a powerful body and head full of thick blond curls—and his words hold sway. He's traveled all over the world training and racing, frequenting Australia, Hawaii, and South Africa, and still, St. Moritz is his favorite summertime spot.

Nearly every Swiss runner I'd encountered had mentioned St. Moritz, a ski resort and Olympic training center in southeast Switzerland. Located in one of the most beautiful parts of one of the most beautiful countries in the world, it's "THE place to be in summer," according to Astrid Leutert. Its appeal includes three hundred days of sun per year, lake water clean enough to bottle and drink, and mountains that attract both world-class skiers and photographers. If that weren't enough, St. Moritz's legacy as host of the 1928 and 1948 Olympic Games, and elevation of 6,000 feet, make it a favorite destination among endurance athletes of all types.

Altitude training has become increasingly popular since 1968, when Mexico City, sitting at 7,349 feet of elevation, hosted the first Olympic Games—summer or winter—at altitude. Still the only Summer Olympic site at altitude, performances there, particularly in track and field, exposed on the biggest stage of all altitude's deleterious effects on endurance events. (It had the opposite effect on explosive events like sprints and throws, evident in the many records that were broken, albeit with an asterisk, that year.) In 1967, foreseeing altitude's influences on the upcoming Games, a group of running physiology researchers including Joe Vigil and Jack Daniels recruited 169 U.S. Olympic hopeful marathoners to Alamosa, Colorado (which has a similar elevation to Mexico City). For six weeks, they administered a litany of tests to each runner, and then offered the world its first comprehensive guide to altitude training.

We know now that living in a state of low oxygen concentration caused by high altitude forces the body to increase its red blood cell production, thus enhancing its oxygen delivery system and resulting in a competitive advantage in races at similar elevations and upon returning to sea level, where oxygen then seems abundant. It generally takes two to three weeks to acclimate to high altitude, at which point hard training can resume, and a rule of thumb upon returning to sea level for a race is to allow yourself fewer than three days (if returning right before the race) or about three weeks. Elite athletes not born with the altitude advantage often seek it at high-elevation training camps in places like Iten, Kenya; Font Romeu, France; Ifrane, Morocco; as well as U.S. destinations in Mammoth Lakes, California; Flagstaff, Arizona; and various cities in Colorado, where I spent half of my summers in college.

After very little convincing, Ueli and I booked our train tickets from Zurich to St. Moritz, set our alarms for 5 A.M., and packed a breakfast of muesli, yogurt, bread, figs, and a bar of chocolate. Candy for breakfast aside, getting there was half the fun. The four-hour ride gave Ueli and me plenty of time to get to know each other and to exchange some vital language lessons. (If I'm ever in a situation that requires me to tell someone in Swiss German that "a small crab is creeping over a small kitchen cabinet," I'll be set.) At one point the train stopped on a bridge where it seemed like one move would send us toppling over the edge into the river below. I was a little worried when a serious-looking, uniformed man came down the aisle and made an announcement in Swiss German, but Ueli kindly translated for me, assuring me that there was nothing to worry about—our parachutes would be delivered shortly.

After we'd barreled through 59 stone tunnels, crossed 196 bridges, and rushed past 20 villages, we finally entered the railway station at St. Moritz. The train screeched to a halt in front of a beautiful crystalline lake, sprawled between a tree-covered, snowcapped mountain on one side, and a multicolored cluster of buildings sloping up the other. First Ueli and I trekked around the perimeter of the lake, fall's first leaves crunching beneath us, as our legs loosened up from the train ride and our lungs got their first exposure to the thin air. From the youth hostel where we stowed our backpacks, he led me on a forty-five-minute run on the dirt trails that branched off in every foreseeable direction. They were neatly groomed and well marked, with options for any type of run: flat, rolling, or straight-up mountainous. The effects of the high altitude were apparent, even though we were only jogging, so Ueli and I took it easy, making the run more of a landscape tour than a workout. The mountains towering overhead were a welcome distraction from my heavy chest and burning lungs.

Ueli Bieler and me at St. Moritz, a two-time Winter Olympics host, popular ski resort, and altitude training spot in southeastern Switzerland.

Backpacks retrieved, we trekked onward, and it became even easier to imagine holing up in St. Moritz for weeks, even months, of training (provided the price tag was not an issue): restaurants for different tastes; swanky shops in the Vail, Colorado–esque downtown; numerous public transportation options and a bike rental program; an affordable youth hostel; apartments available for rent; and an even higher-altitude hotel, located at the tip of the tallest mountain and accessible only by ski lift. The past summer had been an especially busy one at St. Moritz, with a handful of Olympic teams preparing for the Games, on top of the usual crop of summer visitors. While it would have been exciting to see the town buzzing with world-class athletes, the tranquility of our mid-October visit—right between the summer vacation and ski season surges—would still have been hard to beat.

By the end of the afternoon, Ueli and I had covered practically every inch of town and much of the trail system, too, and we'd also done a few strides on the track. I couldn't imagine a more inspiring place to train, and I so appreciated Ueli's insistence that I experience the magic of St. Moritz, even if just for a day. The only negative was that with my new standard for scenic running spots, any future training grounds were already at a disadvantage.

TEN RUNNERS APPROACHED the line wearing long sleeves and tights that blended in with the Zurich twilight. A most unusual competition was brewing, and Ueli and I arrived just in time to dart across the infield to the farthest corner of the track. There, next to the bell ringer, we'd have prime viewing of the TV Oerlikon Track Challenge, Ueli's track club's end-of-season tradition.

Following the last track meet, members of the club compete in a medley of ten races, each one ranging from one to four laps on the 250-meter track. That night, nine men and one woman turned up to race, while Ueli and a few other members did the officiating. By the end of the evening, each person would have raced 4×250 meters, 3×500 meters, 2×750 meters, and 1×1,000 meters to complete the challenge, with a five-minute break in between races.

Members of the Zurich-based track club TV Oerlikon toe the line for the annual Track Challenge.

But there was a catch; the order of the races was a mystery to all but the bell ringer, who drew a slip of paper from a basket before each race, and then gave the signal when half a lap (125 meters) was left in that particular contest. The only result that mattered was place—time was irrelevant—and competitors racked up points depending on where they finished in each round (first place got 14 points, second got 12, third got 10, fourth got 9, and so on). The person with the highest point total at the end of the night would walk away with a cash prize and, more important, a year of TV Oerlikon bragging rights.

During the first few races, the runners had their antennas up, trying out different tactics and gauging those of their competitors. Two men, both middle-distance specialists, set the tone early by charging off the line each race as if they were running the shortest distance (250 meters). If the bell rang that lap, they were in luck, and simply had to maintain their speed for another half lap. If the guys approached the second curve in silence, they settled into a more comfortable pace, fading more and more each lap (like a reverse tempo run) but still jostling for position whenever they neared the bell ringer's post. The long-distance-oriented runners took a more cautious approach, hanging behind the two rabbits in the first lap and relying on their aerobic capacity to help them bridge the gap in all but the shortest races. Still others changed strategies with each start, guessing in advance which distance had been drawn, positioning themselves accordingly, and hoping their speculations weren't too far off the mark.

The true distance runners stole the 750- and 1,000-meter races, as expected, and the guessers snuck in a victory or two. But by the end of all ten races, the middle-distance guys had the win locked down, suggesting that the competition rewarded gamblers, strong kickers, or both. (As a long-distance runner myself, I thought it was a little unfair that only one race extended up to 1,000 meters, but four all-out sprints were included. Where's the love for the slow-twitchers?) I also would have loved to see more females out there, but it was hard to complain about that one from the sidelines. Maybe a split-gender competition or different scoring system would attract more women in the future.

The Track Challenge took just an hour from start to finish but was loaded with drama, risk taking, and humor—a little bit like those bizarre Japanese obstacle course competitions on TV. To fully experience the suspense with the competitors, I resisted asking the bell ringer which distance she had drawn, and I was on pins and needles the entire time. The experience was so far removed from ordinary track meets that I wondered whether the standard all-day format, with similar schedules and long gaps, might be holding our sport back. A few events in the United States like the FloTrack Beer Mile World Championship and the Dallas Marathon Duo to Rio Relay are challenging convention with creative spins on traditional races; and like them, the TV Oerlikon Track Challenge, if imported and publicized, could help bring excitement back to the track.

BEFORE THIS LEG OF MY TRIP, I was right in assuming that I'd be swept off my feet all month long by Switzerland's natural beauty; the majestic mountains, crystal-clear streams, endless trails, and dense, fragrant forests provided an unforgettable backdrop for the hundreds of miles I logged in the land of the Alps. But I'd also come to Switzerland expecting to find a structured and rule-following running culture, on par with my lifelong attraction to rigid routines and meticulously logged training details. Instead, my time there inspired me to be more creative and less habitual in my approach. Each of my hosts—Livia, Astrid, Beat, Julia, Lisa, and Ueli—contributed to this revelation; with them, I conquered intimidating workouts, performed unfamiliar drills on varied surfaces, fueled up with new recipes, ventured to unique training grounds, and rethought traditional competition formats. I never would have anticipated that Switzerland, land of clock towers and Rolexes, would teach me so much about spontaneity—but with nine months of traveling ahead of me, I was grateful for each of those lessons.

And in the name of spontaneity, I swerved deliberately off track before heading to Rome, the departure point for my flight to Ethiopia.

My journey to the Cavicchioli family in Verona, Italy, was an extension of a friendship begun forty years earlier, between my dad, a recent college graduate backpacking around Europe, and Bruno, a charming Italian architecture student. A week after they became fast friends on a train in Italy, my dad pried himself away from Bruno's family's home, a few pounds heavier and one friend richer. After decades of phone calls and letter writing, and one reunion in Texas, the two men passed the torch to the next generation when Bruno's daughter Sara visited my family in Dallas. Four years later, my older siblings visited the Cavicchiolis on *their* European backpacking trip. Now it was my turn to rekindle the Cavicchioli-Wade connection while I was in the vicinity.

So with a week to spare before I was expected in Ethiopia, I finally got a taste of the family (and food) so firmly imprinted on my dad's and siblings' memories. Sara and I made up for lost time with Swiss-Italian Zumba lessons, frequent espresso runs, and late-night discotheques, fueled by Bruno's otherworldly meals. One night he treated us to six rounds of his legendary wood-fire pizzas, crafted with local ingredients and thirty years of practice, and served alongside an epic cheese board and a batch of home-brewed beer. I'm glad I didn't turn down a slice of the last pizza he served, even though my stomach warned me against it; the combination of apple, Gruyère, and cracked pepper was easily the best pizza I've eaten to this day, well worth my discomfort for the rest of the night.

My runs that week were entirely solo, none of them hard— and I was surprisingly okay with that. Normally, I'd be eager to keep my string of good workouts rolling, chasing steady drops in times and jumps in workouts, and illogically fearing a loss of fitness in a few short days. But I decided to treat my limited time with the Cavicchiolis as a vacation for myself and a mini taper for my legs, keeping in mind that two months of thin-aired, blistering runs awaited me in Ethiopia. So as I meandered through vineyards, under archways of old stone churches, and along a slippery lake path, trying my best not to calculate mileage or estimate paces, I could almost sense the Coach Bevan beam—that wide, teeth-baring smile that reveals itself after especially good races or other signs of progress in his athletes.

ON THE EVE of my departure from Rome for Ethiopia, my host Alessio Punzi (former communications officer for the Rome Marathon) led me on a night tour from his apartment. As he pointed out the landmarks—the Colosseum, the Arch of Constantine, and archaeological sites illuminated by the night sky—each looked more like a scene from *Gladiator*. Carefully choosing my steps as we walked, I wondered how the cobblestones beneath me would feel without shoes. The size variation was enormous and the cracks between them gaping—but that didn't deter barefoot Ethiopian marathoner Abebe Bikila from winning the 1960 Rome Olympics on that very road, and announcing the arrival of East Africans to the world of competitive distance running.

Since then, Ethiopia has cultivated an unprecedented depth in long-distance runners, along with its next-door neighbor, Kenya (off-limits to me by Watson Fellowship rules due to a U.S. travel advisory in place at the time.) Consider this: Among the fastest fifty marathons run in 2014, twenty-six were run by Kenyans and twenty-four by Ethiopians. The first non-Kenyan or non-Ethiopian doesn't even appear on the list of top marathoners until number seventy-two, and if you consider Essa Rashed a Kenyan (his original citizenship), the first non–East African barely cracks the top one hundred (with Kohei Matsumura of Japan in the eighty-sixth spot). Since 1981, those two East African nations—whose combined populations account for less than 2 percent of the world's inhabitants—have won every IAAF (International Association of Athletics Federations) World Cross-Country Championship on the men's side, and all but one on the women's side (the lone blemish on their record coming from a surprising Portuguese victory in 1994; Ethiopia and Kenya finished in a close second and third).

Even while touring one of the most historically significant cities on Earth, running along the trails surrounding Rome's Appian Way, and sampling the addictive gelato, my mind was preoccupied. I couldn't stop thinking about the warm, talon-shaped country sitting just above the equator in the Horn of Africa: my home for the next two months.

Rösti (Lisa Gubler, Switzerland)

This traditional Swiss dish consists mainly of potatoes, a staple of runners across the world, which are boiled, shredded, and pan-fried into crisp pancakes and are enjoyable as a breakfast side or dinner entrée.

1½ pounds white potatoes
1 teaspoon salt
1 tablespoon oil (sunflower seed or olive)

1. Steam or boil potatoes (to soften), preferably the night before.
2. Peel and grate potatoes. Mix with salt.
3. Heat oil in a small pan over medium-high heat.
4. Add potatoes to pan, turn heat to high for a few minutes, and then turn to low, stirring and patting occasionally.
5. Cook potatoes until firm and golden brown on each side.
6. Slice into wedges and eat immediately.

4

FOLLOWING THE LEAD OF THE YAYA GIRLS

Ethiopia
552 miles

"FATASHA! FATASHA!"

As a bright blue minibus barreled down the road toward us, the young man riding shotgun, torso out the window and an arm clinging to the top, shouted the name of the next stop. It wasn't yet 5:30 A.M. and seats in the twelve-passenger vans headed to Addis Ababa from the neighboring town of Sululta were a hot commodity that, depending on traffic, the driver's level of risk taking, and his relationship with the local police, might be crammed with twice the legal number of passengers. A week into my visit, I'd had to sit on a chain saw motor during one ride, but usually was jammed in the back, squeezed between strangers or on the lap of a fellow runner. Today, Meseret, Derartu, and Banchi—the "Yaya Girls" and my eventual closest girlfriends in Ethiopia— were taking me and two others to run at Mount Entoto.

"FATASHA!" the conductor called once more, and we hurried into the road as the driver slowed the vehicle just enough for us to slip through the sliding door. It reminded me of a rolling track start, jogging to the line rather than starting from a standstill. Onward we charged, the unwieldy van making moves I'd be scared to attempt in a Ferrari, occasionally offering alarming views down the side of a cliff. With each swerve, the tangled swath of pink fur that hung from the van's ceiling swayed in unison with the passengers, while the collage of bridal portraits, saints, and Ethiopian pop star Teddy Afro stared back at us from the dashboard. This particular driver had the foresight to honk his high-pitched horn every time we approached a curve, warning other drivers of his presence before charging through it, usually in the dead center of the road. Without stop signs, stoplights, or designated lanes, and with droves of pack animals plowing through the streets, it seemed to me a miracle that every ride didn't end in catastrophe.

Ten minutes later and seven birr (about thirty cents) lighter, the six of us leapt out of the van at Fatasha, a neighborhood with a single market stall and a cluster of thatched huts. Our real destination—the village we would start our run from—was still one hour of strenuous, vertical hiking away, via a road unfit for cars. With the sun barely creeping over the horizon, we started the trek up Mount Entoto: 10,500 feet at its peak and the training grounds of some of the world's most decorated distance runners, including Meseret Defar, the Bekele brothers, the Dibaba sisters, and Haile Gebrselassie. Along the way, we passed uniformed kids hustling to school, adults flocking to morning mass, shopkeepers opening their stalls, and Addis-bound workers heading down the mountain. My lungs were burning and my quads were shot by the time we finally reached Entoto Maryam, the multicolored, circular Ethiopian Orthodox church located in a village on one of the mountain peaks. Our workout was about to begin.

DAYS EARLIER, when I'd emerged from the plane at Bole Airport into throngs of boisterous minibus drivers seeking passengers, I felt worlds away from the sacred city I had just left. But as promised, waiting in the baggage claim area was Joseph Kibur, an Ethiopian-born, Canadian-raised businessman—and my saving grace for this part of my trip. A little overwhelmed by my new environment, I breathed a sigh of relief when I saw him.

Earlier that week, my original plans for Ethiopia had gone from perfectly organized to worryingly uncertain. I'd been thrilled to discover Running Across Borders (RAB), a nonprofit social enterprise supporting grassroots athletics and sports travel in East Africa, and had built my itinerary around it. But in a last-minute Skype conversation, the cofounder had informed me that RAB was "experiencing some issues"—specifically, the apartments for visiting athletes, where I'd planned to live for two months in Addis Ababa, were indefinitely unavailable. My good luck with hosts was bound to run dry eventually, I thought, heart sinking at the prospect of beginning the most anticipated leg of my trip alone in a hotel, with no plans and no connections.

In a moment of desperation I e-mailed Joseph Kibur, whose name I'd come across months earlier while searching for a place to stay. After living through the 1983–85 famine in Ethiopia, which resulted in hundreds of thousands of deaths and left millions of citizens destitute, Joseph relocated to Canada and charted a path of unusual success, winning the 1993 Canadian Cross-Country Championship and cofounding NetNation, a Web hosting service that eventually sold for millions. Unable to forget the jarring inequality in his homeland, Joseph returned to Ethiopia, his heart set on improving the living conditions and opportunities for his countrymen. His latest project was Yaya Village, the training camp and hotel complex he cofounded with Ethiopian running icon Haile Gebrselassie, staffed by locals and offering a unique female runners' scholarship program. It sounded like the ideal base for my Ethiopian running explorations, were it not for my limited funds.

I'm not sure what I expected from Joseph's response—perhaps information about a conveniently located hotel, or a family that rented out a spare room. Certainly not an invitation to stay for two months at Yaya Village in exchange for help with the pilot phase of the Yaya Girls Program. But there he was at Bole Airport when I landed, this impossibly generous, optimistic, and pragmatic man, larger than life yet barely taller or heavier than I. As I rode in Joseph's car through Addis Ababa—the most populous city in Africa's most populous landlocked country—and witnessed the chaotic roads and fearless drivers for the first time, my concern was not for my life, but that the proposed arrangement in our brief e-mail exchange was too good to be true.

Forty minutes later, my worries gave way to excitement when we pulled up to a marble sign announcing my home for the next eight weeks: YAYA VILLAGE, sitting almost 9,000 feet above sea level in Sululta, the capital's smaller, rural neighbor. The disparity between the world-class training camp and hotel complex and its surroundings was glaring. Sululta is mostly dry, barren land, dotted with stick-and-mud huts and patches of eucalyptus plants. Thin, barefoot locals are always on the move as they guide animals, work the land, and travel to church and school. Against that backdrop sits Yaya Village, a destination for international visitors and well-to-do Ethiopians, featuring comfortable hotel rooms, a restaurant and bar, conference center, outdoor cabanas, and a horse trail. For runners it also offers a one-kilometer dirt track, backdoor access to both flat and hilly runs, sports fields, a fully equipped gym, visiting masseuse, and sauna. I felt a mix of guilt and gratitude whenever I entered the big iron gates.

Our first stop was the restaurant, to meet the Yaya Girls: Meseret, Derartu, and Banchi. By finishing at the front of a local Yaya Village–sponsored race, advertised by word of mouth and on the radio, the three women had earned four-month scholarships that covered room, board, and English and career-skills classes, and had entered their very first structured running environment.

The youngest and fastest of the Yaya Girls was Meseret. Tall and thin, Mesi wore her hair in tight braids and had a cross tattoo in the center of her forehead and a stitchlike pattern along her right jaw, symbols of Ethiopian Orthodoxy. Although shy, she had a quiet confidence and an exceptional work ethic. Derartu, twenty-two years old and only a hair above five feet, was strong and kindhearted with an infectious laugh. A natural nurturer, she quickly took to scolding me for not wearing pants on brisk morning runs, encouraging me to eat more each time I shared meals with the girls, and showing her affection by linking arms with me when we walked. And Banchi, the "house mother," with ringlets always tied back in a ponytail, was dependable and generous, eager to share whatever she had, from her food to her possessions. Banchi was also the best English speaker of the trio, having completed part of high school, an unusual feat for an Ethiopian female.

The six-foot-two blond guy towering over three slight, coffee-colored girls was the "long" Brit, as the locals described him: Daniel Price, a twenty-three-year-old 1,500-meter runner with a master's in exercise physiology. Like me, he wanted to travel and continue training after college, and Yaya Village had crossed his radar at the right time. Daniel had been there for six weeks already, would stay for six more months, and was loaded with tips—telling me that local time is six hours earlier than Ethiopian international time, "but it doesn't really matter because no one pays attention to time around here"; not to be alarmed by the loud, low wailing coming from the neighborhood church from 4 A.M. until noon every Sunday; and finally, "If you hear any comments about, say, the kilograms you've put on, even when you've *really* just added some muscle to your frame, don't be offended. Ethiopians are extremely friendly and extremely honest."

A few days later, a second Brit, Julia Bleasdale, joined the mix. Five foot six, lean, and thoughtful to her core, she'd trained in East Africa before and was back for six weeks of preparation for the U.K. World Cross-Country Trials. Julia was a few months past her Olympic debut, where she'd finished eighth in both the 10K and 5K, the second non-African in both events. She was Cambridge-educated (a former champion of the Blues Cross-Country Race) and currently training alone, though technically a member of the Melbourne Track Club, based in Australia. With a wealth of experience on the track as well as in the mountains, where her passion for running began as a child, Julia became my stand-in big sister and completed our Yaya posse.

WHEN BANCHI, Derartu, Mesi, Dan, Julia, and I finally reached Entoto Maryam Church on that early morning my first week in the country, the elevation hit me hard. Although the lightheadedness forced me to my knees for a quick rest, I knew there was no use waiting for acclimatization; it could take weeks at that height. Dan, Julia, and I stripped down to shorts and T-shirts, preparing for the quickly rising temperature, while the Yaya Girls stretched on a nearby boulder. Like the Kenyan runners in London, they generally preferred to run in full tracksuits, even in the warmest months of the year. We approached a market stall where an older lady sat amid the usual street goods: candy packages, cookie tubes, soda cans, water bottles, and an abundance of trinkets— neon hair scrunchies, Chinese finger traps, and other items suitable for an arcade vending machine.

"Selam!" the woman said, revealing a mostly toothless grin. Julia had built a relationship with her on an earlier trip, and the woman clearly was delighted to reunite. After exchanging greetings, we handed her two backpacks stuffed with our warm-ups and water bottles. Our unspoken agreement was that, in return for the safekeeping of our bags during our run, we'd buy drinks and snacks when we got back—a post-run snack for Dan, Julia, and me, but always the Yaya Girls' first bite of the day, since they preferred to run on empty stomachs.

"Amasegenallo!" we yelled, thanking her in unison as we started down the dirt path that began as a narrow alley before expanding into a wide, rolling mountain road, even more unfit for cars than the one we'd hiked up.

I'd been in Ethiopia only a week but had run enough (once or twice per day) to know what to expect. The captain of the day— today, Derartu—would take off into the forest like a mother duck with her chicks in a single-file line behind her, choosing any pace and any route, no matter how serpentine or perilous. It didn't help to ask for specifics in advance; rarely was the distance or speed predetermined—as I learned on my very first day, when the thirty-minute run I'd requested lasted over an hour, and no one but Dan and I seemed to notice. The girls were unable even to estimate their weekly volume. ("Twenty miles?" Banchi had responded when I asked her how many miles or kilometers she typically runs in one week. Sensing my shock, she said, "Maybe one hundred?")

Beyond dictating the logistics of the run, Derartu's primary responsibilities as the line leader were first, to warm everyone up gently—the pace after that was up to her discretion—and second, to set off the chain of snaps and finger points whenever an obstacle such as a root or a crack in the dirt arose: the warning system among Ethiopian runners. I assumed that the incessant snapping I heard ahead of me was for rhythm, like an oddly calibrated metronome, and my first couple of runs there, before I'd caught on, were among the most challenging of my trip. *Why on earth are we zigzagging through this uneven field of eucalyptus plants, circling the same tree over and over, when there's a perfectly good running path just a few meters away?* I'd wondered, feeling more and more flustered. With limited visibility, and the ground in front of me packed with crevices and holes, I kept kicking roots, tripping over rocks, and coming dangerously close to twisting an ankle.

Amente leads Derartu, Meseret, Banchi, Dan, and me through a eucalyptus forest in Sululta.

But now, ten Ethiopian runs deep, I stopped hoping for smooth routes, and treated every snap as a red flag. As the six of us continued our ascent up Mount Entoto, my focus shifted from the incline ahead to a flash of movement in the forest to our right. A brightly clothed figure, a bundle of branches on her back, was also trekking up the mountain, not at our pace but much quicker than our earlier hike. I made out a woman's silhouette beneath the patterned cloak, a headpiece covering her hair but nothing between her bare feet and the rough carpet of earth below her.

"A firewood carrier," Dan explained from one position ahead. "These women hike up and down Mount Entoto every day, dawn to dusk, collecting eucalyptus branches to be sold in the marketplace. For less than a dollar a day." The torturous work can permanently cripple them from a very young age, bending their torsos ninety degrees even as they remain nimble. But as contorted as some of their bodies were, most of the firewood carriers I saw moved with extraordinary strength and grace. *How fortunate I am to get so much enjoyment from running,* I thought. Exercise to these women meant something much different: an obligation, a livelihood, and an arduous and backbreaking means to survival.

For this run, Derartu kept the pace comfortable, not ramping it up as we went, as the leaders sometimes would do. She made up for going easy on us by seeking out every creek, crack, and fallen branch to hop over—good steeplechase practice without the hassle of setting up any wooden barriers or filling up a water pit. Julia's footwork was impressive, as quick and effortless as the other girls, while Dan and I clumsily tried to both keep up and remain upright. Joseph Kibur had explained to me that the Ethiopian running style and preference for rough terrain was a major reason that they consistently performed so well in international cross-country meets. Experiencing it day after day, averaging about one fall per run, I wholeheartedly agreed.

After ninety minutes or so, with Entoto Maryam Church signaling the end of our descent, Derartu stopped our convoy. Maintaining our line, she led us in the exercise sequence I'd been learning since I arrived, which capped off every single run, no matter how short or lengthy. Following Derartu in a closed circle, beginning a new exercise after each rotation, we hunched our shoulders and swung our arms side to side; opened and closed our arms to make the "touchdown" symbol; alternated kicking each leg straight up; twisted our torsos, clasping one hip with both hands every other step; and practiced quick arm swings with slower, coordinated footsteps. Afterward, Derartu led us in a few stretches, not unlike the ones I'd done with my teammates in Texas. And finally, we walked the last ten minutes back to the market stall, our run officially complete. One more hour of walking and a final minibus ride would put us right back at Yaya Village, where we'd begun nearly four hours earlier.

I CAME TO KNOW the Yaya Girls through a variety of activities. Our daily runs—or, more conducive to conversation, the warm-up walks, mid-run stretching breaks, and post-run exercises—were just one of them. On the weekends, we spent hours vigorously scrubbing our clothes in the sun, using a set of colorful plastic buckets and soap purchased at a market stall. And each day, Dan and I spent at least one hour in the room Mesi and Derartu shared on the other side of the Yaya campus. As their English teachers, we focused on basic words and phrases that we hoped would come in handy for future jobs in tourism. The classes doubled as an art period when we brought along coloring supplies one day, and realized that in their education—for Mesi and Derartu, through middle school—they'd never been taught how to draw.

About once a week, the girls invited Dan and me to their room for a coffee ceremony, a cherished Ethiopian tradition. My first invitation came the weekend after I arrived. Dan and I approached the girls' door, hoping we weren't interrupting a nap—a guarantee after morning runs and often in the afternoons, too. Before we had a chance to knock, Derartu burst out, gripping our hands and guiding us to our designated seats on the girls' beds. Also present were Atersaw, the hotel receptionist who had recently discovered Facebook and was obsessed with capturing the perfect profile picture; Berhanu, the gym manager with a soft laugh and a chinstrap beard; and Amente, Yaya Village's kind and masterful running guide for foreign guests.

"Welcome!" Derartu said, proud of using the word we'd recently taught her, and returned to the upturned crate in one corner. The room was awash with the smell of candles and incense, and a fresh layer of long grass carpeted the wood floor. In another corner, a tiny electric stove propped up a pan, and a pot sat on a small coal fire. A black box with six miniature porcelain cups, one full of pure white sugar, rested on top of the grass in the middle of the room.

"Welcome," Mesi repeated quietly, vigorously shaking the small yellow kernels in the pan atop the stove. "Shimbra!" she said, identifying the tiny bits.

"First," Banchi said, "clean." She walked around the room with a plastic pitcher and a bucket with a bar of soap inside, and invited each of us to wash our hands while she trickled water over them. We dried our hands on the towel draped over her arm, and then Banchi and I traded roles so she could wash her hands as I poured the water. This was the way that each coffee ceremony and meal began and ended.

"Now, food," Banchi said, while putting a paper plate brimming with popcorn, orange slices, a single Oreo, and a few caramel candies on one of the beds. I recognized the food from the market stalls all over the area. "Belu! Belu! Eat! Eat!" Banchi exclaimed, alternating commands in Amharic and English as she scooped up a small handful of popcorn and brought it to my lips. This was my first *gursha* experience—being fed a mouthful of food—and though odd at first, I learned to appreciate it as an intimate act of friendship. For the next half hour, the girls continued to replenish our plates with more popcorn, orange slices, and the hard, popcorn-like shimbra kernels Mesi had toasted. Every few minutes one of the girls would wave her hand toward our plates, urging us, "Eat! Eat!"

"Eshi," I responded over and over, *Okay,* as I put to use the stomach-stuffing skills I had honed from Bernie in Ireland and Bruno in Italy.

As we ate, Derartu roasted coffee beans over coals until they blackened and popped, then ground them to powder with a mortar and pestle. She brewed the grounds with water over a fire, frequently testing the drink's doneness with quick slurps. Once satisfied, she dumped two heaping spoonfuls of sugar into each tiny cup and poured the steaming, syrupy black liquid over it, adding another hefty dash of sugar to the top for good measure.

Derartu and Mesi prepare coffee and shimbra in their room for my first Ethiopian coffee ceremony.

Mesi and Banchi served Dan and me our drinks, then Atersaw, Berhanu, and Amente, and joined us on the two beds with their own cups of coffee. Each time one of the girls handed out a cup, she extended one arm out straight and touched the inside of that elbow with the other hand (forming a number six), followed by a slight bow. My first few meals in the Yaya Village restaurant, I felt uncomfortable being on the receiving end of this gesture. But as time passed, I began to use it myself, while also mastering the shoulder bump (tapping right shoulders with a friend as an informal greeting, and sometimes going back for a second bump) and the traditional Ethiopian handshake (a symbol of respect similar to the restaurant gesture, with the left hand supporting the right elbow).

As Dan had warned, the coffee tasted nothing like the American drip or European espresso I'd grown accustomed to. It was much sweeter and more viscous, meant to be sipped rather than gulped. The ceremony itself, not so much about the caffeine buzz or food, was a special tradition that revealed a small part of a beautiful, communal culture. As my friends and I sipped, nibbled, and laughed until the coffee ran dry and "Eshi" (*Okay*) turned into "Baka" (*Enough*), I knew that, for me, coffee would never again be just another morning staple, afternoon pick-me-up, or pre-race ritual.

CAPTIVATED BY THE COFFEE CEREMONIES in the Yaya Girls' room—nearly a daily occurrence for them—I made finding coffee a priority each time I ventured to Addis Ababa. At first I was disappointed. I'd heard the legend that an Ethiopian goatherd named Kaldi discovered the coffee bean after his goats ate them off a tree and broke out dancing, and I knew that the country exports some of the finest beans in the world. But it was impossible to find big cups of strong, black coffee like the ones I drank daily at home (unless I went to Kaldi's Coffee, a Western transplant and nearly identical copycat of Starbucks).

In time, the Ethiopian coffee culture won me over, glass by glass of the sugary (or, in some parts of the country, salty) brew. On my first outing to Betty's Buna, a hole-in-the-wall establishment and my friend Xavi's morning stop on his way to work, it became clear that the social connection was as important as the coffee itself. Four birr (approximately twenty cents) bought a steaming cup like the ones I shared with the Yaya Girls, and a seat on one of two wooden benches so close together that bumping knees with the person across from you became part of the experience.

While I ate the majority of my meals in the Yaya Village restaurant, which caters to both Western and Ethiopian tastes, my favorite food explorations were led by Xavier Curtis, a go-getting

Washington, D.C., native who was a few months into a five-year stint in Ethiopia. He's the Yaya Girls program coordinator on top of his daytime job, and along with his girlfriend, Eliza Richman, his ongoing mission is to unearth the capital's most delicious and authentic eateries, which has since evolved into a popular walking food tour called AddisEats.

My first weekend there, Xavi and Eliza introduced me to nearly every Ethiopian dish that would fill my plate over the next two months. Along with Dan, we went to a restaurant down the road from Yaya, sat beneath a straw hut, and shared a feast composed of many layers, served hot on a platter reminiscent of an oversize Frisbee. Injera, the spongy, pancake-like, slightly sour Ethiopian staple made of teff flour and loaded with nutrients, was spread across the bottom of the tray and rolled up around the edges. Covering it was an array of colorful, textured mounds: beef and goat tibs (pieces of sautéed meet); doro wat (stew with chicken); goben (boiled, buttered, and spiced collard greens); ayibe (a drier, crumblier cottage cheese); shiro (a deep red stew made of ground chickpeas, onions, tomatoes, and a spice called berbere); and a boiled egg in the middle.

A small bowl of mitmita (a mix of African bird's eye chili peppers, cardamom, cloves, salt, and often other spices like cinnamon, cumin, and ginger) came on the side, along with a paste made of berbere, and I became hooked on both during that first meal. By the end of my stay, I was liberally dousing most dishes with them—shiro, tibs, wat, and even rice and omelets. In Ethiopian style, Xavi, Eliza, Dan, and I crowded around the platter, tore off pieces of injera with our right hands—first from the rolled-up border, then from the soggy, flavorful bottom—scooped from the various dishes, and quickly devoured every morsel.

While that meal reflected traditional Ethiopian cuisine, I

found that the runners I spent time with ate differently. When I asked them, all three of the Yaya Girls told me that bosena shiro, chickpea stew with ground beef, was their favorite food. But meat is a delicacy in Sululta, and I usually saw the girls eating either injera and shiro without meat, or some combination of white pasta, white potatoes, and fluffy white rolls from a local market stall. Other than oranges, fresh fruit isn't a substantial part of their diet—there aren't many options available around town—and vegetables don't take up much room on their plates, either.

Such a simple, carbohydrate-ruled diet is typical among Ethiopian runners, whether through habit, preference, or availability. While Americans are quick to swear off bread or whatever food is taboo at the moment, citing health and weight concerns, elite runners from Ethiopia and Kenya—the best in the world—have been found to consume between 64 and 76 percent of their calories in carbohydrate form. As one article posits, that's like "'carbohydrate loading' every single day of training." The difference is that East Africans, unlike some Americans, aren't socialized to eat until they're stuffed or to spend many hours a day sitting at a desk, nor are they inundated by addictive, processed foods at every corner. I was surprised to hear from Joseph that food is actually a limiting factor in Ethiopian running, especially in rural areas; because many runners simply aren't able to consume enough calories to fuel high mileage, their volume may be lower than their counterparts' across the world.

One of the most memorable meals of my trip occurred after an hour-long run with a new friend I met running on Mount Entoto. Zewdenesh appeared to be a strong runner, but for one limitation: Every few minutes, she had to bend down and scoop out the rocks that had slipped into her tattered shoes. When we finished our run, I insisted on a shoe swap, and after many refusals, she squeezed my size sixes onto her much larger feet before wrapping me up in a comparably tight hug. In return, Zewdenesh invited me to lunch at her nearby home, a small structure with dirt floors, low ceilings, and upturned crates for seating. She then proceeded to use up almost every item in her pantry for our meal of injera, shiro, lentil wat, and rolls. After preparing a full coffee ceremony to finish off our meal, she stuffed little candies in my pockets as I walked out the door.

Like coffee, food in Ethiopia is not just sustenance or energy for training or work. It's infused with meaning, and three times a day brings friends, families, and sometimes total strangers together to socialize and relax.

When I became comfortable running off-road and hurdling objects in my path, I decided to make my first solo trek up Mount Entoto. Heeding Coach Bevan's reminders to "respect the altitude," I'd been taking it easy as I acclimated, occasionally running alone to ensure a leisurely pace. If I wasn't in line behind one of my friends, I usually went to Satellite Field, a thick, grassy expanse two miles from Yaya that was a favorite among locals, and felt welcomed by the running groups that brought it to life in the early mornings. The runners, who ranged from teenagers to young adults and all looked blazingly fast, flashed me smiles as we passed one another and cheered me on in their language or mine: "*Aizosh!*" "*Berta!*" "Don't give up!" "Be strong!"

Aside from the altitude and running style, I had a couple of other adjustments to make—to the dirty, stray dogs that roamed the area in packs, and to the curious neighborhood kids who greeted me in one of three ways: "Moneymoneymoney," "Ferengi! Ferengi!" or "CHINA!" (Light-colored skin bears an association with money in Ethiopia, and also with the industrial plants that

Chinese companies are building in Sululta and elsewhere.) A couple of the bolder kids occasionally threw pebbles in my direction, but mostly they just ran next to me for a few steps or poked me curiously. When I was with Derartu, always the protector, she could be counted on to put them in their place with a menacing glare and a threatening kick in the air.

Stray animals and pesky kids, I could handle. Two hours of hiking with a ninety-minute run in the middle, in the thick of Entoto's sprawling forest, was more daunting. I feared encounters with wildlife such as hyenas and monkeys, a fateful misstep without my friends' warning snaps, or one of the long, unintentional detours I'd become known for and that had earned me the nickname "Magellan" from Coach Bevan. Tackling Mount Entoto alone, in my mind, was a rite of passage in Ethiopia, and I was eager to make the leap.

The climb from Fatasha to Entoto Maryam was straightforward and easy enough, if you don't count my labored breathing, leaden legs, or sweat-dampened brow. The woman in the market stall was in the same place she'd been every other morning, ready and eager to stash my belongings. I took off down the path and, like the start of a race after an anxious buildup, my worries abated with the rhythm of the run.

About a mile in, once I'd made it through the village and onto the open dirt road, the gentle slope gave way to the most difficult segment of the mountain I'd experienced so far: a roughly 400-meter, near-vertical climb, a stretch of road that was at least as steep as the hardest part of my uphill tempo in Switzerland. I started my ascent, taking short, choppy steps that felt like high knee drills with ten-pound weights on each leg, and again was distracted by something in the woods on the side of the road. This time, though, it wasn't firewood carriers (though they were never far away if I looked hard enough). It was a single-file line of runners, two men and one woman, weaving up the mountain in a zigzag pattern. The line leader, a man decked out in a green and yellow Adidas sweat suit—typically the sign of a sponsored runner, though sometimes just a friend of one—spotted me around the same time, and steered the group across the hill toward me.

"America?" he asked. As I clicked the stop button on my watch—an ingrained faithfulness to the exact length of my run and the day's mileage total—I noticed that, like the Yaya Girls, none of these runners wore watches. They seemed unconcerned about the brief pause in their run, making no effort to hurry or to continue moving as so many U.S. joggers do while waiting for red lights to turn green.

"Yes! I'm from Texas," I responded, wondering what gave me away.

"Wow! Welcome to Ethiopia!" the leader said, introducing himself as Yosef. The two runners behind him looked at each other and then at me with curious grins.

"Come!" The female, tall by Ethiopian standards and wearing a long-sleeve cotton shirt, waved emphatically and glanced back at the forest from which they'd come.

"Yes, please run with us," Yosef said, and the two others filed behind him in line, this time leaving a middle spot open.

With a little apprehension but no easy way out, I tucked in line and uttered a silent prayer. I'd struggled enough running at my own relaxed pace on the mountain, and had no idea what to expect with this fit-looking group of locals. But as we reentered the forest, my practice with the Yaya Girls kicked in, and I yielded to the Ethiopian style of running—finger snaps, loops, swerves, follow-the-leader formation, and all. As the locals tend to do, we stayed in the forest, hidden from the road I'd been following before I met them, and silently grinded our way up the mountain.

When we reached the peak, 3,000 meters above sea level, we stopped again, this time to peer over the side of the mountain and down onto Addis Ababa, the capital city of Ethiopia and the unofficial political capital of Africa. I enjoyed the view from that perspective much more than from the seat of a teetering minibus. Amid the colorful disarray—boxy homes, clusters of skyscrapers, wide roads, streetside market stalls, as many half-finished as finished buildings, and masses of people buzzing around like bees on a fruit salad—a few landmarks stuck out, which Yosef identified: Bole Methane Alem Church, yellow-tinted with huge arches and three turquoise domes on top; Meskel Square, a public gathering spot and track of sorts, with rows of concrete seating used as running lanes at sunrise every morning; the main Addis Ababa University campus, one of thirteen in total; Holy Trinity Cathedral, the ivory-colored, Gothic-looking Orthodox cathedral; and legions of minibuses in motion.

Back in line, we resumed our run once more, flying across and down the crest we'd just worked so hard to climb in a fraction of the time. Running hills in Ethiopia reminded me of the dominoes I used to play with at my grandpa's house, my sister and I spending all afternoon making an elaborate train of tiles on the dining room table. The triumphant feeling of pushing the first tile in line—if my brothers didn't get to it first—and then watching, mesmerized, as each tile fell in succession, was akin to the satisfaction of climbing the most circuitous route uphill and blazing straight down, following the lead of a human catalyst. Like Laura Haefeli, my Colorado mountain-running friend, the Ethiopian runners were quick-footed, upward-looking climbers, and fearless, gravity-embracing descenders. With a lot of effort, I could generally keep up with them on the inclines, but no matter how hard I tried to gracefully float back down, I always lost ground on the downhills, lagging cautiously behind.

The four of us wove our way across Entoto, covering unfamiliar areas and more rugged terrain, until we arrived back at Entoto Maryam Church. It was one of my best runs yet, and the Ethiopian approach to running was clearly rubbing off on me: I'd forgotten to restart my watch after our second stop and, for the first time since I started keeping a training log ten years ago, put a big fat question mark in that day's mileage box.

AFTER MY SUCCESSFUL FIRST "SOLO" RUN at Entoto, I made a habit of returning there by myself once or twice a week. Occasionally, I came across a scavenging hyena or small, long-tailed monkey, much preferring the latter. More often than not, I was invited to join a group like Yosef's. I only got lost once, due to a fateful missed turn that turned a one-hour run into a three-hour one. (Premature marathon preparation, I called it, though it was certainly unplanned.) But my favorite and most memorable runs were led by the Yaya Girls.

One evening, Banchi, Derartu, Mesi, and I trooped off into the forest across the road, where an uneven dirt road divides a eucalyptus forest into two and eventually leads to a greener hillside. We left at twilight, the Ethiopians' second favorite time of day to run, for its cool air and limited sun exposure. Derartu chastised me from the start for wearing only my Ireland singlet and shorts, markedly underdressed compared to their long pants and windbreakers.

The girls invited me to lead, assuring me that they'd point me in the right direction if (and when) I got turned around. I reluctantly accepted, much preferring to shut off my brain, follow their footsteps, and pass on rather than initiate the chain of warning snaps. From the front, a straight dirt path never looked so enticing, but instead I went with the local style, trailblazing through the eucalyptus forest and seeking out every boulder, stump, and ditch I could find, doing my best to correctly time the snaps and points. The girls seemed pleased with my route and cheered whenever I hurdled an obstacle without a stutter-step or scrape.

After a couple of miles, I passed the torch to Banchi—on easy runs, trading leaders was acceptable—who shook up the rhythm with a surge up a steep hill followed by an easy descent. A while later—fifteen minutes, perhaps, but again, no watch among the group—we came to a halt at a junction of four large fields. Banchi scanned the area for a few seconds and then bolted off on a path to our right, in between rows of big green stalks. Keeping our line intact, we followed her along a thin groove in the earth that was just wide enough for one foot. As I tried not to twist an ankle, both feet planting on one narrow plane, I wondered what Banchi had up her sleeve. I'd followed her down plenty of unexpected routes, but a field like this one was a first.

A few minutes in, we ran straight up to a woman working in the field. Banchi, Derartu, and Mesi had a quick conversation with her and then began foraging, yanking bundles of the green stalks from the ground and piling them up in their arms. Soon I, too, had an armful of branches, the girls helping me with my own pile once their collections were complete. I assumed we'd come to help this woman, perhaps a relative of Banchi, with her fieldwork, so I walked toward her and pushed the stalks in her direction.

"No, Becky!" Derartu yelled at me from a few rows away.

"This? Eat!" Banchi chimed in, pulling off what looked like a small green pea from one of her branches and popping it in her mouth. "See? Eat!"

So I followed her lead, not knowing what exactly we were munching on, but also not wanting to miss out on a mysterious delicacy. The "peas" were flavorless and crunchy, but the girls made sure that I had my fill before we continued on our way. I looked down at my stash, so bulky it obscured most of my top half, and I hoped I wasn't expected to pluck every little pea from those branches and swallow them before we headed home.

That actually might have been better than the alternative, which I soon learned was trudging back home in the dark with the massive, spiky bundles in tow. I could barely hang on to my branches, much less run comfortably or smoothly. I thought of my poor dad, who covered countless miles while pushing four fidgety toddlers two to a seat in a double baby jogger. Fortunately Mesi, the leader on the way home, took us over only a few creeks and ditches, and even treated us to a short stint on an actual dirt path.

Just over a mile from the Yaya gate, Banchi and Mesi suddenly stopped, feeling tired and deciding to walk the rest of the way. Derartu and I continued on another few minutes before agreeing our arms could use a rest, and waited for them to catch up. The abrupt ending to our run caught me off guard—my instinct said, "We're eight minutes from home . . . Why not just finish up?"—but it impressed me, too. My whole life, it had seemed taboo to cut a workout or run short, even when my body gave me signals to stop. But to these girls, an easy walk home was the obvious solution to a recovery run that wasn't doing its job.

When we finally reached Yaya Village, I was still waiting for an explanation. "Your mom, Banchi?" I asked her, pointing to the stalks and giving my best impersonation of the woman whose field we had just raided.

"Nooooo," she replied with a laugh. "My mom? No!"

"Then who? An aunt? A friend?"

"No, no, not friend," Banchi replied. "Met first time tonight."

Then we walked around the complex, passing out the branches to our friends, who seemed unsurprised but excited about our gift. For all I knew, passing out unplucked pea plants was as common as offering someone tea in Ireland. Dan was the only one who seemed as confused as I was, not understanding how I could run with huge branches for miles without the slightest inkling of what they were or who we'd taken them from. I couldn't offer him an acceptable explanation, but I could—and did—offer him a tasty nightcap of hard, green pods.

The Yaya Girls and me with the stash of mysterious plants we'd collected in a stranger's field.

WEARING AN ADIDAS SWEAT SUIT color-blocked in green, yellow, and red, with ETHIOPIA spanning his shoulder blades, Haile Gebrselassie stood at the entrance of his mansion ready to greet every visitor. Dan, Julia, and I were guests at his annual party following the Great Ethiopian Run—Africa's largest 10K, one of Haile's many investments, and a stepping-stone for many up-and-coming runners. Along with Mesi, who was one of the top finishers, I was offered a spot in the elite corral on behalf of Yaya Village. Unlike her, I spent most of the race in no-man's-land, positioned between the fastest women and the nearly forty thousand recreational runners behind us, a Christmas-colored mob thanks to that year's red-and-green race shirts. The race was an eye-opening experience—soldiers barricading the starting line, ensuring no false starts; more females ahead of me than any race I could remember; and the streets of Addis overtaken by runners, instead of the usual cars, animals, and vendors—but the party that followed was even more so.

Haile's mansion rests halfway up Mount Entoto on the opposite side of Sululta, with a panoramic view of Addis Ababa. The backyard party featured a live band, shimmering pool, shaded tables, extravagant buffet, ongoing coffee ceremony, and a handful of running superstars. Among them, I recognized Tiki Gelana, reigning Olympic Marathon champion, and Tsegaye Kebede, bronze medalist in the 2008 Olympic Marathon.

Many of Haile's guests were foreigners—international runners, members of the media, and VIPs—and all of us were in awe of this lean, five-foot-five giant of a man who gave no indication that he's one of the most decorated and formidable distance runners of all time, only six days away from running a major marathon in Tokyo. A natural host, Haile strolled around his backyard, mingling with his starstruck guests, posing for pictures, and even serving drinks. "In a marathon, there are only drink stations every few kilometers," he said at one point. "But at my house, there are drinks every meter—so please, drink up!" Haile is beloved and revered in his home country, having earned 27 world records, 2 Olympic gold medals, and 5 World Championship titles, and run an astounding 10 sub-2:07 marathons. Not only has he given Ethiopia something to rally behind and inspired legions of younger runners, he's constantly funneling money back into the Ethiopian economy through a number of business ventures: the Great Ethiopian Run, Yaya Village, the Alem Center (a multipurpose building with a gym in Addis Ababa), his namesake race in the city of Hawassa, and even the very first cinema designed to play local movies exclusively.

Dan, Julia, and I ate our fill from the buffet, stuffing our stomachs with rarities for Ethiopia such as grilled Nile perch, whole chicken breasts, vegetable curry, and carrot cake. The only dish I didn't sample—my single refusal of the whole year—was kitfo, a minced raw beef dish that usually appears at special events like weddings and holidays. I'd heard stories about Westerners getting sick from it, and the thought of spending part of my trip bedridden diminished my curiosity.

A few hours into the party, I noticed a flurry of activity on the far side of the backyard. I rushed over to see what was going on, and heard traditional Ethiopian music looping through the speakers and a rhythmic clap keeping time with it. Next to a cluster of shaded tables stood a ring of men performing a fluid, bouncy dance: shoulders popping, feet tapping, fingers wiggling, and arms loosely blending the hula with the Soulja Boy dance. One enormous man dominated the group and regularly took to the center of the circle to let his jiggly body and flailing arms loose. Every few seconds, when the big man leaned to one side or squatted down low, I caught a glimpse of a man less than half his size, dancing gracefully with a clear sense of rhythm and an enormous grin.

Haile Gebrselassie: runner, businessman, host, dancer.

THE CLOCK WAS TICKING, and I hated to leave a country I'd fallen in love with without seeing more than the area surrounding its capital. So with Xavi and Eliza's help, Dan and I planned a week-long trip to the northern region of the country, beginning with four days of hiking and camping in the Simien Mountains.

Our starting point—reached by plane from Addis Ababa to Gondar and then a three-hour taxi ride—was Debark, the official registration point for the Simiens. Dan and I dashed around the small town, renting well-used camping gear and buying food at the open-air market. We hired the mandatory scout—ours was an elderly, turbaned man who spoke no English—and a slight young man named Ishoo as our guide. Both men wore thin pants and jackets and brightly colored jelly sandals, the type that were all the rage among young American girls in the nineties. In sharp contrast to the sandals was the big gun slung over our scout's shoulder. "For people! Not animals," Ishoo assured me, pointing at the gun. That didn't make me feel much better.

When we were ready to go, Ishoo set the pace up front, while our scout—whose age had to be closer to one hundred than fifty—trod effortlessly behind us, breathing quietly and balancing on the edge of enormous cliffs as if they were city curbs. Ishoo was also an impressive athlete, sometimes inadvertently gaining a little distance on us. He built in breaks every hour or so, urging us to sip from our water bottles and pointing out interesting elements of the landscape: a tall tree used for medicinal purposes and a green tomato relative that makes great soap for washing clothes. At the crest of one hill, if everyone was silent, we could hear beautifully haunting music swelling faintly from the villages below. Ishoo explained that it came from farmers singing a traditional harvesting song.

When we reached Sancobar, our first campsite, a few hours

later, Dan and I pitched our tent and spread out our sleeping bags, and then rummaged through our food sack so Dan could start cooking dinner while I ran. After all the hiking we'd done, I still craved a run, no matter how slowly, and knew my body would benefit from the shakeout. When I told Ishoo my plan—to go for a jog, but to never run more than ten minutes away from our campsite on either side—he gasped. "You are a runner? Oh, wow! Becky!"

I took off down the dusty dirt road, the elevation noticeably higher than Sululta's, and my legs and aerobic system worked hard to maintain a respectable pace. When I flipped around at the ten-minute mark and approached the campsite again, Ishoo and two of his friends, guides for another group, were perched on a large boulder. "YAY BECKY! GO BECKY! YOU ARE SO STRONG! AIZOSH!" They clapped and yelled as I ran by, as if I were chasing down a competitor at the end of a race, and did the same each time I passed them again. Ishoo was the proudest of them all. After I finished, he said, "Becky! I appreciate you so much! I have never met a white person like you. You are so strong! I think you will be the champion in the next Olympics." He might have been less impressed if he had been taking splits on that run, but I appreciated the encouragement nonetheless.

Midway through our hike the next day, Ishoo stopped abruptly. "Wait!" he exclaimed, crouching down, shading his eyes, and squinting as he scanned the horizon. "There they are," he said quietly, too focused to notice the nervous looks Dan and I exchanged. As we waited for an explanation, I tried to keep my thoughts from lingering on our scout's gun and the people Ishoo casually mentioned it was meant for. I moved closer to Ishoo and followed his gaze to a hilltop in the distance. The grassy slope looked alive, tiny brown figures scampering and somersaulting all over it. As we got closer, the figures took on furry, four-limbed shapes, and their shrill cries echoed through the mountains.

"Gelada baboons only live here, in northern Ethiopia," Ishoo explained, "and they are so friendly and playful. Like babies! You can get very close to them, and some might even let you touch them. Try it!" Cautiously at first, Dan and I crept toward the baboons. Technically monkeys, not true baboons, this was clearly a social species, as nearly every one of them was engaged with another: wrestling playfully, engaging in flipping competitions, chasing after each other with high-pitched roars, carrying babies on their backs or stomachs, and picking bugs out of each other's hair. They were all so busy that they hardly noticed the two large biped creatures strolling through their territory. Careful not to interfere with any downhill somersaulters, I plopped down in a patch of grass and sat silently among them. As badly as I wanted to pet one, the sharp teeth they bared with each shriek—daggers really, gums flipped back for full effect—made me rethink Ishoo's suggestion.

Gelada baboons, friendly and playful creatures, live only in the Simien Mountains.

Throughout our hike, we passed smaller troops of gelada baboons as well as ravens, lammergeiers, ibex, and bushbucks; tiny villages comprised of circular, straw huts; shepherds of all ages, gripping staffs and guiding sheep and cattle across the land; and enterprising kids selling crafts and playing homemade instruments. When we reached the peak of one monstrous incline, a group of eight children capitalized on my euphoria by selling me two small incense bowls woven out of hay. They nearly sold me a colorful hat with a single stick sprouting from the center and a furry ball on top, but my backpack was already a struggle to zip, and so I declined, despite Dan's enthusiastic prods.

Our evening campsite stops were as entertaining as the hiking itself, and not just because Dan and I were forced to get creative with our meager food supply. (Our options had been limited at the market, and we did a poor job of rationing the food we bought.) At Geech, our second campsite, the hut owners welcomed us with a coffee ceremony over an open fire pit and, after dinner, passed out beakers of tej, a homemade honey wine and a popular alcoholic drink in Ethiopia. The tej was equally sweet and bitter, not really my style, but I may have stomached more than a few sips were it not for the little black bugs floating around in the glass.

When Dan called my attention to the row of guides sitting in folding chairs behind us, I thought the tej was deceiving my eyes. Like our guide, they were all older, stern-looking men, with massive guns slung on the chairs behind them. But their bottom halves told a different tale; in addition to wearing the same model of plastic jelly sandals, each man held a small paper cone of popcorn like the ones I used to get on field day in grade school, every so often bringing the cup to his lips and tossing back a kernel or two.

On our last day of hiking, we reached Imet Gogo, a plateau

standing 3,900 meters (12,800 feet) above sea level and offering a 360-degree view of the Simien Mountains. After five full days of hiking and subsisting on minimal provisions—our last dinner was like an episode of *Chopped,* using only penne, hummus, and a crunchy snack mix called kolo—getting there felt like a victory. We made our final descent and said goodbye to our trusty scout and to Ishoo, who by that point was ready to crown me the world cross-country champion.

THE END OF OUR SIMIEN MOUNTAIN TREK marked the beginning of Christmas week and my final one in Ethiopia. Though Christmas falls three weeks later on the Ethiopian calendar than in the West, Dan and I still wanted to celebrate on the same date as our friends and family back home—but with a local twist.

Our tour of Lalibela was the perfect kickoff to the holiday. Nicknamed "the New Jerusalem," this high place of Ethiopian Christianity attracts pilgrims from all over the country, who turn it into a sea of white muslin robes. Eleven churches are scattered about the city, each carved in the twelfth and thirteenth centuries by angels, according to popular belief, out of a single underground rock, and further chiseled into doors, tunnels, elaborate designs, and small offshoot rooms.

Many of the people Dan and I encountered in Lalibela were nearing the end of their days, having saved up for a lifetime to make the journey to the Ethiopian Holy Land. Barefoot and clutching wooden staffs, they meandered slowly from church to church, making three signs of the cross and bowing at each entrance, and pausing to pray silently on the ground in between services. We learned to watch where we stepped, as many pilgrims were curled up on the floor into tight motionless balls, their entire bodies covered by their robes.

At our last church visit to Bete Giyorgis (Church of St. George)—perfectly carved into the shape of an Ethiopian cross with a top that is level with the ground—Dan and I got to sit in on the end of a mass. A woman who couldn't have been much younger than ninety or much taller than four-feet-eight escorted us up the stairs and into the church, where the deep, monotone chanting, strong incense, and dim lighting moved me profoundly. I thought back to my first run in Ethiopia, seven weeks earlier, when Banchi explained that Derartu couldn't finish the workout because she was consumed by the Devil. Sitting on the pew during that cryptic, stirring service, in a city full of devout individuals, put Banchi's explanation into context.

Dan and I made it back to Addis Ababa just before Christmas Day, and saw only a few signs of my favorite holiday, mostly in establishments frequented by Westerners like Kaldi's Coffee and the Hilton hotel. We arrived at Yaya in time to witness the Christmas Eve sheep slaughter, in which Amente slit the throat of a sheep purchased from a neighboring farmer, drained the blood out of its neck, hung it upside down from a tree branch, and peeled its skin off before sending it to Chef Ermes in the kitchen. I don't anticipate a new Wade family tradition, but the respect shown to the animal and the generosity shown to those of us who feasted on it made for a special first experience of yet another Ethiopian custom.

While sharing holiday traditions and memories with the other Yaya guests, I felt a tangle of emotions when my turn arrived. I talked about my mom's decorations that make our home look like the inside of a snow globe, my dad's continual stoking of the fire no matter how warm it is outside, and the dinner that my family would share for my dad's birthday on Christmas Eve. While I felt wistful imagining them sitting around our kitchen table with one empty seat, I was happy knowing they were all together, and I tried to savor the rare opportunity for a simple, inward-focused Christmas.

December 25 was still full of gifts, but not as I traditionally knew them. The morning began with one for myself: a solo sunrise run at Mount Entoto, twelve miles bookended by two hours of reflection and thanksgiving. The people I passed on my way up the mountain were going about their days as usual, and the holiday felt like my own little secret. I gave myself a second gift once I stashed my bag with my vendor friend at the end of the hike: freedom to run as fast as I wanted, or at least as fast as my legs and lungs would propel me across that sky-high mountain range. I knew that it was my last Entoto run—I would fly to my next country the following day—and I wanted to challenge myself a little more than usual.

After a post-run nap, I joined Dan, Julia, Julia's partner Kevin, and Richard and Celia Taylor (another British running couple) for lunch at Banchi's home across the road. I didn't know that she was aware it was Christmas according to the Western calendar, so I was surprised to walk inside and find Banchi and Tsigereda, also a Yaya Village employee, kneeling on the floor with an elaborate display of food in front of them and a coffee ceremony with popcorn, shimbra, and incense nearby. The feast took over Banchi's tiny living room, with its cracked and slanted floors, two religious posters taped to the wall, a makeshift kitchen in one corner, and a few miniature animal figurines and family pictures on top of a dresser.

Banchi and Tsigereda doled out cups of coffee and servings of food—injera, shiro (by then my favorite Ethiopian dish), rolls, and a salad of carrots, potatoes, and lettuce—and didn't stop until all of the food was gone. While the other guests and I ate on Banchi's mattress, taken from her bed and placed on the floor, our two hosts entertained us with traditional Ethiopian dancing, featuring the female version of the torso-twisting, shoulder-popping, and body jiggling I saw Haile Gebrselassie and his friends perform weeks before. Banchi seemed to think that I might have a hidden talent for that style of dancing, but about thirty seconds into my attempt she realized her error. Nonetheless, Julia, Celia, and I shimmied away with them for a couple of songs, trying to mimic their synchronized moves while acknowledging that ours were more comical than coordinated.

Before we left, our hostesses presented each girl with a small wrapped box. Inside mine was a brown, beaded necklace, which Banchi fastened around my neck as I fought back tears. How much this party, including the food and gifts, would set my friends back, I couldn't bear to calculate—at least a few weeks' worth of paychecks from their jobs as waitresses—but I felt as thankful and loved then as I did on any holiday in my memory.

AFTER I BECAME INTERESTED IN RUNNING, East Africa grabbed my attention. It was impossible not to notice the slight-framed, dark-skinned athletes at the front of major marathons, and to wonder how they train and where they come from. The Kenyans in London had given me some clues in their slow warm-ups, communal meals, and run-by-feel philosophy. But it wasn't until I lived in East Africa that I began to understand the forces behind the world's supreme distance-running region.

In the last two months, I'd seen that Ethiopia is much more than a running factory, churning out world record holders and marathon champions through a system refined in the fifty years since Abebe Bikila's Olympic Marathon victory. What this country has over the rest of the world (and shares with its neighbor Kenya) is a culture that breeds many of the qualities that happen to make good distance runners: discipline, resilience, self-awareness, and most of all, a desperate drive to succeed. The role of poverty cannot be ignored, as running is for many an attempt to rise above it, with ultrasuccessful runners like Haile Gebrselassie and Kenenisa Bekele (who was building his own hotel and track next door to Yaya Village) offering both a measure of inspiration and false hope. For every person who successfully makes a career out of running, there are thousands of others who remain in obscurity in the forests. But the fact that those running stars, and dozens more, are household names reflects the cultural significance of the sport in Ethiopia.

Spirituality is also a factor in Ethiopia's running success. Ethiopians are a people of strong faith, with 75 percent of them practicing Ethiopian Orthodox Christianity or Islam. For most of the country, faith seeps into every aspect of life—running in-cluded. While Sunday is a standard long run day in many parts of the world, there it is a day of rest; Sunday was the only day I couldn't count on seeing other runners at Satellite or Entoto. The inseparability of running and religion, first demonstrated by the story of Derartu and the Devil, was confirmed again and again during my stay, as I saw runners brush off bad workouts with conviction that God would provide on His own terms; utter quiet prayers on the starting line of the Great Ethiopian Run; and drop to their knees in thanksgiving after especially good workouts.

I was surprised to discover that running is not a big recre-ational sport in Ethiopia. In fact, with the exception of the Great Ethiopian Run, I didn't see recreational runners, at least in Su-lulta. Those whom I ran with or passed on my daily runs to Satel-lite Field, through the fields near Yaya Village, and up and down

Mount Entoto appeared to be athletes who were taking their training very seriously. As I learned, many families discourage their children from running because it cuts into their fieldwork and the family's food supply. I met one female who snuck away in the early mornings to run before she was expected in the field, in the hopes that she'd eventually be able to provide for her family with her legs rather than her hands.

My experiences in Ethiopia transformed me, both personally and athletically, and I was afraid of undoing the progress I was making. It was clear that I was becoming fitter—my runs hardly felt easy, but at least now I could keep up with my Ethiopian friends when they unleashed their speed at the end of some runs, and my Entoto outings got longer and longer each week (though I never surpassed that accidental three-hour run).

I'd also made strides in other areas, influenced by the locals I spent time with. Flexibility, in my daily schedule as well as on runs, a necessity in a watch-free society. Patience, for waits at minibus stations, severed Internet connections, and multiple loops around the same eucalyptus trees. Elevated work ethic, in grueling, oxygen-deprived runs and in everyday life, as I hand-washed my clothes and purified every drop of water I drank. Body awareness, gleaned from the Ethiopians' confidence to take days off, stop runs short, and run at speeds that felt right in the moment. Cohesion, in shared meals, group runs, and hours of bonding in the Yaya Girls' room. And generosity, learned by example through Banchi and Tsigereda's Christmas party, my local friends' insistence to pay for my minibus rides to Fatasha and Addis Ababa, and Zewdenesh's elaborate home-cooked meal. My friendship with Dan, who was by my side throughout my two months in Ethiopia, helped me keep the challenges of this new existence in perspective, and went unmatched by any other of my trip.

It was hard to leave knowing I wouldn't be able to reunite with my Ethiopian friends anytime soon—not only because of the inconvenience and expense of my getting to East Africa but also the barriers to securing an Ethiopian passport, the lack of a reliable postal system in Sululta, and the rarity of computers in rural Ethiopia. I hoped that I might see Banchi, Mesi, or Derartu on the international racing circuit someday, perhaps at one of the World Marathon Majors. But the reality was that, like the vast majority of Ethiopian runners, the odds were against them, and our reunion would be dependent on my return.

In typical fashion, the Yaya Girls were nowhere to be found when I was loading up Joseph's car for Bole Airport. I'd tried to explain the night before that I was leaving for good the next morning, and to *please* let me tell them goodbye before I left at 9 A.M. (three o'clock Ethiopia time), but clearly they hadn't understood. Even when I asked Amente to translate my words, they just laughed, wrapped their arms around my shoulders, and said, "No, Becky! No." Either my recent trip to northern Ethiopia confused them, or, as I began to fear as I finished my rounds of Yaya Village, thanking and hugging each of the staff members, perhaps I had overestimated the relationship I'd built with Banchi, Mesi, and Derartu.

I scanned the Yaya campus one last time, and out of time to procrastinate further, began to get into the car. Before I made it all the way inside, three figures entered the big iron gates and came sprinting my way. If they hadn't understood before, my tear-filled eyes and luggage got through to them now, and they yanked me out of the car and into a tight group hug. As I tried to hold back my tears, and then just let them roll, it became clear that the country and the people who long ago had captured my attention had, in the last two months, captured my heart, too.

Kolo

A crunchy snack mix available in Addis Ababa market stalls and grocery stores, kolo is the Ethiopian version of trail mix. Delicious by the handful or in a cup of yogurt, it's a great snack for a hungry runner to keep on hand.

1 cup barley kernels
¼ cup peanuts
¼ cup dried chickpeas
¼ cup sunflower seeds
¼ cup dried soybeans
Olive oil
Salt
Optional seasonings: 1 tablespoon berbere (Ethiopian spice mix, available at ethnic grocery stores or on Amazon) for savory kolo, or 1 tablespoon honey for sweet kolo

1. Preheat oven to 350° F.
2. Toss barley, peanuts, chickpeas, sunflower seeds, and soybeans in olive oil until lightly covered. Dust with salt and optional seasonings, and toss to coat evenly.
3. Spread mixture onto a baking sheet and toast in preheated oven, tossing occasionally, until the mixture becomes crunchy and starts to crackle (20–30 minutes).
4. Remove from oven, let cool, and eat plain or on top of yogurt or oatmeal.

5

STRIKING A BALANCE AND TACKLING THE TRACK

Australia and New Zealand
1,058 miles

The scene was familiar: a dozen of us scattered around a cabin, kicking back after a tiring day; a boisterous card game unfolding in one corner; a few people dozing off, books propped up nearby; an eclectic playlist filling the background; snacks dwindling by the minute . . . I was even finishing up a stack of postcards for my family.

But instead of the preteens who surrounded me at the Pines Catholic Camp for two weeks every summer of my youth, my peers were in their twenties and thirties; and copious gum trees took the place of towering pines. Our exhaustion wasn't from a full day of canoeing, arts and crafts, and zip-lining, but from our long morning workout—kilometer repeats for most of us—and afternoon shakeout. And though the hot sun and pesky mosquitoes evoked those East Texas summers, we were actually in the middle of a New Year's training camp. I'd connected with another club that had welcomed me to their ranks—the Melbourne University Athletics Club (MUAC)—and had tagged along on their annual team trip.

A few days before, as 2012 turned into 2013, I flew across the Indian Ocean and dropped from 9,000 feet of elevation in Ethiopia to nearly half that in Falls Creek, Australia, to begin the next leg of my journey.

According to my itinerary before I left the United States, I was scheduled to be in New Zealand, my third out of five countries. Instead, the prospect of visiting a different altitude camp, joining another track club, and exploring one of the world's most running-friendly cities (according to some locals and travelers I'd met on my trip) prompted me to carve out room in my schedule for the Land Down Under. Australia's proximity to New Zealand and near-perfect January weather didn't hurt, either.

After a thirty-six-hour journey from Ethiopia, with stops in Dubai and Kuala Lumpur, and then a four-hour drive from Melbourne, I arrived in Falls Creek ready for quality rest and quality running. By this point of my trip, nearly halfway through the year, I was eager to run workouts with purpose again—to gauge my fitness after months of high mileage and low intensity, and test myself in a competitive environment. I knew that I'd be in New Zealand during the summer track season, so I anticipated that Australia would be a month of transitions: from high to moderate to low elevation, from an African to a Western society, and from a looser to a more structured training program.

Like St. Moritz in Switzerland, Falls Creek is a popular ski resort that swells with athletes in warmer months as they train in a high-altitude, low-distraction environment. It's been a magnet for runners for more than twice my lifetime and my early January arrival meant I'd be sharing the trails with two or three hundred other runners. Some were recreational athletes seeking a social running holiday; others, like the Melbourne Track Club, with a handful of Olympians on its roster, were serious runners sharpening up for Australia's World Cross-Country Trials, held at the end of the month. I'd be sharing a lodge with MUAC, a 120-year-old running club (only loosely affiliated with the university), which strikes a happy medium: Its membership spans self-dubbed "hobby joggers" all the way up to Olympic champions (including Herb Elliott, who went undefeated in the 1,500 meters and the mile a half century ago).

At an elevation of 5,250 feet, Falls Creek is about half as high as my training grounds in Ethiopia and made a great segue to my next sea level stint in Melbourne. The nice part about moderately high locations like Falls is that they still impart some benefits of altitude—forcing the body to increase its production of red blood cells, which boost the delivery of oxygen—while allowing for more intense speed sessions than higher elevations allow. In Ethiopia, because of the extreme altitude and difficult terrain, I found the act of running challenging enough without incorporating specific workouts. I spent those two months logging lots of easy miles with weekly 100-meter strides and hill sprints, and the occasional second-half surge. Now, with the lower elevation, I was excited to add intensity and speed work to the aerobic base I'd been building. I also looked forward to the veiny web of smooth dirt trails Falls is known for, not so different from the trails in Ethiopia. (The difference being that in Australia, we actually used them.)

Trail running wasn't the only difference from Sululta. While it took me weeks to adapt to the disregard of time and distances in Ethiopia, running up to an hour shorter or longer than I'd have chosen, the Falls Creek training schedule has barely changed in the last fifty years. "Fitzy's Hut run tomorrow at 9:30 A.M., easy runs from the village for the next two days, 1K repeats at Langford's Gap on Saturday, Pretty Valley long run at 9 A.M. on Sunday, and optional doubles at 5:30 P.M. every evening, starting on the aqueduct path just above the village," Hamish Beaumont, president of MUAC, informed me when I arrived. I had to admit, while the Ethiopian style had its benefits, I appreciated the routine I found at Falls Creek.

The culture shock from Ethiopia to Australia went beyond running. Shiro and injera were replaced by sandwiches slathered in Vegemite, a salty, yeast-based food spread (Australia's peanut butter equivalent), and thick, sugary coffee gave way to flat whites, larger drinks with espresso and a thin layer of velvety microfoam. More noticeably, the Australian-English dialect was a big departure from the Amharic- and Oromic-tinted English I'd grown accustomed to. With the Yaya Girls, I spoke in simple, choppy English while also becoming a skilled mime. This new country required a different sort of translation. "Chrissy," "prezzies," and "rellies"—Christmas, presents, and relatives—were hot topics following the holiday, as were "stressies" (stress fractures) and "sunnies" (sunglasses) among the running crowd. After three months in non-English-speaking countries, Australian English was a sweet symphony of abbreviations and slang.

Other aspects of the Falls Creek training camp took more getting used to, as I discovered in my first hard workout. The easy group runs were relaxed and social, the hundred or so runners who showed up—mostly Australians but a few from Switzerland, the Netherlands, England, and Ireland—offering excellent company. There was no shortage of paces, distances, and conversations from which to choose, and switching between groups was encouraged.

During hard workouts, however—like 8×1,000 meters a few days after I arrived—the atmosphere intensified. Still unsure of my fitness level and wanting to be cautious, I began in the second group of females and helped lead the first few repeats. Feeling comfortable and confident, and assuming that moving between groups was still permissible, I decided to test my fitness with the faster group—a few girls whom I recognized from NCAA podiums—so I cut my recovery jog short to join them on the line. Over the next four intervals, I sensed through silence and subtle surges that maybe I should have asked permission to run alongside them. I clung silently to the back of the small pack until the workout ended.

I finished each hard workout that week either unsatisfied by my effort, having run with a slower group than I would have liked, or feeling self-conscious and intrusive after latching on to the front group. For the first time on my trip, I felt like I'd entered a territorial atmosphere. I'm a competitor at my core—I wouldn't have made it far as a runner if I weren't—but to me, racing should be reserved for special occasions, the mental strain that goes with it tapped into infrequently and deliberately. During those Falls Creek sessions, I better understood why Coach Bevan usually placed my teammates and me in groups for hard workouts, moving us around as he saw fit and requesting specific splits. Taking the race out of the workout prevented the strain I was feeling now, and preserved friendships that otherwise might have suffered; Allison Pye, my main training partner and suitemate at Rice, is still one of my closest friends, thousands of shared miles later. My creative high school coach, Maureen Shinnick, had her own method of team building: "banana runs," scavenger hunts along our practice routes for fruit she'd inscribed with inspirational messages (assuming the squirrels didn't get there first). When I finished that weekend's long run with the top female group—fourteen miles with hills, sand, and a burning 100-degree sun—without sharing so much as a high five or a "good job," I felt homesick for my wise coaches and encouraging teammates.

Fortunately, the competitiveness at Falls Creek started and ended on the trails, and was mostly confined to a handful of the best runners. Whether they were gunning for spots on Australia's World Cross-Country Team or just not used to having visitors around, I tried not to let those workouts dampen my experience and, thanks to the MUAC crew, they didn't. The ten or so members of MUAC whom I shared Cooroona Alpine Lodge and many easy runs with kept the mood lighthearted and easygoing— exactly as I think a training camp should be. Taking things too seriously can be just as destructive as being too relaxed, and that group had found a healthy balance. We filled time between runs with ice baths in a creek, dips in a watering hole, potluck dinners, and idle coffee dates at Milch, a local cafe with a wide selection of board games.

By the end of the week, I had relaxed as hard as I had trained— the beauty of Falls Creek and other training camps done right. With so much free time and so few distractions, there were no excuses for dodging an ice bath or a second run, opting for fast food over a home-cooked meal, or forgoing a nap or long night's sleep. And a change of environment, even from one running sanctuary to another, can do wonders for a runner's spirit—especially when there's a group like MUAC around to keep things fun.

Back in Melbourne, after almost ten weeks at elevation, it would have been nice to feel light-footed and super-oxygenated, and to immediately reap the benefits from my stints in Sululta and Falls Creek. While my first few runs felt great, by the fourth or fifth day, I felt flat and fatigued. Altitude has a way of doing that, I knew, the reason for the recommendation to return to sea level either three days or three weeks before a race (to avoid the shock that comes after a few days at a lower elevation or to give oneself enough time to adapt beforehand).

During those daily or twice-daily trudges, as I awaited my body's signal to resume hard training, the MUAC members were again the perfect sidekicks. Club members Neil and Mel Sampson—dubbed "the New Zealand Consulate" for their generosity in hosting foreign runners for long stints (including Alan Webb, American record holder in the mile)—provided me with a base in Melbourne, lending me a spare room in an ideally located part of town. Their home is just a short run to the Yarra Trail, a long concrete path that zips alongside the Yarra River like Houston's bayou and Phoenix's canal, and eventually connects to what I'd consider the Central Park of Melbourne: the Tan. Circling the Royal Botanical Gardens, the 3.8-kilometer dirt trail is the most popular place in town for joggers, walkers, sunshine seekers, and serious athletes alike. The course record is an impressive 10 minutes and 12 seconds, clocked by Olympian and Falls Creek regular Craig Mottram in 2004. The Tan quickly became my go-to spot, too.

While the Sampsons honeymooned in Thailand (and trusted a stranger in their lovely home), Hamish Beaumont and David Paroissien, both MUAC members, highlighted the best of their hometown from a runner's perspective. In addition to club practices at the Melbourne University track, I tagged along with Hamish and Dave for runs at Princes Park, a group of football fields near campus that are bordered by a dirt path; Yarra Bend National Park, with single-track trails, a thriving bat population, and at least one large lizard with a blue tongue; and Yarra Flats, a shaded, woodsy area where we covered nineteen miles with former Rice runner Lachlan McArthur and his wife, full-time consultant and Olympic marathoner Lisa Weightman.

For a longer trek one weekend, Zacca and Mark, also MUAC guys, took me to the unofficial long run spot for generations of Aussie runners: Ferny Creek, a village about an hour's drive from Melbourne with dozens of trails and the feel of a rain forest. Though it's not as much of a hot spot today—the Sunday of our visit, we saw fewer than a dozen other runners—in the 1970s and '80s, up to a hundred runners used to meet at one main trailhead each weekend. The regulars back then included Rob de Castella (winner of the 1983 World Championship Marathon) and Ron Clarke (Olympic medalist and 17-time world record holder). Landmarks like Clarke's Hill connected us to that past. The forest was both beautiful and eerie, so dense at times that I couldn't see farther than a few feet ahead, and the single wombat and large group of crimson parrots I spotted made me wonder what other creatures were lurking in the trees.

Between runs, Hamish, Dave, and other MUAC friends introduced me to Melbourne's coffee and food scene, one of the most vibrant in the world. Following our bat colony run, we went for flat whites at the Abbotsford Convent Farm Cafe, an old monastery that had been converted into a coffee shop, restaurant, and petting zoo. Before one track practice, we walked through downtown's narrow laneways, a labyrinth of lanes and arcades full of one-of-a-kind cafes that reminded me of brick-and-mortar versions of Austin, Texas's food trucks. Dave treated me to a recovery meal of pho in the Vietnamese part of town, and Hamish arranged an outing for club members ("Friday follies," according to his e-mail title) at Joe's Shoes, a shoe store turned bar with a wood-fire pizza parlor next door.

And finally, we brunched, well and often. The Aussies introduced me to fancy toast before the trend had reached the United States: thick pieces of bread, often sourdough, toasted and adorned with a variety of toppings such as smashed, citrus-infused avocados; feta, rocket, olive oil, and cracked pepper; poached eggs, spinach, and roasted pumpkin; and my favorite, carrot hummus, tomato relish, goat cheese, tomatoes, and lettuce on pumpkin sourdough. Brigette Vallance, a Melbournian whom my brother Matt met in Aspen, Colorado, continued my education by taking me to coffee shops with names like Friends of Mine and Gypsy & Mosquito, as well as two markets where I would have loved to become a regular: the Queen Vic Market (the largest open-air market in the Southern Hemisphere) and St. Kilda Night Market (enhanced by a band, food stalls from around the world, and a colony of small penguins in the ocean nearby).

After three weeks, Melbourne had become one of my favorite places to run, and my very favorite to eat and wander. The city maintained its distinction as the most personally livable place I visited all year. Patios are abundant, live music is always an option, and restaurants and cafes stand out with creative themes and unusual décor (like church pews for seating or sheet music wallpaper). For such a big city—Melbourne's population of 4 million makes it the second largest in Australia—it's amazingly green and natural, with plenty of open spaces and a vast trail system. You can be in downtown or on the Melbourne University campus one minute, and in a national park the next, never far from a scenic run. It was the perfect place to let my legs—used to running slower at altitude—catch up to my lungs. Within the second week, without forcing anything, they finally did.

A big part of Melbourne's allure was the friendly group that included me from my arrival in Falls, took me under their wing in their city, and treated me like a long-standing club member. The MUAC team has a knack for turning group runs into all-afternoon and evening events, and collecting friends along the way. Like the members of the Finn Valley Athletics Club in Ireland, rarely were my Aussie running partners (and friends like Brigette) too busy to grab a bite to eat and socialize, even—*especially*—after long, energy-depleting runs. To them, hard efforts and small victories were worth celebrating, not an in-grained mindset of mine, but a worthwhile reminder. By the end of my visit, I had entered dangerous territory with the MUAC group by coming to expect a social outing at the end of each run. It wasn't economically sustainable, but it was fun while it lasted.

From the Falls Creek aqueduct to the Melbourne trails, my running friends in Australia were skilled at balancing full social lives, dedicated training programs, and demanding careers. I rarely heard complaints that investment in one area required a sacrifice in another. If they wanted a couple of beers the night before an interval session, fine! If a run had to be pushed back because a workday ran long, no big deal. And if one person in the group craved a post-workout bakery run for lattes, scones, or Anzac biscuits, he or she wouldn't be left stranded. While some parts of a season certainly require more rigidity than others, the MUAC attitude seems to me like a formula for a long, gratify-ing running career. In future moments of discouragement or questioning the path I've chosen, I know which country—and club—to revisit to find my way back to the joy of running.

IN FEBRUARY, I picked up where I'd left off on my agenda, and traveled eastward to New Zealand. My original intent was to explore the roots of the first global jogging boom, along with the hometown and training philosophy of famed coach Arthur Lydiard. My arrival a month later than planned allowed me to add another purpose to that list: to participate in New Zealand's summer racing season. While I'd needed a break from competition right after graduating from college, all of the low-intensity weeks I'd strung together in the first half of my trip, many at altitude, had to be doing *something*. I felt anxious to race and curious about my fitness level.

I owed a lot to New Zealand before I even landed. Though jogging has been part of my life since birth—first from the double baby jogger my dad pushed around Dallas's White Rock Lake, then on my own two legs for a mile or two, and finally as a competitive runner—jogging is a relatively new concept. Until the 1970s, it didn't really exist in most developed countries, and running was mainly reserved for young or serious athletes, individuals in a hurry, or fugitives on the lam. Enter Arthur Lydiard, a running coach in Auckland with a background in rugby and a desire to test the limits of the human body. First drumming up local interest when three of his athletes—Peter Snell, Murray Halberg, and Barry Magee—medaled in the 1960 Rome Olympics, Lydiard transformed New Zealand's entire athletic environment in two decades' time.

With his country's attention turned to running, Lydiard began showing that the health and social benefits of running were available to the masses, too: first converting a few friends into joggers and eventually, in 1962, forming the Auckland Joggers Club, the first organization of its kind in the world. Rumor has it that Lydiard met his cofounder, eventual Auckland mayor

Colin Kay, on a plane; Lydiard gave Kay "a hard time about his visible paunchiness and lack of fitness"; and Kay's subsequent enthusiasm for jogging spread to his colleagues in the business world. One February day, Lydiard and Kay led "a motley bunch of about 30 unfit men, some quite old and some unable to manage more than 100 metres," on the club's first run, "because Arthur had convinced them it would do them nothing but good." Though Lydiard initially hoped the club would whip unhealthy businessmen into shape, he eventually decided that his clientele was far too narrow. The world was full of potential joggers—they just didn't know it yet.

Later that year, famed U.S. distance coach and Nike co-founder Bill Bowerman visited Lydiard in Auckland and brought along some of his athletes. Upon arriving at One Tree Hill (now called Cornwall Park), Bowerman was so impressed with the wide-ranging turnout and excited about the concept of recreational running that he bought in entirely. He joined the jogging movement himself and then imported it back to Oregon, in the form of classes, clinics, Sunday morning runs, and a popular manual titled *Jogging*. The American jogging boom followed and was bolstered by Frank Shorter's 1972 Olympic Marathon win in Munich, the first American victory in that event since 1908. By the time American Joan Benoit became the first women's Olympic Marathon champion in 1984 in Los Angeles, "the sight of runners in the park or on the sidewalk no longer raised eyebrows."

The buzz begun by one man from a small island nation set into motion a worldwide running phenomenon. Fifty years later, the marathon is one of the most international and diverse sporting events in the world, and still gaining momentum. I'm no physicist, but I understand that, barring interruption, an object in motion stays in motion. Considering that global marathon participation increased 13 percent between 2009 and 2014 (with females experiencing a 26.9 percent growth), the future of running looks bright.

SHORTLY AFTER I ARRIVED IN AUCKLAND, I witnessed the ongoing extent of Lydiard's reach—his push to get the masses out the door. No longer satisfied simply to run, or even to compete in standard road races like marathons and 5Ks, many active Kiwis have turned to creative spin-offs that capitalize on New Zealand's natural beauty.

Simon Bucknell, an Auckland native and former Rice University runner, needed a third support staff member for one such race, and the timing of my visit made me a perfect candidate. Very loosely, the Speight's Coast to Coast Multisport Race is a cross between an ultra-marathon and a triathlon (a kayak through fierce rapids replacing the swim), with a short night's sleep in a tent, only an occasional spectator or course marshal, and a huge array of stunning landscapes. Each person (or relay team) brave enough to compete cycles 140 kilometers (87 miles), runs 36 kilometers (22 miles), and kayaks 67 kilometers (41 miles) in total, either in one day for those competing in the World Multisport Championship; in two days, as Simon chose; or on a double-day relay team. Whatever the format, the athletes ultimately race 243 kilometers (150 miles) across the breadth of the South Island, from Kumara Beach on the Tasman Sea all the way to Sumner Beach on the Pacific Ocean, following race founder Robin Judkins's original 1982 route.

The logistics of the race are nearly as complex as those of

my trip around the world but are condensed into a few days and require a lot more equipment. In the days leading up to Coast to Coast, Simon checked, tinkered with, and rechecked his gear, and finalized lengthy checklists for the transition points where his parents and I (his "roadies") would meet him. The mid-February weather meant potentially brutal heat, necessitating thorough hydration and nutrition plans and sacks full of energy bars, sports drinks, and portable snacks like bananas and bagels. (One competitor even dared to stuff a burrito in his spandex shorts.)

On race morning, a familiar, charged atmosphere filled the starting area in Greymouth, as Simon and more than eight hundred other athletes relished the final still moments of the day, the sun not yet risen. As soon as the two-day competitors began the first leg, a 3K run, Simon's parents and I made a run for it ourselves, competing, in a way, with the other support crews hustling to the transition points. Per tradition, support crews wear loud, easily identifiable attire for quick spotting by their athlete; the Bucknells and I donned neon yellow wigs, like a circus family on the loose.

We saw Simon for a few minutes at each transition (the shorter, the better for him), as we waited for him to enter the chute; led him to the equipment, clothing, and fuel we'd arranged on a tarp; and helped him prepare for the next leg. Before we knew it, he was off, and we were, too, as soon as we'd cleaned up our station. The rest of the competition followed that pattern, the action we saw limited by our ongoing duties. Some of the transitions were more challenging than others—lugging a kayak across a sandy stretch nearly a mile long with a few sharp inclines and steep staircases, for one—so I made the most of our drives from point to point, as the landscape changed from sea to mountains to plains and back to sea.

Coast to Coast finishing chute for one cycle segment of the multisport race.

The night between race days was nearly as action-packed as the daytime. The athletes entered the last finishing chute of day one haggard and hungry, and it was their crew's job to ensure an adequate cool-down and plentiful fuel replacement. Resting his legs for the first time since morning, Simon lent moral support as his parents and I set up the campsite. With two of us squeezed into his one-man tent—his parents slept in their car—our anti-bacterial wipe "baths" wouldn't mask the evidence of a long, hot, physical day. But the stars above us, the mountain range behind us, and the field full of tents, campers, and makeshift kitchens created a striking environment nonetheless.

By the time we cooked and ate dinner, the moon hung high in the sky, and it dawned on me that I hadn't yet run. In an extremely unusual lapse, I'd been so occupied that I'd forgotten about my own running plans for the day. I'd taken a day off a few days before, when Simon and I had flown to the South Island, so

I was determined to get in at least a few miles. Running in the dark on a full stomach is never ideal, but inspired by the racing and scenery I'd seen that day, I settled on a forty-five-minute jog.

The road was blocked off for the competition, leaving me with two options. I chose a riverbed of sharp rocks instead of a steep, rugged rise into a forest, viewing a twisted ankle as a better consequence than an unrecoverable wrong turn. But as I staggered back to the still, black field of tents barely over half an hour later, I wasn't so sure I'd made the right choice. After running over a sea of chalky, jagged rocks of varied sizes, I now felt little muscles in my shins and foot arches that I didn't know existed.

After a fitful night's sleep, I woke well before dawn to prepare Simon's gear and to clear out our campsite, while he squeezed in another hour or so of much-needed sleep. Throughout the second day, as his parents and I rushed from stage to stage, worrying about beating him to each one and nailing the setups, my appreciation for the simplicity of running grew. The only equipment involved is a pair of shoes, *maybe* a watch, but even those aren't necessary, as my Ethiopian friends taught me. Of course, there's always the possibility of injuries, but flat tires and leaking kayaks are nonfactors, as are flawed transition plans and unreliable crew members.

The very reasons I'm not a multi-sport athlete make other personalities a good fit for events like Coast to Coast. Simon's serious running days ended when he graduated from Rice, but his track background gave him a leg up on his competition here, and this race allowed him to train with purpose, but not pressure, once again. It was an opportunity to set new goals, test his toughness in different contexts, and chase the rapid improvement latent in new endeavors. Long-distance adventure racing is more about tolerating an extended, varied, and calculated grind than performing a single discipline at maximum capacity; completion, not mastery, is the badge of honor. I respect those adventurous athletes, but after my short-lived stint as a roadie, it was clear I'd chosen the right sport for me. I'm consumed enough by the pure act of running; I'd drive myself crazy if I were to add more disciplines to the mix, always wondering which one I was slighting. (I guess the heptathlon was out, too, even if I had an iota of javelin potential.)

AFTER REENTERING THE RACING SCENE as a support crew member, it was finally time to get competing myself. New Zealand's summer racing circuit, both on the roads and on the track, offered yet another link to Arthur Lydiard. In the 1960s, his athletes ascended the international running hierarchy on the same surfaces on which I'd be training and racing.

My look into Lydiard's legacy as a world-class coach began with two of "Arthur's Boys": Peter Snell and Barry Magee, both medalists in the 1960 Olympics. Before I left the United States, I spent an evening with Snell and his wife, Miki, in their Dallas home, and once in Auckland, I paid a visit to Magee. The remarkable list of accomplishments between the two men is a testament to each of them and their coach. Snell is a three-time Olympic champion (two from the 800/1,500 double in the 1964 Tokyo Games), the holder of many world records during his career, and the winner of New Zealand's Sports Champion of the 20th Century award. Magee, best known for his bronze medal in the Olympic Marathon, also earned a number of world number-one rankings, from the 4×1-mile relay to the 10K. While Snell has been lying low in the track-and-field world since his 1965 retirement, Magee remains involved, still coaching forty to fifty young Kiwi runners in the Lydiard style.

Like most experienced runners, I was familiar with Lydiard's periodization-of-training model, which has seeped into most of today's distance training systems: a pyramid anchored by heavy aerobic conditioning and topped by the targeted event, with a 4-week strength phase (with hills), a 4-week interval phase, a 4-week speed and skills phase, and a 3–4 week taper phase in between (from bottom to top). For his own athletes, the coach's foresight went even deeper. "He said it takes three to ten years to make a champion, and six months to peak for one race," Magee told me. Lydiard's Boys trained at high volumes, primarily on roads, grass tracks, and horse tracks (as opposed to running tracks as we know them in the United States), and spent summers at the beach, using sand as resistance and logging two runs a day.

Lydiard bred runners who were as mentally tough as they were physically fit. Magee mentioned that he raced his former teammate Murray Halberg around 100 times and lost 95 of them—but he set out to win every single time. The weekly 22-mile run that Snell, Magee, and their teammates did all year long, according to Snell, brought many men to tears—but was a "*must*-try" when I was in Auckland. "It was impossible to be coached by Lydiard and not be mentally strong," Magee recollected, before recommending that same 22-miler. It seemed there would be no getting around it.

Much more than just the mastermind behind their running, Snell and Magee remember their coach as an advocate of meaningful, balanced lives—not unlike what I'd just witnessed in Australia, but with less emphasis on the social aspect. During his most competitive years, Snell biked around town and ran to and from his full-time job, refusing to own a vehicle until he retired from running. Even Lydiard himself, while coaching, co-owned and worked in a shoe factory, moonlighted as a milkman, and served as his own guinea pig for training ideas, once logging

402 kilometers (250 miles) in a single week. In our conversation, Snell echoed his coach's recommendation that elite runners always hold a job and his belief that a productive, well-rounded athlete will go further than a single-minded, mentally unstimulated one. A few years later, as I set out to balance running with writing, volunteer coaching, and nonprofit work, those words ring true.

I FELT REVERENTIAL as I entered hallowed running territory in Auckland; but more than that, after six months of training and no serious racing, without the direct oversight of a coach, I was a little uneasy about my return to competition.

Fortunately, my next hosts, whose homes I alternated between for six weeks, were willing training partners and skilled stand-in coaches. Kyle Barnes is an American runner and distance coach who was working toward a Ph.D. in exercise physiology at the Auckland University of Technology (AUT) and training for the Boston Marathon during my visit. Hayden and Charlotte Shearman, native Kiwis, are also active in the running world, Hayden as a competitive runner, running form coach, and publisher of running guides to international cities, and Charlotte as a recreational runner and racer, between nursing shifts. Their homes provided easy access to some of Auckland's best training spots: oceanside trails and the AUT track; the Domain, an enormous field with a 400-meter grass track and a smooth dirt path; and Cornwall Park, the preferred long-run spot for Kiwis, dating back to Lydiard's era.

I figured that a road race would be a nice reintroduction to competition—large crowds, low pressure—so I chose to begin my season at the Round the Bays 8.4K, the 1972 brainchild of Lydiard's Auckland Joggers Club. Under Coach Bevan's instructions and Kyle's guidance, I eased my way back into hard work-outs in preparation for the race. The morning after I moved in, Kyle took me on a long run on a trail that, in true New Zealand fashion, traversed dense, lush forests, breezy marshland, and sandy beach paths—three starkly different environments. Most mornings, we ran along an elevated stone path that cut through the ocean at high tide, and a few times a week, Kyle and I pushed each other up the massive hills scattered throughout his neighborhood. The more I saw of Auckland on foot, from the seaside runs to the pretty, remote paths, the better I understood why New Zealanders were the first members of the jogging boom. In that setting, alongside my positive training partner, fitness gains came quickly.

Race day arrived sooner than I would have liked, which is usually the case. I expected a big crowd and some local elites, but the 70,000 participants who turned the starting area into a half-mile-long mosh pit caught me by surprise, and officially stamped Round the Bays as New Zealand's largest mass partici-pation sporting event. To put it into perspective, the largest race on U.S. soil, the Atlanta Peachtree 10K, attracts around 56,000 entrants—a full 14,000 fewer than Round the Bays. Coach Lyd-iard's running revolution is charging on, at the recreational level at least.

Standing beneath the start banner, I was catapulted back in time to my very first race, at the age of nine: the 1998 Jingle Bell Run, a 5K fun run through downtown Dallas. I remember very little of the actual race—my dad had me at "free T-shirt and jingle bells"—and I'm sure that my three siblings and I held up the rear. But that event was significant enough that almost two decades later, I still have my race bib taped to my bedroom wall, now joined by bibs from nearly every organized race I've participated in since then.

After the gun fired, I tinkered with my pace for the first mile and a half as we exited downtown, eventually falling into a nice rhythm behind the lead pack of men and slightly ahead of the other women. The weather was cloudless and the temperature was rising, and it seemed that all of Auckland that wasn't out racing was watching from the sidewalks and outdoor cafes that lined the course. On my own at two miles, now winding along the ocean, I turned the race into a game: How many guys could I catch before the finish? A few who'd gone out hard were already falling back, and the heat and humidity gave me confidence to hunt them down.

One by one, I made my way up the field, appreciating the contrast of each bay we ran through. When I reached Mission Bay, Hayden, as promised, caught up to me on his bike and spurred me on in the final miles, letting me know my position in relation to my competitors. St. Heliers Beach finally came into sight and the finish banner sparked one last push—holding off the other women, I crossed the line in 28:18 (a 5:25-minute mile pace for 5.22 miles, exactly the kind of effort Coach Bevan had wanted). Happy with my win and feeling part of something special, I celebrated at beachside barbecue pits with the thousands of other racers.

AFTER I SHOOK OFF THE COBWEBS on the roads, the oval beckoned. Unlike many others of its kind around the world, New Zealand's national track association allows foreigners to compete in its yearly championship meet, though the title of national champion is still reserved for the top Kiwi in each event. Though low-key compared to the U.S. championship, which features a who's who of track athletes each summer, the meet still promised good competition and an opportunity to mix it up with the locals.

After six months of uninterrupted base training, working my way up to 95-mile weeks (about fifteen miles more per week than I ever logged in college), I felt stronger, aerobically, than I ever had before. But spiking up and running fast, timed intervals on a track was a different kind of animal. In my first couple of workouts in Auckland, I felt awkward and uncoordinated bumbling around the track, regaining my feel for faster paces. Fortunately, other than Kyle and me, only one other person was regularly using the AUT facility: Valerie Adams, a shot putter with 2 Olympic golds, 2 Commonwealth Games wins, and 7 indoor and outdoor world champion titles to her name. Her training couldn't have been more different than mine, but her gigantic throws, hurled with audible effort, created an exciting training environment nonetheless.

My training progressed, and a couple of weeks later, the track gained a bubbly, blond addition when Callie Thomas—a great friend and a former Rice teammate—came to visit with her husband, Paul, an equally joyful Rice graduate and football player. After some less than subtle encouragement, here they were, my first visitors from home and a training partner I knew and loved.

For one week, I happily toured greater Auckland and much of the South Island with Callie and Paul, combining outdoors adventures like paragliding over Queenstown and stargazing from the base of Mount Cook with a heavy dose of running (and some first-class refueling) each day. Callie was preparing for the upcoming track season in the United States, and as we explored new cities by foot, we fell right back into our side-by-side formation from college, pushing each other in workouts and easily filling long runs catching up on the news from the last six months. Alongside Callie, a champion kicker and one of my role models, I finally started seeing glimpses of my speed, which had gone untapped throughout my trip thus far. The value of a training partner who's also a close friend can't be overstated.

Soon after Callie and Paul went home, leaving me with my college racing spikes and some fresh trainers, it was time to dust off the spikes. Not feeling quite ready to take on the steeplechase, I entered the 5,000- and 1,500-meter races at the National Championship. The 5K was my focus: It's closer to my specialty events and was first on the schedule, meaning I'd be rested and fresh; the 1,500 would be a nice bonus, a test of speed after months of aerobic training. Kyle timed my final track workouts, also pacing me for parts of them, and kept me company on a few easy oceanfront runs—an abbreviated taper.

Moments before the start of the 5K, I looked around the call room and saw only five other competitors—a far cry from the U.S. Championships. It was odd not knowing any of them or their credentials, but freeing too, since I was even more of an unknown. Stealing a tactic from the TV Oerlikon Track Challenge I watched in Switzerland, I used the beginning of the 5K to gauge the competition as I sat on the leaders for six laps. When Kyle, who was taking splits from the backstretch, gave me the command, I took control, first putting in a big surge to shake all but one pursuer and then settling into a comfortably hard rhythm. As planned, I pressed hard in the last kilometer and finished in first with a negative split. If you heard nothing besides my four raucous housemates who came out to support me—Kyle, Scott, Erin, and Grieg—you would have thought I'd set a world record. In reality, my 16:25 was about 30 seconds off my personal best, and much slower than the fastest Kiwi 5Kers, who didn't compete. But it was a successful return to the track, and an honor to share the podium with three fine New Zealand runners.

The podium at the New Zealand National Track and Field Championships, where the highest Kiwi finisher and I shared the 5K victory.

With a day between my events and a desire to stay occupied before races, I spent the next day relaxing at a beach with my housemates. I'm not sure that sunbathing and snorkeling are recovery activities that most coaches would condone, but it put me in a positive frame of mind going into the 1,500 nonetheless. Back at the track for my second race, I warmed up a little longer than usual, making sure my legs had time to work through the stiffness they felt from the race two days before. The warm-up area was much livelier than I remembered it, and checking in, I discovered that the field was over twice as large as the 5K, with thirteen runners participating. The race began and, not wanting to dictate the pace, I settled into a position where I was still in touch with the pack, but able to watch the race unfold. I realized the error of my patience when, around the 800-meter mark, I realized I was in last place. Used to having another 10 or 20 laps to make up ground and correct mistakes, I'd put myself in a bind over such a short distance. With Kyle and the others urging me on, I picked it up over the last half mile, treating it as an extended kick to the finish. By the time I reached the bell lap, I'd reconnected with the field and I managed to pass almost half of them over 400 meters. Four runners held me off in the end, including Lucy van Dalen, a New Zealand Olympian and Stony Brook University graduate, who finished so far ahead of everyone else, it almost became an exhibition.

Despite getting handily beat in the 1,500, I was pleased with the way my legs responded to just a handful of track workouts. My six months of accumulated mileage had, as expected, translated better to the 8K and the 5K than to the 1,500, an event that felt short to me even in college, when I was doing less mileage and more speed work. I had no way of knowing what another half year of consistent, varied training would do, but I was getting more and more excited to find out.

My track season wrapped up at Nationals, but I still had one race to run. My short summer season would end on the roads where it started, in an unparalleled, marginally dangerous event: the Queen Street Golden Mile. First contested in 1972, the downhill course has been the setting of some "terrifying" performances, according to Kiwi great and former mile world record holder John Walker, who finished fourth in the race in 1982. (Former U.S. mile record holder Steve Scott won that year in 3:31.25.) Kenyan Mike Boit, 1983 Olympic bronze medalist in the 800 meters, ran a jaw-dropping 3:28.36 the following year—still the fastest mile ever clocked.

The Golden Mile was revived during my last week in Auckland after a thirty-year hiatus. The course was almost the same as the original version, with one safety-related change: The start had been pushed down the road, eliminating the steepest segment of the previous route and ending with a flat quarter mile instead of a continued drop. Regardless, it was slated to be an insanely fast event. I wanted in.

The race was open to the public and, to accommodate a range of abilities, all participants were assigned to a particular wave based on one's estimated mile time. Thanks to one of Kyle's connections, I'd received an invitation to the International Women's division alongside an impressive lineup. The entries included three women who had run 4:30 or faster for a flat mile, and two who had competed in the London Olympic 1,500 meters. My mile PR was a comparatively modest 4:45, clocked indoors a year before; I truly had nothing but a personal record to lose.

After evaluating my last race and examining the road, Kyle helped me map out a plan. Given the course, we decided that I needed to hammer the first quarter mile; even with the lowered start, the first 400 meters had the largest elevation drop and we predicted that my competitors would take advantage of it. From there, the plan was to hang on to the leaders for as long as possible, saving one last gear change for the final flat 400. For this last race in New Zealand, I dropped all caution and committed to our strategy.

After a gentle warm-up with a few subtle downhill strides to get my legs spinning, the gun fired and the field quickly split into two. As planned, I stayed attached to the front group, running at a pace frighteningly more akin to my 300-meter hurdling days in high school than to a normal distance race. When we approached the half-mile mark, one of the runners made a move that two others matched. I tried to go, too, but the trio pulled away, leaving three of us in their wake. As the course flattened out in the final quarter, our group began to string out, too, and I found myself in sixth place. I heard Kyle yelling at me to increase my turnover (footstrike frequency), and keying in on my closest target—who happened to be a former Conference USA rival—I turned on the gear change Coach Bevan and I had worked hard on during my last year at Rice. She looked over her shoulder with a few strides to go, giving me just enough time to nip her at the line. My finishing time was 4:32, about 13 seconds faster than my flat-course best; Susan Kuijken of the Netherlands won in 4:17, followed by Zoe Buckman of Australia and Lucy van Dalen of New Zealand.

Finishing in fifth place against a stacked field was even more satisfying than winning the sparsely contested 5K a few days before. I loved the road race mile format, which blended the precision of a track with the lighter atmosphere of the roads, and I felt privileged to participate in the revived Queen Street Golden Mile. Even though the downhill advantage prevented me from claiming a new mile PR, I savored the time attached to my name and left confident that an honest sub-4:40 mile was within reach.

Two DAYS LATER, racing season complete, I finally got to take a crack at something that had been tugging at me for months, even before I'd left the United States: Arthur Lydiard's Waiatarua Circuit, the 22-miler that his athletes used to run every Sunday. Both Peter Snell and Barry Magee considered the loop an essential element of Lydiard's program and of their physical and mental training; while in Auckland, I couldn't *not* run Waiatarua. Despite the paved roads that replaced the quieter dirt roads of the 1960s, it was still possible to trace the footsteps of Arthur's Boys. When Hayden, who'd run the course before, offered to keep me company on his bike, I jumped at his invitation. My directional skills as shaky as ever, I also wrote out directions to tuck in my sports bra as a backup; there were eighteen turns in total, and I didn't want to risk an unplanned separation from my guide.

Legendary coach Arthur Lydiard's former home in Auckland, and the start and finish of the 22-mile Waiatarua Circuit.

Around 7 A.M. on my final day in Auckland, Hayden and I parked in front of the starting point for the run—Lydiard's old house, surprisingly unassuming for such a global coaching giant. Following Hayden, who biked ahead of me to signal upcoming turns, I ran the first part of the route on the sidewalk of a busy road, the flattest part of the run. A few miles in, we turned off onto a more peaceful, empty stretch, enclosed by green fields that I imagined was much more like the setting during Lydiard's day. Soon the course began rolling and after a few gentle hills—and a friendly reminder from Hayden to pace myself—we approached four kilometers of a steady, grinding climb. I kept pressing upward and finally, after a handful of deceiving bends, we reached the Scenic Drive signpost, pointing left to Titirangi and right to Piha: the Waiatarua Summit.

The second half of the run was as much downhill as the first was uphill, with one more surprise series of rolling hills in between the peak and the finish. At one point, Hayden swerved to the shoulder of the road and waved me over, revealing an obscured water source where Lydiard's athletes used to rehydrate. We both cupped our hands and took a few sips—if there was any magic in the water, I wasn't leaving without it—before making our final descent to the coach's old home. We reentered the city and the last few miles were a blur, mixed with euphoria from nearing the end of *the* Waiatarua Circuit, and exhaustion from the climbs and the distance.

My finish at Lydiard's house marked my longest run ever by two miles (not counting that accidental Ethiopian detour), and I felt a personal connection to the guys whose careers took off on that road. Peter Snell had told me months before that Lydiard believed that a person's time, running all out, on the Waiatarua Circuit was a rough marathon predictor. If he was right, my comfortably hard 2 hours and 37 minutes boded well for the future and made me even more impatient for my 26.2-mile debut.

NEWLY PAVED ROADS and Lydiard's passing aside, the running climate in New Zealand has changed since its zenith in the 1960s and 1970s. Whereas the tiny country once "punched above its weight," as Barry Magee put it, it now performs about how you'd expect for a population of 4.5 million people (compared to the United States' 319 million and Ethiopia's 94 million). A few Kiwi runners, such as Nick Willis—national record holder and Olympic silver medalist at 1,500 meters—and Kim Smith—long-distance runner with 6 national records and 3 Oceanian records—are threats on the global stage. (Interestingly, both Willis and Smith went to college in the United States.) But if distance running was once king in New Zealand, it's since been usurped by the throwing events, with athletes like Valerie Adams and Tomas Walsh leading the way.

While Arthur Lydiard made a groundbreaking impact on running, I wondered whether his introduction of the sport to the masses might have had an unintended effect on the future state of the country's elite running. The huge turnouts at Coast to Coast, Round the Bays, and the Queen Street Golden Mile, compared to the small fields at the New Zealand National Track and Field Championships, suggest that casual athletes form the bulk of the country's current running community. But by the end of my trip, I saw the transformation from Lydiard's era less as a running decline and more as a reflection of New Zealand's robust and active outdoors culture. International podium presence isn't every athlete's aim, nor is it necessarily an accurate measurement of a country's running environment. I think Arthur Lydiard would be pleased rather than dismayed to see the repercussions of the movement he started a half century ago, both in New Zealand and throughout the world.

With its diverse and gorgeous landscape, ideal summer weather, and numerous racing opportunities, Auckland turned out to be the perfect setting to return to competition. My generous hosts—Kyle Barnes and his housemates, and Hayden and Charlotte Shearman—helped ease my transition from training to racing, while also becoming some of my closest friends of the year.

Coach Bevan ingrained in me that it's neither healthy nor possible to stay sharp year-round, and this trip was shaping up to be one big experiment in the benefits of an Arthur Lydiard–style base. I wouldn't get to fully reap those benefits until I returned to the United States six months later, but the New Zealand summer racing series had been a telling midyear checkpoint. Though no races were planned for my next stop on the map, Japan promised some tests and challenges of its own.

Anzac Biscuits

These cookies, popularized during World War I by wives of the Australian and New Zealand Army Corps (ANZAC) and a favorite treat of Mel Sampson, can be made with ingredients found in most athletes' pantries and pair nicely with afternoon tea or coffee. I adapted this particular recipe from taste.com/au.

1 cup all-purpose flour
1 cup rolled oats
1 cup desiccated coconut
½ cup brown sugar, firmly packed
¼ cup granulated sugar
8 tablespoons butter
2 tablespoons golden syrup (can use honey or molasses)
2 tablespoons water
½ teaspoon baking soda

1. Preheat oven to 325° F. Line 2 baking sheets with parchment paper.
2. Combine flour, oats, coconut, and both types of sugar in a large bowl.
3. In a small saucepan on a stove set to medium heat, stir butter, golden syrup, and water until smooth. Stir in baking soda. Add wet to dry ingredients and stir well.
4. Roll dough into balls by the tablespoonful and space evenly on prepared baking sheets, flattening gently.
5. Bake on two racks in preheated oven, switching baking sheets halfway, for 15 minutes or until biscuits turn light golden brown.
6. Remove from oven. After 10 minutes, transfer to wire racks to cool completely.

6

POUNDING PAVEMENT, RETHINKING RECOVERY

Japan
297 miles

As I dipped a toe into the gold-flecked hot tub, I felt remarkably unrelaxed. The purpose of the *onsen*, I knew, was healing and rejuvenation. And from the look of things—women rotating between ten pools, each one catering to different preferences in temperature, scent, jet intensity, and, apparently, mineral content—it worked.

But as I tiptoed around the public bathing house, faking confidence and trying to blend in with the cream-colored bodies around me, I found it impossible to unwind. It didn't matter that, nearly nine months and as many countries into my trip, I considered myself a cosmopolitan young adult; I felt more like an eight-year-old giggling at nude grandmas in the YMCA locker room. Nor did it help that I was exhausted from my recent journey from Auckland to Tokyo and a ten-mile, jet-lagged run. My tense body and stark tan lines stood out like chopsticks in a bowl of ramen.

Fortunately, the ladies of Namban Rengo, the international running club I joined for the month, were there to help. The most important thing, they told me as we finished our run under a canopy of the season's last cherry blossoms, was that I follow the body-washing protocol before entering the pools. And so I did, copying their every move as they squatted on short plastic stools, scrubbed their bodies multiple times with warm water, soap, and washcloths, and then sprayed down their stations. Even if I couldn't loosen up completely, at least I'd be in the running for cleanest traveler on the circuit.

Once I actually submerged myself in the first pool, and twisted my wrung-out washcloth on top of my head like the bathers around me, my anxiousness melted away in the jet streams and bubbles. I became more concerned about which pool I wanted to try next—the lavender-scented one? The hot tub or the *hot* hot tub? The one with built-in recliners?—than with how exposed I felt in a room full of naked strangers. And as I lazed the hour away, my own birthday suit resembling a big raisin, the irony of my situation sank in: I had come to Japan to witness one of the most regimented and disciplined running systems in the world, and yet my first run was overshadowed by the long, leisurely onsen session that followed it.

My interest in Japan's running culture was first kindled by a group of monks, of all people, the subjects of John Stevens's *The Marathon Monks of Mount Hiei* and the seekers of an unusual path to enlightenment: seven years spent in isolation in the mountains, working their way up to covering a marathon or more for one hundred days straight (for those who are successful). During the fifth year of their endurance challenge, the monks spend more than a week sequestered in a dark room, without eating, drinking, or sleeping, the goal being to maximize the window of enlightenment through a close encounter with death. In former centuries, monks who gave up before finishing the *kaihôgyô*—the name for the challenge—had to take their own lives.

To outsiders, distance running in Japan seems, in a word, intense. Training systems emphasize extreme discipline, unquestioning obedience, and colossal work ethic. One of the highest compliments available to a Japanese athlete is to say that he or she has *makenki,* roughly translated as "the spirit not to lose." Female marathoners commonly log 60K (37-mile) long runs, while males run over 200 miles in one week—and some do much more. Yuko Arimori, an extreme but not isolated example, won silver and bronze medals in two women's Olympic Marathons off 750-mile training months (averaging a marathon a day), once stringing together two 20K (12.4-mile) time trials in one day; a 31-mile run the next day; and three 10K intervals the third day.

As serious as they are about high volumes, the Japanese are equally purposeful about taking their recovery runs easy, abiding by the belief that every minute spent running accumulates in the end. While shuffling is hardly considered training in the United States, and many runners I know limit their exertion away from practice in fear of compromising their workouts, slow, low-impact activity is perceived differently in Japan. Some elite Japanese runners even prepare for long races by wearing weight vests and walking up to 180 miles per week in the base phase. That unhurried mindset reminded me of the East Africans I'd run with so far—the Kenyans in London and the Yaya Girls in Ethiopia—only much more methodical and intense.

I found Japan's unparalleled public interest in long-distance running almost as intriguing as the running itself. Japanese running stars are household names; some, like Yuki Kawauchi, "the Citizen Runner" who works forty hours a week as a government clerk and so far has won 23 of 51 marathons, garner cultlike followings. Even Haruki Murakami, author of the hit book *What I Talk About When I Talk About Running,* is widely known both as a recreational runner and a novelist. In the United States, by contrast, a disconnect exists between recreational runners and professionals; I'd be afraid to find out how few non-elite runners would recognize even Galen Rupp or Shalane Flanagan if they passed them on the streets. The Japanese public doesn't just like to follow running though; they get in on the action, too. In light of its enormous applicant pool, which is now upward of three hundred thousand—meaning a one in ten chance of gaining entry—the Tokyo Marathon recently became one of the World Marathon Majors (a prestigious title shared only with Berlin, Boston, Chicago, London, and New York). When I visited, Japan was in the process of bidding (successfully) for the 2020 Olympics.

Runner's World's Brendan Reilly contrasted Japan's running climate with that of the United States by noting, "While U.S. marathon broadcasts rarely creep above 1 percent ratings, in Japan a 10 percent rating for a major ekiden or marathon would be a disappointment; certain athletes and events can bring Super Bowl–like 40-plus percent rankings." The Boston Marathon, the oldest annual 26.2-mile race still contested, is one exception; Marathon Monday attracts 500,000 live spectators, and the race's stringent qualifying standards have made "BQs" (Boston Qualifiers) the litmus test for a marathoner's seriousness. Imagining that kind of interest in multiple road races back home was comical; comparing the enthusiasm for distance running to the mega-popularity of the NFL was downright hilarious.

But there was one more purpose for my trip to Japan.

"Miss Becky Wade! How is your workout in NZ. Big information for you! Team SHISEIDO has interesting for you. SHISEIDO is cosmetics company. Can you stay in Tokyo until December from April? for EKIDEN. But SHISEIDO will be able to pay as income that a contract worker. And you must teach English to Japanese at her office. You will be able to receive good treatment for your room. If you hope the conditions of SHISEIDO, it will welcome. It do not accept short term. Please tell me your answer Yes or No? Take care."

From what I gathered, this was a generous offer and a chance to experience Japan's one-of-a-kind corporate-sponsored running culture. The invitation came by e-mail from one of Coach Vigil's connections, the coach of a male corporate team who had found a women's team willing to take me on board. While it's rare for an American runner to receive significant sponsorship from non–running stores or brands—and hard enough to earn those—many professional Japanese runners are financially supported and employed by companies ranging from department stores and automakers to cosmetics manufacturers (like Shiseido) and lingerie shops. Once an athlete gains membership to a team, often straight out of high school, he or she is given nearly every resource imaginable to succeed as a runner: housing, food, a stipend, coaches, nutritionists, physical therapists, and a rigid schedule. Teams typically meet for a morning run, put in a half day's work at the corporate sponsor's office, and meet again in the afternoon for the main workout; logging around 620 miles per month (20 per day and 140 per week) that way is typical. Team members also attend regular training camps around Japan and abroad—I served members of one Japanese team at the bakery I worked at one summer in Boulder, Colorado—and represent the corporations in races, with a heavy emphasis on peaking for the major *ekiden*.

The ekiden, unique to Japan, is a long-distance road relay modeled after the ancient communication system in which mail was delivered through a chain of messengers. In 1917, on the anniversary of the relocation of the capital from Kyoto to Tokyo, the first ekiden was staged between teams covering over 300 miles in a three-day event. Today, there's no uniform distance or number of legs in an ekiden; the National High School Ekiden is composed of half-marathon legs for women and full marathons for men, while the New Year Ekiden features 7-person teams running stages between 8 and 22 kilometers to cover a total race distance of 100 kilometers. The common thread among them is extreme competitiveness and massive public interest, which consumes the country during ekiden season. These races are taken so seriously, in fact, that they're partially blamed for Japan's weak presence in international running, relative to the true depth of the country's runners. I kicked myself for missing the peak of ekiden season in January, having lingered in Australia and New Zealand as I chased summer around the world. But the next time I visited Japan, I decided, I'd either be standing on the sidelines of an ekiden, or even better, wearing one of the sacred *tasuki* sashes, fighting for a U.S. victory.

Unfortunately, I had to decline the Shiseido team offer—Watson Fellowship rules strictly forbade employment, and I wasn't willing to eliminate my final destinations in order to spend April through December in Japan. But the invitation substantiated my research about the disciplined, structured lives of my Japanese running counterparts. It was an interesting contrast from the runners I encountered in Ethiopia, who worked hard but with little sense of time or schedule. Yet both countries had very strong running traditions, Ethiopians consistently manning the podium after international races and Japan showing incredible depth in the marathon and half marathon; in a single month in 2007, more than 90 Japanese men ran halves faster than 65 minutes, the standard to compete in the 2016 U.S. Olympic Trials marathon with a two-and-a-half-year qualifying window. The "best" way to train was becoming more baffling with each stop on the map.

BECAUSE MEMBERSHIP in a corporate-sponsored training group wasn't possible, I scoured the Internet for an alternative, one that would allow me to learn about the Japanese running scene without signing a binding contract. My e-mails to local clubs went unanswered, our language barrier the likely culprit. But Namban Rengo, an international running club whose name loosely translates to "the Barbarian Horde," stepped up, Chairman Bob Poulson leading the way. In addition to meeting me when I arrived in Tokyo, Bob arranged home stays with three members of Namban Rengo and introduced me to many more; he assured me that, though many were expats and none were elite, they'd help me unlock the mystifying world of Japanese distance running.

Fascinated by the colossal volumes that Japanese runners are known for, I chose Yoyogi Park, a training spot with history, as my first stop on the Tokyo running circuit. Toshihiko Seko, two-time Olympic marathoner and former world record holder, was a Yoyogi regular during his prime in the 1980s, logging many of his 200–300 miles per week around the park's two-mile perimeter. I wondered how many of those miles—and of his famous 630-mile week—were run there, how often he changed direction, and whether he counted by laps or by minutes.

I didn't want to experience that for myself, but I did want to test out the footpath Seko helped carve around Yoyogi's circumference. So I tagged along with Bonnie Waycott—my first host, who grew up in London in a Japanese home and worked for NHK, the Japanese equivalent of the BBC—to her workplace one morning, conveniently next door to Yoyogi. For our lunchtime meeting point Bonnie chose a big metal structure on the edge of the park that looked like it had been plucked from a high school hallway.

"Public lockers," Bonnie explained, "where people can stow their purses or backpacks while they're in the park." A rental costs between 100 and 500 yen (80 cents to $4), depending on the size of the locker and the length of the reservation; a small one for my backpack set me back less than two dollars for the morning. Once Bonnie pointed the lockers out, I began spotting them all over the city—near trails, parks, train stations, and tourist attractions. Active individuals were never far away.

As my host headed to her office, I approached the single-track dirt path on the edge of the park, only a couple of feet wide. From the middle of Yoyogi, you wouldn't notice the path, but once on it, you have prime viewing of the park's interior. Much of what I ran by confused me, and each run brought new surprises. Dogs, for example, were often dressed like humans. In one afternoon alone, I saw pooches dressed in skinny jeans, overalls, tank tops, and army garb, a few even wearing clothes that matched with their owners. I also observed the opposite at Yoyogi: humans dressed like animals. One scene I jogged by consisted of a man wearing a panda mask, holding the attention of at least a hundred people sitting cross-legged on a tarp and decked out in bunny ears, wands, alien heads, tails, and bumble bee antennas. The panda and I made eye contact on my second loop, and the third time I passed by, the entire crowd turned my way, waving and cheering with the gusto of a marching band.

The park wasn't all fun and games, however. A few runs into my stay, I spotted my first corporate-sponsored team running in the distance at Yoyogi, identifiable by their crisp, matching black and white uniforms. For a moment, I feared that they were the Shiseido team I'd been invited to join; I hoped they wouldn't put the pieces together and feel disrespected by my rejection. Instead, when our paths collided behind a pond, the all-male group ran right by me without a single glance in my direction, looking focused and serious. We passed each other a few more times that day, and I never did muster up the bravery to wave hello or hop in with them for a mile or two, as I might have in Ethiopia. The team's intensity was intimidating, and made even the atmosphere during Falls Creek workouts feel light.

The monotony of the Yoyogi loop, barring amusements such as humans and animals dressed as each other, could be difficult at times; but that was part of the appeal to Toshihiko Seko and other elites who trained there. A large component of the Japanese running philosophy is mental strength, harnessed in many cases through extreme mileage and grueling repetition. If you can push yourself for 10 or 15 laps of a single park, I'd imagine you feel like a claustrophobe emerging from a closet when you covered the same distance on an open road. Loop courses like Yoyogi are also popular among Japanese runners because not only do they allow for precise pace monitoring and continual self-assessment, they also give coaches multiple opportunities to see their athletes, critique their form, and give them instructions.

Though far from a running treasure like the Tan in Melbourne or Cornwall Park in Auckland, the Yoyogi loop became my favorite route in Tokyo. It required a couple of train exchanges to reach, but in a city so congested and developed, the park offered a rare connection to nature and a soft, uninterrupted circuit. It also linked me to Toshihiko Seko, the king of repetition; on my fifth or sixth lap, when the inevitable boredom started to creep in,

I simply thought of him and the performance-enhancing power of repetition.

A SHORT JOG away from Yoyogi Park is Oda Field, a track-and-field venue named after Mikio Oda, Japan's first Olympic gold medalist (in the triple jump in 1928). Bob Poulson told me that Namban Rengo and some other clubs practiced there every Wednesday at 7 P.M. and invited me to come check out this popular Tokyo training spot.

When I showed up, however, it looked as though the practice was conflicting with a track meet. At least three hundred runners, most of them wearing pristine windbreaker sweat suits, filled the track, the infield, and the stone steps near the facility's entrance. Not actually a meet, Bob explained, this was just an ordinary Wednesday night, and one of only a few time slots in which the centrally located track was open to the public. Numerous teams, including Namban Rengo, corporate-sponsored groups, and university clubs, claimed it as their home track and miraculously, it worked.

As the evening wore on, what would have caused pandemonium on every other track I'd run on—dozens of workouts and paces happening at once—was organized chaos on Oda's track. An unspoken rule ensured that the fastest runners got the inside lanes, while everyone else politely jostled for position around them. Although it seemed as though each lane was hosting a separate workout, the participants of one were respectful of the others. Rather than adding another workout to the mix, I watched while jogging around the comparatively peaceful infield, and was shocked that I didn't witness a single collision all evening.

The orderliness I saw at Oda Field, unfortunately, did not extend to Tokyo at large. While I ran at Yoyogi Park as much as I could that first week, my high volume necessitated running from Bonnie's urban apartment for many of my main runs and all of my two-a-day sessions. My best option was a one-mile stretch on a sidewalk that started at one major highway and ended at another, and put me within arm's length of cars on the road. Unlike the United States, where walkers and runners stick to the right side of a sidewalk or path, and runners run against traffic while in the street, Japan has no such rules. I learned not to expect others to move out of my way, meaning I had a 50 percent chance of dodging the right way when faced by an oncoming pedestrian. I also learned (through disapproving looks) that when it comes to traffic laws, runners are no different from cars and pedestrians. Even if the path ahead was clear, I was expected to stop at every stop sign and stoplight and wait for the signal to order me forward.

At the start of those runs, I was less than inspired; by the end of them, I felt flustered and tight, the impact of the pavement shooting up my legs and the constant stopping, starting, and cutting interrupting my flow. I could handle the Yoyogi repetition, but by the time I moved on to my second host in Tokyo, all of my sidewalk running was catching up to me.

THE CALF STRAIN that cropped up during my second week in Japan—my first setback of the trip—was almost predictable. Though I replaced my last few runs from Bonnie's with double Yoyogi days, a slight limp and increasing discomfort while running indicated that, according to my training log, the damage had been done over almost 70 miles on that one-mile stretch of road in a week. (*Overdo things? Me??*) I mentioned but downplayed it to Coach Bevan; had I been under any other roof, I might have continued running and risked further damage.

Luckily, Mary Eckstein, my next host, was a competitive runner, biker, and triathlete—not to mention one of two sets of twins, an upstate New Yorker (where my maternal roots are), and a fervent globetrotter—and I met her at just the right moment, when my pavement-pounding runs and fatigued muscles were conspiring against me. Before I even had time to protest, she'd set up a cross-training station in her living room where I could ride her mounted bike while helping her judge *American Idol* contestants and complete *New York Times* crossword puzzles.

Mary also encouraged me to seek an outside opinion on my calf. She knew of an acupuncturist in the area who was popular among both Japanese and visiting runners (including the great Joan Benoit Samuelson, the American marathoner and 1984 Olympic gold medalist). I was still a bit uncertain about alternative medicine; a few stubborn injuries during college had me trying nearly every healing mechanism in the book, usually to the effect of conflicting opinions and deeper frustration. But if an Olympic Marathon champ and personal heroine like Joanie trusted the practice, I certainly wasn't above trying it myself.

Other Namban Rengo members confirmed that in Japan, acupuncture—which involves the insertion of thin needles into specific points of the body—is as ordinary a healing technique as massage and chiropractic care in the West, and the preferred treatment for banged-up runners. Unlike my limited experiences with it in the United States, they told me that rarely is acupuncture an isolated approach; depending on the location and cause of the damage, it's usually accompanied by massage, realignment, or physical therapy. Nearly all of the runners I asked about it in Japan had tried acupuncture at some point, and nearly all of those believed in its healing power. So I booked the earliest appointment available with the acupuncturist Mary recommended and did my best to muster up the same optimism and trust I'd take to an orthopedist's office.

Hiroshi Kawaguchi, a compact, soft-spoken man dressed in a white coat, didn't ask many questions—lots of prodding and head nods, followed by a request to lie flat on my back and relax completely. He gently stuck six or eight small needles into my affected leg—all along the side and front of it, rather than the aggravated calf itself—and then connected them to a machine, fiddled with a few knobs, and left the room. About thirty minutes later, I was startled out of a daydream.

"Good. You're relaxed!" Kawaguchi said approvingly. After dislodging the needles from my skin, he spent about ten minutes massaging the knot in my calf and the arch of my foot. His touch was purposeful and experienced, neither too aggressive nor too soft, and he lingered on the tender spots without my having to point them out. As he worked, he told me that my body was the master healer, and that his acupuncture work was just pushing it along. "Rest for a few more days, and then slowly return to running. I think you will like how you feel."

Before I left, Kawaguchi showed me some things to work on as I healed. I was to stretch my calf in two ways: the normal standing calf stretch, heel hanging off a ledge; and a squatting one, my left shin entirely on the ground, right foot flat on the ground, and torso leaning forward. He also wanted me to roll my foot on a golf ball a few times a day until the tenderness subsided. And finally, Kawaguchi taught me a simple two-step exercise for self-aligning my pelvis, which was off-kilter when I came to see him. First, lying on my back with my knees bent and feet flat on the ground, I let my knees fall together to the floor on my right, and then to my left (ten times on each side). Next, lying on my stomach with my quads flat on the ground, knees bent at 90 degrees and feet in the air, I let my feet fall together to the floor on my right, and then to my left (again, ten times on each side). I started following Kawaguchi's advice that night, and continue to revert back to it whenever I sense misalignment.

I stayed on Mary's bike and in her gym's pool for the next few days as I let the acupuncture and exercises work together to begin repairing my calf. During my first afternoon in the Tokyo Metropolitan Gym, despite my Japanese illiteracy, I became an expert on the facility's no-nonsense rules, a list so long and precise I would have thought it was a joke had every other patron not been dutifully following it. First, I was chastised for water jogging without wearing a swim cap (never mind that my neck stayed above water). Minutes later, a lifeguard came charging my way, furious that I'd gotten past him wearing a watch in the pool. Without a visible clock in the room, I wasn't sure how people kept track of their intervals or splits, other than by laps (which meant nothing to a water jogger). But I wasn't about to protest, especially when, shortly after, I was asked to relocate to a different corner of the pool. I didn't dare ask which rule I'd violated now.

Later that week, I got a break from the indoors (and the rules) when I took my cross-training to the mountains, along with Mary's husband, Peter, and two of his friends, Mika and Murphy. They were doing a 100K charity walk the following month, and to prepare, were traversing the entire course in segments. They wanted to cover 25 kilometers that day, meaning a predawn start to catch all of our train connections and finish before dark. I've never met an early morning I didn't like, and the opportunity to see a different area of Japan was enticing after a couple of weeks of urban chaos.

I acknowledge that 15.5 miles of hilly hiking (over about six hours) isn't a common form of recuperation. But Peter's invitation reminded me of a conversation I'd had with Julia Bleasdale back in Ethiopia about her untraditional approach to healing. When she has to take time off, she slowly works her way back into running, bit by bit, until she reaches a certain point (45 minutes or so of continuous running). At that point, Julia escapes to the mountains, feeling unchained and inspired in the natural setting. She believes that running uphill, especially, activates muscles that can get neglected on flat surfaces, while also keeping her speed in check. If an injury has already begun to heal, Julia prefers to let the endorphins and variation offered by the mountains finish the job.

As I followed my hiking buddies up and down hills, between green tea plantations, and past traditional Japanese homes—with colorful koi windsocks flapping in celebration of the upcoming holiday, Children's Day—Julia's logic resonated with me. I was using my legs, and my aggravated calf in particular, in a slower, more deliberate way than I had been while running, and I was feeling invigorated. The landscape offered pleasant, ever-changing distractions, including, every once in a while, a hazy peek of Mount Fuji, the highest mountain in the country and a still-active volcano. While enjoying my surroundings, I admit to being a tiny bit preoccupied in trying to figure out the ideal way to consume the rice balls we brought for lunch: triangular mounds of rice wrapped in *nori* (dried seaweed), with tasty morsels (salmon, in my case) buried in the middle. Just like the Toaster Strudel dilemma of my youth, I eventually accepted that the corner bites would not have any of the precious filling, and I savored the salmon bites for as long as I could.

I woke the next morning stiff and achy but felt ready to put my calf to the test. In the spirit of my Kenyan friends and the Japanese marathoners who walked as training, I took a leisurely stroll from the Ecksteins' home to Yoyogi Park, and then let my legs get to spinning. I was careful not to get carried away—a habit I've fallen victim to before—so I faithfully followed Coach Bevan's instructions to take a short break every mile, filling a couple of minutes of rest with Kawaguchi's stretches. Thirty minutes in, all signs pointed to a much-improved calf. Whether the fix was the acupuncture, the cross-training, or my open-minded optimism, I don't know. But I was no longer limping, or an alternative medicine or therapy skeptic.

First injury of the trip: averted. *Had I ever dodged an oncoming injury before?* I racked my brain and couldn't think of a single instance in which I had. The fear that my body is doomed to break down, no matter how careful and attentive I try to be, was finally vanquished.

PEOPLE-WATCHING IN YOYOGI, or during the famous Shibuya Scramble (when pedestrians completely flood the world's busiest intersection), was one way to get an authentic taste of Tokyo. Another was sampling directly from the city's cuisine.

Tim and Susan Griffen, my third and final hosts in Tokyo, masterfully took the reins. Hardly considered American expats after living in Japan for twenty years, Tim and Suse immediately impressed me with their annual sushi party, featuring a kaleidoscope of ingredients so delicately arranged that I felt guilty disturbing it: vinegared sushi rice, sheets of *nori,* a dozen types of seafood (including tuna, salmon, shrimp, scallops, eel, crab, sea urchin, octopus, and salmon eggs), avocado slices, pickled plums, cucumber and daikon radish spears, and *tamago* (thin omelets), alongside accompaniments like shiso leaves, wasabi, soy sauce, and ginger.

The bounty of seafood came from Tim's weekly shopping trip to Tsukiji, the world's largest fish market, which employs 65,000 people and brings in $7–8 billion each year. When I joined Tim on his next Tsukiji trip, I was mesmerized by the competitive tuna auction, with carcasses as big as hogs, endless rows of straight-from-the-sea catches, and an entire street devoted to kitchen and restaurant supply goods (the knife makers were particularly captivating).

Japanese cuisine goes far beyond sushi. When I landed in Tokyo, Bob Poulson took me to a hole-in-the-wall *yakitori* restaurant, where we tried an assortment of skewered and grilled vegetables and meat: sautéed mushrooms, grilled shishito peppers, charred lines of ginkgo nuts, and a few chicken varieties, my favorite of which was marinated in a slightly salty and sweet sauce called *tare* (made of mirin, sake, soy sauce, and sugar). While feasting with members of Namban Rengo, I became hooked on soba noodles and ramen, which I was relieved to see bore little resemblance to the microwaveable cups popular in college dorms. Both meals were delicious, slurp-friendly, and enhanced by intensely flavorful broth, the soba noodles hearty and dark, and the ramen noodles delicate and slippery. Tokyo also offered an unexpected rival to the treacle bread I savored in Ireland: the delicate, croissant-like *hokkaido* milk bread we bought at Suse's favorite bakery.

No matter where I went or what I tried, my enchantment with the Japanese food culture continued to grow. I was constantly sidetracked by the intricate, handmade replicas of dishes that restaurants displayed in their windows (many purchased at Tsukiji), and I could have spent days in the food gardens below Tokyo's major department stores. Each display cabinet presented produce, candy, bento boxes, and of course, seafood, as if they were luxury goods on sale. Some were ordinarily priced, while others—like the two-hundred-dollar cantaloupes—might have been a better fit for one of the more extravagant sections upstairs.

As a health-conscious athlete, I deemed Japanese food the most nutritious and quite possibly tastiest of my destinations so far. Because Japan is an island nation, its cuisine revolves largely around seafood, which, if recently caught and handled properly, requires little tinkering and few frills. Don't get me wrong—the food industry there is ruthlessly competitive, with sushi chefs taking as long as twenty years to master their craft—but it almost requires a different skill set when the quality of the food depends more on the masterful selecting, cleaning, and presenting of ingredients, than the transformation of them. Combined with the small portion sizes and use of chopsticks—a natural barrier to gorging—it's no wonder that the Japanese obesity rate is among the lowest in the world.

FORTUNATELY, while eating my way through Tokyo, I was also reaping the benefits from Kawaguchi's acupuncture and my week of rest. After a few days of easy running, starting with thirty minutes of jogging with breaks, I gradually increased my load, my calf strengthening and compensations subsiding as I went. And once again, I found myself in good hands with running-savvy hosts. Jogging is Suse and Tim's preferred method of socialization, with thirty-eight marathons between them (including every Tokyo Marathon since its 2007 inception). When I felt ready to tackle pavement, having run mostly on Yoyogi's grass interior the week before, my hosts and I hit the ground running.

My first long run back in action was along Tokyo's canal path, one of the Griffens' standard running spots. It's concrete and occasionally interrupted by car crossings, but well maintained and much more pleasant than my stop-and-go sidewalk runs earlier that month. I gave up on trying to navigate through Tokyo by myself—the absence of signs in English and the different system for addresses threw me for a loop—so I hopped on the canal when I wanted to branch out from Yoyogi. Suse also took me for a morning run at the Imperial Palace, known for housing Emperor Akihito and the rest of the imperial family, as well as for the popular jogging trail that borders it. Five kilometers around and void of any traffic lights, the path is nearly always packed with joggers, walkers, and bicyclists. Our run was no exception, even at 10 A.M. on a weekday, though the system of counterclockwise running made the loop seem much less crowded. From the path, we could see the moat-surrounded, low-walled white palace, and I wondered if any members of the imperial family had ever ventured onto the path for a quick run around their home.

I was delighted when, toward the end of my stay, Suse—a self-professed running nerd—asked me if I had any interest in watching the London Marathon. I'd already been planning on paying to stream it from my iPad, I admitted, and was surprised when she told me that in Japan, major road races happening both domestically and overseas were commonly broadcast on national television, *live and for free*. I didn't have any personal interest vested in the race, but on the women's side, Suse and I cheered for Japan's own Yukiko Akaba, the eventual third-place finisher, along with Tiki Gelana, the London Olympic champion who was slammed by a wheelchair athlete in the first half of the race, but still managed a sixteenth-place finish.

If running—and watching running—was a national pastime in Japan, such an active country needed a leisurely diversion; hence the institution of public bathing facilities. A handful of my runs with Namban Rengo ended with an onsen, and the more I visited, the more comfortable I felt in my own skin. I don't think I was ever mistaken for a local—my pigment and tan lines gave me away—but by my last spa outing with Suse and her daughter Heidi, I felt cultured and accomplished when I undressed and dipped in without hesitation. Suse suggested we cap off my visit with a dip in a special pool, meant to work wonders on our feet, and upon entering, I lost my composure entirely. The three of us spent the better portion of our fish therapy session howling in laughter at the incessant pecks on the soles of our feet and in the nooks between our toes. After about ten minutes, a group of women speaking Japanese walked into the room and I quickly stifled my laughter so as not to appear disrespectful of the ritual. But the moment their own feet touched the water, the room erupted into a cacophony of shrieks and squeals and the three of us laughed right along with them. Though fish therapy is intended to cleanse and refresh, I found it just as rejuvenating for my soul as it was for my body. If hot-tubbing naked is the best introduction to a country, getting your feet nibbled by fish, I decided, was the best way to say goodbye.

Susan and Heidi Griffen and I share some big laughs during a fish therapy session in Tokyo.

From a tourist's perspective, Tokyo was a dream: delightful, electric, interesting, and bewildering (like the baby doll costumes seen on many grown women, and the infiltration of Hello Kitty into every corner of society). But it hadn't been the running hub I anticipated, with training venues limited and elite runners rarities in the crowded, concrete-laden capital. So before I left Japan, I was determined to run in a city that was calmer and more hospitable to the purpose of my trip.

My first thought was to travel to Mount Hiei, located northeast of Kyoto, to visit the mysterious Marathon Monks. I imagined tracking them down in their mountainous hideaway and gleaning wisdom from the monks in training and the few still living who have completed the seven-year endurance challenge—only 46 men in the last 130 years. The *kaihôgyô* was the most reverent embodiment of movement I'd come across, and I couldn't wait to witness it in person.

The only problem, as I learned from my research, was that meeting the monks apparently had to be on *their* terms, not mine. As badly as I wanted to talk to those dedicated men, I didn't have time to wait for their invitation. I'd have to look beyond Mount Hiei.

Another option hovered in the background, becoming more and more enticing with each photograph I scrolled through. Google Mount Hiei and you'll find Kyoto, the former capital of Japan, filling the foreground of many pictures. The Kamogawa ("Kamo") River, flanked on both sides by a wide dirt path, rivaled the famous peak above it for my attention, and visitors confirmed that Kyoto was as friendly to runners and walkers as it looked on my computer screen.

Kyoto it was. As a bonus, I'd received an invitation from a Japanese family to spend the weekend in their home in Yokohama—a town just outside of Tokyo but on the way back from Kyoto—and to bring a friend along if I wished. I quickly e-mailed Celeste Miles, a high school friend who'd recently moved to Singapore for work, and she opted in immediately. (Only later did we realize that the "quick trip" from Singapore to Japan is seven hours by plane, about the time it would take to fly from Mexico to Canada.)

CELESTE AND I ARRIVED in Kyoto at night, so naturally, our first priority was to get in on some karaoke, one of the city's most popular pastimes. Our opportunity arrived when, while strolling around town, four young Japanese men came stumbling across the street, arm in arm, singing at the top of their voices and making a horrible racket. Our karaoke partners had arrived, whether they knew it or not. None of them spoke much English, but Celeste and I were either great at charades or they were so confused that we tricked them into joining us. Either way, a few minutes later, the six of us were crammed onto two couches in a tiny room, passing drinks and a songbook around while warming up our vocal cords. They insisted that the ladies start first, so Celeste and I nervously approached the mic.

Within the first three notes of Justin Bieber's "Baby," I knew we were in for a riotous night. Our friends exploded off the couches and into position, as if they'd been waiting all their lives for the chance to perform this song. We nailed the first number as a group, our passion making up for the horrendous noise spilling from the speakers. The next thing I knew, Celeste and I were engaged in a back-and-forth battle with the guys, each team trying to outdo the other with song selection, volume, and dance moves. By the end of the hour, we'd given them memorable renditions of Christina Aguilera's "Come on Over," Destiny's Child's "Say My

Name," and Miley Cyrus's "Party in the U.S.A.," while the gentlemen wowed us with Japanese pop and rap and American hits such as Fergie's "Big Girls Don't Cry."

The end of the hour neared, and there was still not a clear-cut champion. Then, seizing the moment and the mic, and waiting for total silence, one of the men broke off in a pitchy, heartrending version of "Let It Be" that would offend every Beatles fan who's ever lived. That performance alone justified my purchase of a nice video camera for this trip, while also clinching the win for the male team. After the applause died down, one of our fellow crooners handed me and Celeste his phone, a Google-translated message on the screen: "Do you want to extend?" As much as we did, we didn't dare end the night on any note but the ones still ringing in our ears.

Kyoto's all-star karaoke crew, featuring Celeste Miles and our four unabashed new friends.

ALWAYS THE GOOD SPORT and with little time to spare, Celeste, a former soccer goalie at the University of Virginia, agreed that running around Kyoto would bring us the most bang for our buck. Dozens of temples, shrines, and gardens stood in between our hotel and the Kamo River, so the next morning we began our crooked beeline to the river, taking breathers whenever we came across a worthy site (using the volume of selfies being taken nearby as a quick indicator). We lingered longest at the Golden Pavilion (Kinkaku-ji), a three-story, gold leaf–adorned Zen Buddhist temple with a history reaching back to 1397. The pond beneath it and the deep green forest in its shadows made the temple look as if it had been dropped straight from heaven.

By the time we reached the Kamo River, Celeste and I had logged a solid run, a few miles since we'd left the hotel, and at least that much remaining. But the clear skies, wide-open trail, gently flowing water, and runners scattered on both sides of the river lured us in for more. We decided to run in opposite directions this time, and as I took off down the path, my spirits soared, feeling energetic and balanced for the first time since my calf flared up. The surface—loosely packed dirt—reminded me of my old stomping grounds around Rice University, and on a nice day like that one, restaurants on the river opened up their balconies, allowing diners to keep tabs on the activity below and hungry runners to scope out their eating options.

In Kyoto, for the first time all month, I was able to "run free," Coach Bevan's cue to disregard my watch and run as fast as I wanted to without straining. My feeling on the river path was as powerful as when I sensed something was off on the one-mile stretch in Tokyo, but this was the opposite, an indication to press on. Self-discipline is a valuable tool, and an important and admirable component of the elite Japanese running culture. But equally crucial to me are the runs that uplift and inspire me, that make me want to both run forever and freeze-frame time. In Japan, I experienced runs on both ends of the spectrum, and learned about myself from each of them.

MY CONNECTION TO THE HATTORI FAMILY, whom Celeste and I were going to stay with in Yokohama, requires some explaining: Mr. and Mrs. Hattori's son Daisuke (in Mexico at the time) is a friend of Sara Cavicchioli, the daughter of the Italian man my dad befriended on a train in Italy forty years ago (and whose family I visited in September). More of a squiggle than a line, with the potential for our visit to either capsize or swim, Sara connected Mrs. Hattori and me by e-mail, and soon I had an invitation to be the Hattoris' honored houseguest. Two follow-up questions set the tone for the weekend: "What kind of dishes do you like? Do you have any difficult foods?"

The only difficulty I had at the Hattori table was prying myself away from it after each meal. Machiko, a kind, motherly woman with a wavy bob of black hair, insisted that she wasn't going out of her way for Celeste and me, but—like with Kieran Carlin in Ireland—I had a hard time believing that each time she laid out a feast of no fewer than eight courses, with that many dishes at each place setting. After an introduction over matcha tea and sweets (mostly gelatinous and neon), I got the Japanese cooking lesson I'd been waiting for. First, Machiko showed us how to make pork, ginger, and bamboo dumplings, a process that requires thorough mixing, precise filling, and careful crimping. Next, we marinated slices of cucumber and bamboo shoots in sesame oil, vinegar, and garlic, and helped her chop and stir-fry the main dish of chicken and vegetables (red and green bell peppers, eggplants, and onions). Finally, we made a flavorful rice medley with mushrooms, bamboo, and seaweed, and then washed and chopped an assortment of fruit for dessert. The rest of our meals were as elaborate as the first; our 6 A.M. breakfast spread the next morning included salted and grilled salmon filets, bowls of miso soup, rice, side salads, pickled radishes and cucumbers, fried eggs, a fruit platter, green tea, and coffee.

When she wasn't cooking or serving, Machiko was busy ensuring that Celeste and I were experiencing the best of her culture and the most of her hospitality. In addition to Michelin-star-worthy meals, Machiko prepared comfortable, plush beds for us atop straw tatami mats on the guest room floor, and let us choose from her daughters' patterned pajama sets left over from their teenage years. Celeste picked a rainbow striped one, and I settled on a pastel flowered one—the perfect ensemble for a middle school sleepover. Along with her husband, Akio—who also treated us as honored houseguests, insisting upon wearing a suit throughout our visit—Machiko devoted a full day to showing us around Yokohama, taking us to a foot bath spa (not of the fish variety) with a view of Mount Fuji; a tempura restaurant, where I feasted on battered and fried vegetables; and the Landmark Tower, the tallest building in Japan, with a 360-degree-view of the metroplex below and a Pokémon gallery battling for attention on the top floor. At the end of our stay, Machiko and her thirty-two-year-old daughter, Shugoku, again outfitted Celeste and me, this time in kimonos that the Hattori girls had worn when they were younger. They spent a good half hour wrapping, cinching, and tying, until they agreed with delight that we looked "very, very fine."

Mount Fuji looms behind the Hattoris, Celeste Miles, and me during a full day of sightseeing with our Yokohama hosts.

Machiko's parting gifts were as thoughtful as she was. In addition to a set of three hand-painted ceramic dishes, she gave each of us a square board that she'd adorned with a *kanji* (Japanese character). Celeste's stood for "destiny" and "many connections," which was appropriate given the circumstances of our reunion; the character she chose for mine meant "dream." Referring to the Olympics, which I'd told her was my ultimate goal, Machiko told me, "You have a big dream and I hope you will reach it," her words piercing my heart like Ishoo's had in the Simien Mountains of Ethiopia. As badly as I've always wanted to succeed in running for myself and my family and friends, my desire swelled at each stop on the map, with hosts like Machiko inspiring me to honor my talent and make them proud, too.

WHILE PLANNING MY VISIT TO JAPAN, I had envisioned spending the month with elite runners, dabbling in their extreme training methods and learning new ways to elevate my own discipline and commitment. While casually joining a corporate training group proved to be a challenge, as did breaking through the English–Japanese language barrier, my time was well spent with Namban Rengo, the running group with so many generous, interesting individuals. My hosts from that group—Bob Poulson, Bonnie Waycott, Mary and Peter Eckstein, and Tim and Susan Griffen—shared with me runs and experiences that no other team could possibly have matched.

While I had to learn about many Japanese running traditions by word of mouth—ekiden and Marathon Monks, monstrous mileage, and the system of corporate sponsorships—in the end, my hosts confirmed that Japanese society revolves around honor, humility, duty, and collectivism, and nowhere are those values reflected more than in its long-distance running culture. The marathon is a mass-participation event that thrives on a mass-participation following; Japan has both. The ekiden is "the ultimate team sport," the tasuki worn by each runner symbolizing the sweat and dreams of the whole group. And the traits cultivated by high-level Japanese distance runners—stoicism, discipline, and tunnel-vision focus—are the same that make noble citizens.

The intensity of many facets of the Japanese culture, running included, is lightened by traditions designed for relaxation and rejuvenation. Acupuncture, which thwarted my first injury scare of the trip, along with yoga and other Eastern customs, promotes healing and lessens the stresses of daily life. Japan's emphasis on fresh, nutritious food—on display at Tsukiji fish market, food courts, sushi restaurants, and my hosts' tables—aligns with the Japanese runner's mentality of honoring one's body and living purely. Onsen, the public bathing houses that baptized me by fire, and karaoke, an endlessly entertaining form of leisure, allow individuals to compartmentalize work and rest. With Namban Rengo, Celeste, and the Hattoris, I learned that both are not only possible in Japan but essential to a satisfying life. I hoped to carry that lesson with me to the last region of my trip: Scandinavia.

Ozoni (Bonnie Waycott, England and Japan)

Bonnie Waycott shared her mom's ozoni recipe with me—a light and flavorful Japanese soup that's enhanced by the addition of a rice cake or two and is warm and comforting after chilly runs.

2 garlic cloves, minced
½ white onion, diced
Olive oil
2 packages of chicken cutlets, with skin peeled (or 2 large boneless, skinless chicken breasts)
2 large carrots, peeled and chopped
½ head of cabbage, cut into thick slices
6 shiitake mushrooms, sliced
2 leeks, cut diagonally into ½-inch pieces
1 tablespoon fresh ginger, minced
Fish stock and soy sauce, to taste
Mochi (Japanese rice cakes, not to be confused with the dessert version; available at ethnic grocery stores or on Amazon)

1. Sauté garlic and onion in olive oil.
2. Add chicken pieces and brown.
3. Add carrots and cover with water.
4. Add cabbage and mushrooms, and then simmer for about 15 minutes, adding leeks and ginger in final 5 minutes.
5. Stir in fish stock and soy sauce to taste at the very end of cooking.
6. Heat rice cakes in toaster oven or on a pan.
7. Ladle soup into bowls, add 1–2 rice cakes to each, and eat hot.

SPEEDING SWEDES AND FLYING FINNS

Sweden and Finland
573 miles

I've run in some unusual places since entering the sport at the age of nine. A chicken farm in the Cayman Islands. Colorado's white sand dunes. A slum in Tijuana.

Even so, as I tore across a purple carpet rolled out like a tongue through a Swedish shopping mall, with DJs spinning records on the side, I couldn't help but laugh. I was racing in the Skärholms-loppet 5K, an annual race through a Stockholm suburb, and the atmosphere felt more like a disco than an athletic competition.

Adding to the excitement, running next to me was my older brother Matt, the first family member to visit me on my trip. Fresh out of his first year of law school at Harvard during our reunion in Sweden, he's nearly as absentminded as he is brilliant. The same guy that staged his first filibuster at age ten and kicked himself for missing one question on the LSAT has been known to lock his keys in the car with the engine running and once suffered second-degree burns from a skirmish over hot Bagel Bites with my twin. It was no surprise when, the morning of his expected arrival in Stockholm, he e-mailed me that he'd forgotten his passport *and* driver's license at home and missed his flight. No worries, though—he'd hop on the next one and "see ya in Switz soon!"

I sweated until the moment my olive-skinned, cowboy-hatted brother appeared at Arrivals in the *right* country, just a few hours late. Months earlier, he had agreed to meet me wherever I was in the world at the time, nearly convincing me to book his tickets, tell him when to show up to the airport, and surprise him with the destination at the last possible moment. But I'd traveled enough with Matt before to rightfully assume that even without any planned surprises, he'd contribute a few of his own. I'd also learned through experience not to take a hotel's complimentary breakfast lightly while traveling with him; his strategy was to gorge himself in the morning, pocket a few pastries for later, and buy food only when he became faint with hunger. (He agreed to relax the last stipulation just for this trip.)

Though Matt played club lacrosse in college and hadn't been on a run in months, he'd long since proven his natural talent and uncommon ability to push himself; he lived with me for two summers in Colorado, and both impressed and aggravated me by casually jumping from zero to 100 miles per week during our second stint there (a feat I definitely don't condone). So I took his assurance not to change my running plans to accommodate him as consent to sign us both up for a local road race.

Matt and I showed up to the Skärholmsloppet 5K after a full morning of sightseeing, and settled into the pack behind the starting line. The first mile was comfortable and conversational, as I'd promised, but near the halfway point, the course took a strange detour. The chalk arrows on the sidewalk led us to the parking lot of a shopping mall and straight through the open doors, a purple carpet beneath us, red balloons to our sides, and DJs blasting music ahead.

It was all fun and games until, just on the other side of the mall, we spotted a girl in skinny jeans and high-top sneakers ahead of us on the course. As uninterested as we were in taking the race seriously, and as distracted as we were by the runway atmosphere, we were not about to be shown up by a jegging-clad pedestrian. So Matt and I had no choice but to kick it up a notch until we caught her, and then ensure that we held our lead through the finish. I never actually saw our time, but our victory over that one rival, and our first race through a shopping mall, made it a successful day in our books. It also warranted a round of celebratory pick-'n'-mix candy popular in that part of the world; bumlingar jordgubbs and skumsvampars never tasted so good.

My brother Matt and I race through a Stockholm shopping mall during the Skärholms-loppet 5K.

By this point in my trip—ten months deep—I was starved for family time and happy just to be in the same place as my brother. The fact that we'd be traveling together to Stockholm, Gothenburg, and Malmö, Sweden and Copenhagen, Denmark was a bonus. Each day after a morning run and buffet feast, we let our legs guide our wanderings as we alternated between acclaimed attractions and unplanned detours, such as used-book stores, inviting benches, and usually a couple of coffee and pastry stops. I don't remember the history behind Copenhagen's Mermaid Statue or Tivoli Gardens, but I could paraphrase the conversation Matt and I had about my running goals and his career goals on the train ride to Malmö, and I could paint a picture of the little Stockholm garden in which we picnicked and filled in our training logs.

I could also describe in detail most of the 75 miles we ran together that week—I meant it when I said my brother has a gift—over city streets, bike paths, and forest trails in Scandinavia's pleasant summer weather. Though I tried to get him to hold back, I think Matt would rather have injured himself than let me stumble upon an interesting spot without him. Fortunately, barring one incident—nearly fainting after an optimistic fifteen-mile run, remedied by a few smuggled sugar cubes from an outdoor cafe—Matt matched me stride for stride all week long.

Ten days of trotting around Scandinavia with my older brother left me feeling like a brand-new traveler. When Matt arrived, I was feeling like a fish out of water. My energy and patience levels had dwindled after ten months of bouncing from one stranger's home to another, and I was chronically sleep-deprived from time zone changes, packed itineraries, and a full training load, all while trying to be a considerate and sociable guest. I was grateful to my many exceptional hosts, but traveling for another two months seemed daunting.

During Matt's visit, I was able to fully relax and, thanks to our aimless conversations on runs, walks, and train rides, I also had a clearer vision of what I wanted to do when I returned home. I've gone to my older brother for advice for as long as I can remember, and his support of a life built around running—which interested me before my trip, and by now had me hooked—carried a lot of weight. While I wished that Rachel, Luke, and my parents could have tagged along with Matt, that first reunion with a family member since I left home was just the elixir I needed to sustain me through the final segment of my journey.

MATT'S DEPARTURE MEANT it was time to dive into the running scene I'd come here for. No other region of the world showcases the ebb and flow of athletics like Scandinavia. The story begins with a duel—before Lydiard's Boys, before Bannister, and before the East Africans—between the neighboring nations of Finland and Sweden.

Between the resurgence of the modern Olympic Games in 1896 and the start of World War II, Finland—a nation of fewer than 4 million people—took home a slew of middle- and long-distance Olympic medals, including every 10,000-meter title except one. Three of those golds, all from the 1912 Olympics, were earned by Hannes Kolehmainen, "the Flying Finn." By the 1936 Berlin Olympics, when three Finnish runners swept the 10K, the nickname had been extended to their entire distance contingent. The Flying Finns became the team to beat.

In the late 1930s, the Swedes struck back. Gunder Hägg

and Arne Andersson—best friends and fierce rivals who were both coached by Gösta Holmér—each set three world records in the mile between 1942 and 1945. Hägg's 4:01.4 record stood for nine years—until 1954, when Englishman Bannister finally crashed through the four-minute barrier in Oxford. Along with his four-lap achievements, Hägg set thirteen world records and was the first man to run the 5,000 meters in less than 14 minutes.

A few decades later, with some assistance from New Zealand coach Arthur Lydiard, Finland rebounded from a slow period for Scandinavian runners. Juha Väätäinen's 5K and 10K victories in the 1971 European Championships, in front of a home crowd in Helsinki, began the comeback. With his double-double at the 1972 and 1976 Olympics (victories in the 5K and 10K at both), Lasse Virén officially resurrected the Flying Finns, joined by other successful runners such as Martti Vainio and Pekka Vasala.

After decades of internal jousting—eclipsing and trading world records, and fighting for running supremacy—Finland and Sweden have been mostly absent from the running conversation. Beginning in Stockholm, Sweden, and then making my way to Finland, I hoped to look to the past in order to better understand the sport's tradition on that side of the globe. Without a crew of A-list milers to stalk, as I would have done if this were the 1940s, I took my explorations to the fields, roads, and tracks that played host to a wide array of running events throughout the month of May. The nearly twenty-four-hour summer sun in Scandinavia, though a nightmare for my sleep, promised a pleasant and limitless backdrop for outdoor activities.

After participating in the 5K with Matt, my next race experience was as an assistant race director to Brian Nielsen, my Swedish-but-actually-Danish host father. I'd met Brian in Ethiopia, during one of his work assignments there; while talking at Haile's Great Ethiopian Run after-party, our similar compulsion to see the world through running surfaced. Before he flew home, he scribbled his number and address on a Post-it note, and offered those magical words, "If you ever make it to Sweden . . ." Six months later, I did, slipping Sweden into my agenda before I spent June in Finland, one of the five countries on my original itinerary.

A serious runner (he's run 1:08 and 2:27 for half and full marathons), race director, husband, and father, Brian trains before his family wakes up, refuels with a bowl of twelve-ingredient muesli and a glass of fresh-squeezed juice while he helps his daughters get ready for school, and spends the rest of his day working for two running-related organizations. For the local relay race he was putting on the day I moved in, we sorted the bib numbers and marked the 2-kilometer course before the racers showed up and gathered in a grass field near the starting line. About ten minutes before the gun went off, two young women got up on a portable stage in front of the participants and prompted them to gather round.

To the beat of Swedish pop music pounding from speakers on both sides, the ladies led the crowd in a high-energy routine that blended Jane Fonda aerobics, Zumba moves, and elementary school gym class exercises. Never had I seen grown men and women windmill, run in place, and shimmy so vigorously. It struck me as comical in comparison to my standard pre-race regimen of jog, stretch, drill, and stride; but as my friends from

Kenya, Switzerland, and Ethiopia had demonstrated, to each his own warm-up strategy.

The race began, with relay teams battling it out on the 2K loop while the DJ played on, and many runners replicating the spirited warm-up moves while waiting for the baton. I didn't see blazing speed out there—unless you count Brian, who was darting from one side of the course to the other to ensure a smooth race—but what caught my attention more than the talent was the turnout: about one hundred four-person teams, most individuals showing up straight from their nine-to-five jobs, Brian told me. Had the competitors been of school age, running just another extracurricular event, I wouldn't have been fazed; but these were exclusively middle-aged professionals, unafraid to let loose in the warm-up or the race, and I admired their game attitudes.

A WEEK LATER, I saw the Swedish running populace on the other end of the spectrum; this next group of racers had neither the jobs nor the same fitness goals as the adult relay teams. In fact, a few of them barely had hair, and many hadn't yet graduated from Velcro tabs to shoelaces. The Tullinge-Tumba Friidrott, one in a series of kids' forest races, essentially took place in the Nielsens' front yard. Brian, his wife, Lily, and their young daughters, Isabelle and Amanda, live at the edge of an old military base in Stockholm, and their front door opens up to acres of flat, grassy land surrounded by a thick forest and a well-marked trail network that gets increasingly hillier the farther out you go. The setting is worth five stars to a distance runner, and made it the perfect location for a trail race.

Little racers wait for the start of the Tullinge-Tumba Friidrott, a 725-meter dash through a Stockholm forest.

Isabelle and Amanda were among the thirty kids racing that afternoon, ranging in age from four to twelve years old; Brian, Lily, and I went out to cheer them on. Once the runners were positioned on the starting line, a dad led them in a bouncing warm-up routine that was very liberally followed by the kids. Someone yelled, "Go!" and the diversity of racing styles that followed was a sight to behold. One of the taller boys quickly put a gap on the rest of the field and kept extending it as the race went on. A few of the racers plodded steadily from start to finish, pausing only when their meddlesome fans wanted pictures or high fives. Some of the luckier ones, like Brian's youngest daughter, Amanda, received aid during the race in the form of a parental piggyback ride, which seemed to me the way to go. And at least half of the group, Isabelle included, sprinted off the line like wild banshees before slowing to a walk around the 200-

meter mark. When the finish line became visible, it was back to full throttle, each kid charging through the chute as if he or she were the champion.

It's possible that I saw a world record clocked that day—as far as I know, the 725-meter forest dash isn't contested anywhere else. Whether any of those kids will wind up as competitive runners, I'll never know (unless it's one of the Nielsen girls). But identifying young talent and making serious long-distance runners out of them was far from the point of the race. It was meant to plant seeds for an active lifestyle, expose kids to healthy competition, and teach them about work ethic and sportsmanship. From the post-race hugs and broad smiles on their faces, I suspected that many of those little racers would come back for more.

MY FIRST OPPORTUNITY to watch some serious Swedish runners in action came a couple of weeks into my visit, at the Swedish Relay Championships, an annual track meet in relay format that pits the country's best track clubs against one another. I've run on countless relay teams in my life—from the 4×100-meter relay in fifth grade, one of my first races ever; to the distance medley relay in college, a compilation of 1,200 meters, 400 meters, 800 meters, and 1,600 meters—and always felt honored to be chosen, the shared attention and collaborative effort a special treat. But a meet devoted exclusively to relay races was something I hadn't yet encountered.

Källbrinks IP, the track-and-field stadium in Old Stockholm, was packed with runners when I arrived, most of whom were in groups in the stands or warming up in packs of four. I recognized only two people that entire afternoon: Lisa Naucler, a former San Diego State University athlete I'd met through a Conference USA rival; and a middle-distance male, Middle Eastern by birth but Swedish by citizenship, whom I'd briefly crossed paths with at Yaya Village. Sitting down on a sunny patch of grass near the 300-meter mark, I was mesmerized all afternoon by the batons flying around the track.

Lisa and her teammates ran well in a competitive field; their 4×800-meter team finished third in a time that would have won the race the year before. And the guy I recognized from Ethiopia was the clear star of the men's 4×800-meter race, swallowing up a handful of competitors in his two laps alone. But beyond them, I hardly paid attention to any individual performances, distracted as I was by the battle between teams. It was rejuvenating to watch a team-driven track-and-field meet, and I appreciated the rare opportunity—usually reserved for sprinters—Sweden was giving its middle- and long-distance runners to pass the baton.

MY EXPLORATION of Sweden's running culture had so far been focused on the assortment of races happening throughout May. But something interesting was catching on in one training environment across town. On my last Monday in Stockholm, I got a chance to take part in it myself.

Just before 6 P.M., I arrived at Karlbergs Slottspark, where the presence of at least one hundred workout-ready individuals, mostly young adults and equally male and female, confirmed I was in the right place. I spotted Lisa Naucler, whom I had watched at the Swedish Relay Championship, dressed in fluorescent, logo-emblazoned gear that matched that of many of the other runners. She made her way to the center of the crowd, introduced herself and her fellow coaches—Charlotte Karlsson and Linn Modin, also elite runners—and explained the logistics of the upcoming session. As with every other Monday of the year, barring holidays, a free running clinic would fill the next hour, with both technical training and a structured workout, and options for different ability levels.

After leading the group on a warm-up jog to a nearby field and demonstrating a series of drills and stretches, Lisa, Charlotte, and Linn explained the three workouts they'd be coaching that day. Each coach was responsible for one group, and the options were: 3×5-minute hard efforts (recommended for those gearing up for the Stockholm Marathon the following weekend); 4–6×800 meters around a dirt track, surging the 100-meter backstretch of each lap (designed for those with some running experience); and a 40-minute circuit of jogging, drills, and strength exercises (a good workout for first-timers). The groups headed to separate areas of the field, and I divided the hour among them.

Whether introducing a new runner to proper running form or helping an experienced marathoner with a race strategy, the coaches cultivated an open, nonjudgmental environment. They demonstrated nearly everything they asked the athletes to do, cheered on their runners by name, and kept the energy high for the entire hour. By the end of the session, spirits were soaring, and it was easy to see why Runday had caught fire since its 2011 origin. As more and more people showed up each week, Lisa explained, she, Charlotte, and Linn realized just how influential they could be to recreational and beginning runners. They expanded their concept, and Runday morphed into a whole business model, with full-time jobs for the founders. Along with the free Monday practices—which remain the heart and soul of the organization—the coaches now also offer corporate and personal training, lectures, training camps, and workshops. Like London's

ParkRun movement, Runday is transforming Stockholm's athletic landscape and bringing the sport to the masses. As a bonus, the coaches are connecting with less serious runners, and bridging a gap that's too often overlooked.

MY TIME IN THE SCANDINAVIAN CAPITAL was coming to a screeching halt. And like a perfect parting gift, the Asics Stockholm Marathon took place on my last weekend there. The grand finale of my month of races, it's one of Sweden's premier sporting events, attracting many of the region's best distance runners, 7,000 international competitors, and hundreds of thousands of enthusiastic fans. Lisa invited me to watch the race with her, so naturally, we built our own run around it.

As flocks of racing-bib-clad runners inched toward the starting area and spectators took their posts along the course, Stockholm felt alive and on a mission. Although I was only watching, the nerves and excitement of the marathoners—including my host dad, Brian, and dozens of Lisa's friends and Runday clients—were infectious. Over the last ten months, and especially through my exposure to Stockholm's racing scene, my desire to resume serious racing had been growing. There was something to be learned from each race I saw or participated in, but the marathon was increasingly the object of my attention.

From our first watching spot on the crest of Västerbron, a bridge with a clear view of the city, to the finish line in the 1912 Olympic Stadium—site of eighty-three track-and-field world records, more than any other venue in the world—Lisa and I covered much of Stockholm by foot, pausing every couple of miles to rush toward a new mile marker on the course. Our run evolved into a long fartlek session—a combination of easy running and intense bursts—which was only fitting for my last run in the birthplace of Coach Gösta Holmér's popular speed-play technique. Every landmark we passed on the two-loop course—the woody Djurgården (the Royal Park), City Hall, Norrmalmstorg (the square where the 1973 bank robbery took place that yielded the term *Stockholm syndrome*), the Royal Palace, and finally, Stadion—presented an opportunity to say goodbye to the latest country I'd called home. And each time, Brian, who had so generously welcomed me into the Nielsen family, passed by, I thanked him with my loudest cheers.

ONE LAST AL FRESCO MEAL with the Nielsens—grilled portobello burgers, a salad with watermelon and sunflower seeds, garlicky black beans, and a frozen dessert made of blended berries and bananas—and I was on my way again, heading next door to Finland.

Twice in the last century, Finland has been the epicenter of distance running. My visit began with two men who contributed to the second wave, in Olympiastadion, the stadium in Helsinki where their careers were built. Decades past their prime, Ari Paunonen and Henrik Sandstrom are wonderful, kindhearted men who both have impressive running resumes. Ari holds three national records (in the indoor mile and 5K, and the outdoor 3K, shared with Lasse Virén) and is editor in chief of *Juoksiva* (the Finnish equivalent of *Runner's World* magazine), and Henrik is a former world-class marathoner and cross-country runner who did a training stint in Alamosa, Colorado. Both were eager to reminisce about their teammates and training, but my questions about their individual achievements yielded far fewer words.

Soon after I arrived, Henrik introduced me to Helsinki's Central Park during a pleasant 45-minute run. We began at an office building and within minutes were inside the forest, running along the 10K-long trail that cuts straight through the city, passing sports fields, horse stables, and deep, dark woods. Marked at every quarter mile and as wide as a road, it's popular among Nordic skiers and runners alike, including many of the Flying Finns of old. The surface of the trail makes speed work difficult, Henrik noted, but is ideal for recovery runs and long interval work, not to mention bird-watching and animal-spotting.

When we finished, Ari was waiting for us outside the capital's seventy-five-year-old Olympiastadion: site of the 1952 Olympic Games, the first World Athletics Championships in 1983, a second World Championships in 2005, and Väätäinen's big breakthrough in 1972, which put the Flying Finns back on the map. From the statues of Paavo Nurmi and Lasse Virén in the parking lot, to the official Sports Museum of Finland and the trackside Olympic Bistro, the venue is one big nod to Finnish track and field. Stadium Tower, which stands 72.71 meters high in honor of Matti Järvinen's gold medal javelin throw in the 1932 Los Angeles Olympics, reminds visitors that Finland's athletic supremacy has spanned multiple disciplines; in that same Olympics, Matti Sippala and Eino Penttilä finished second and third behind Järvinen, completing Finland's remarkable javelin sweep.

My Helsinki explorations continued when Ari took me to watch a local meet at Olympiastadion's warm-up track, which connects to the stadium through an underground tunnel. Once the host of many low-key competitions for the Flying Finns, the track is especially significant to the Paunonen family; it's where both Ari and his wife (a former Finnish champion in the 800 meters and 1,500 meters) used to train, and where they now coach their elite-level daughters; Venla and Aina take after their speed-oriented mom, competing in the 400-meter hurdles and 800 meters, respectively. Although the competition at the meet was not particularly noteworthy, the turnout in the stands comprised a small Finnish Dream Team; in addition to the members of the Paunonen dynasty, I sat with Arto Bryggare (bronze medalist in the 1984 Olympic 110-meter hurdles), Tommy Ekblom (two-time Olympian in the steeplechase and "the Head Coach of Everything"), and Joonas "Badger" Harjamäki (one of Finland's top steeplechasers today). All the while, the old-timers exchanged stories about the glory days, poked fun at former rivals, bragged about each other's accomplishments, and projected bright futures for the current crop of runners.

Sitting among some of Finland's greats, in the old stadium where they'd all begun, Olympiastadion looming overhead, the Finnish track world felt small but proud, its history as a powerful running country something to remember and aspire to. Finnish runners had tasted success on the greatest stage of them all, having lived through two separate golden ages. Perhaps more important than knowing how to win, the tiny Nordic nation had shown that it knew how to fall and then fight its way back to the top. A comeback may seem unlikely now, but it must also have seemed that way in the 1960s, just before the second round of Flying Finns stormed in.

"MIND IS EVERYTHING. Muscle—pieces of rubber. All that I am, I am because of my mind."

Of all the Flying Finns, Paavo Nurmi embodies *sisu*, a Finnish word with no perfect translation in English—but roughly meaning guts, bravery, resilience, and hardiness. His resume is unrivaled in the distance world: 9 Olympic gold medals, 3 silvers, and 22 official world records at distances ranging from 1,500 meters to 20 kilometers. Nurmi is the only person to win the Olympic 1,500 meters (1924), 5,000 meters (1924), and 10,000 meters

(1920 and 1928), and two of those races were won 55 minutes apart (the 1,500 meters and 5K in 1924). He accumulated a 121-race winning streak at distances from 800 meters and up, and died in 1973 with an undefeated record in cross-country races and the 10,000 meters. In 1966, *Time* magazine named Nurmi "the greatest Olympian of all time."

I traveled a hundred miles west from Helsinki to visit Turku, Paavo Nurmi's hometown and Finland's former capital. On my first morning, my new host, Juha Hellstén, biked alongside me as I explored the trails in his neighborhood. A young distance coach and talented runner when he is healthy (which he wasn't during my visit, having recently undergone his fourth Achilles' surgery), he was my gateway to Turku's running world. In seventy minutes we covered quiet streets, empty and shaded single-track trails, a serene fishing pond, and a nice stretch of grass next to a railroad track. I took an instant liking to my new home and my new hosts.

That afternoon, Juha's wife, Helena—a tall, friendly brunette with a determination to perfect her already advanced English—introduced me to another important venue of my Turku visit: the sauna. As widespread as showers, saunas are found in nearly every Finnish household, even in military posts and university dorm rooms. They help Finns endure brutal winters, rejuvenate during warm summers, and relax in the company of friends and family. Like Japanese onsen, Finnish saunas are steeped in ritual; and like the Namban Rengo women, Helena led the way for me and her daughters, Mathilda and Melissa, who at one and three years old were not old enough to tie their shoes but were well within the acceptable sauna age.

First, onsen-style, we undressed and took turns rinsing off under the showerhead with soap and water, and then filed into the sunlit sauna room, composed on three sides of oversize wooden steps. In one corner sat a stove topped with stones, and beside it a copper pot protruding with birch branches, a metal bucket full of water, and a giant wooden ladle. As we adjusted to the warm, damp environment, which typically climbs above 200 degrees Fahrenheit, Helena tossed water on the hot stones every couple of minutes, upping the moisture level in the room each time. She then demonstrated the birch-branch-beating tradition and, with a few gentle whacks on my back with the fragrant bundle, revitalized me, despite my cumulative fatigue and the demands that came along with each new resettlement of my trip.

A WEEK INTO MY TURKU VISIT, Juha invited me to Paavo Nurmi's 116th birthday party. Though Paavo died forty years ago, proud residents of Turku pay tribute to him on June 13 each year by visiting his childhood home, now a museum that's open to the public only one day a year, and attending the annual Paavo Nurmi Games, a local track meet held at the Paavo Nurmi Stadium. His most fervent fans can also run the Paavo Nurmi Marathon two weeks later.

The Hellsténs and I kicked off the celebration by adding to the pile of blue and white wreaths beneath the bronze statue of Paavo, midstride, erected on a street median. From there we found the old Nurmi home, modest and timeworn and the last in a row of connected homes encircling a grassy courtyard. Paavo shared the small one-room dwelling with his mother, two sisters, and brother for most of his upbringing. The tiny beds, table, sewing machine, fireplace, and portraits on the walls filled the room, just as they did a century ago. For most of their stay there, the Nurmi family didn't even have use of the adjacent kitchen; they'd rented it out to another family until Paavo made enough money from the 1920 Olympics to buy the whole place, also upgrading to electricity and running water.

The volunteers in the Nurmi home added substance to the history books with personal stories about the Finnish running icon. I learned that Paavo was one of the first runners to take a systematic and analytic approach to the sport, popularizing the use of a stopwatch and demonstrating the value of even-paced racing. He thrived on interval and speed work, both novel during his day, and supplemented his running with walking and calisthenics.

Just before I left, one volunteer told me about the time that Paavo showed up for a meet to find out he was being paid only two-thirds of his promised $1,000 appearance fee—in response, he only ran 1,000 meters of the 1,500-meter race in which he was entered. Nurmi meant it as an innocent jab, but the Finnish Athletic Association interpreted it differently, excluding their greatest runner from the next Olympic team. It's safe to say Paavo wasn't the only loser in that decision.

SO FAR ON MY TRIP, I'd spent countless hours trying to find my way around new cities, a vague set of directions in one hand, a map in the other. So you'd think that, by this point, I'd be a skilled and confident navigator.

That assumption was tested when Juha suggested I take a stab at orienteering. Popular in Finland and elsewhere—the International Orienteering Federation is housed in Helsinki—the discipline combines navigating an unfamiliar and mixed-terrain course with running (when the ground permits it). Participants use topographical maps and compasses to find an ordered list of targets (called "control points"), checking in at each one with an electronic or paper control card, and battle each other and the clock to the finish. To complicate matters, the quickest way around the course is often not the most direct route, due to steep, rugged, wet, and otherwise unpassable territory; that's where knowing how to read the intricate maps becomes important. Because orienteering races often have staggered starts, my initial scheme—to latch on to the best map reader and ride his coattails all the way up the podium steps—sadly wouldn't be possible.

Juha's younger sister, Anna, who'd been an au pair in the United States, generously offered to join me on my inaugural orienteering attempt. She had some experience in the sport and thought a casual competition, beginning at the trailhead next to the Hellsténs' home, would make a great venue for my debut. For this informal race, participants could compete in groups and start whenever they wanted within a certain time frame, provided we clocked in and out. Upon arriving at the trail, I was a little offended when I discovered that Anna had entered me in a competition with a handful of Boy and Girl Scout troops, easily half my age. But as more and more of those hip-high rascals zipped past me toward the next marker, I wondered why she'd thrown me to the wolves on my very first try.

Orienteering is not like driving, in which I have a fifty-fifty chance of making the correct turn. As hard as I tried to make sense of the squiggles, circles, lines, and colors that composed our "map," Anna spent the whole race straightening me out, patiently explaining why going *around* the swamp would actually save us time, and why we couldn't just trounce straight up a jagged cliff. Despite my map snafus, I still hoped to make up time with my talent in the running component of orienteering. But in the end, it took me 51 minutes and 22 seconds to cover 2 kilometers. That's a blistering pace of 41 minutes per mile.

So I didn't show early signs of orienteering greatness. But in addition to its humbling effect, the experience soon came in handy for my first glimpse of competitive Finnish orienteering. Jukola, one of the largest and most historic relay orienteering competitions in the world, fell on the next Saturday, and I watched the first two hours while Juha and Helena commentated for me. Like major ekiden in Japan, the entire hours-long event is broadcast on national TV and attracts massive viewership. The men's 11 P.M. start at Jukola means that competitors and devoted spectators (like Juha) would relinquish their Sunday plans, either trudging through dim woods until morning—Finland was approaching twenty-four hours of sunlight per day—or following the drama from afar.

As Juha explained to me, Jukola is composed of two main relays: one for men (7 per team), and one for women (4 per team). Every man runs between 7 and 15 kilometers, while the women each cover 5 to 8 kilometers. A different Finnish city serves as host each year—this one was in Jämsä, about 125 miles north of Helsinki—but regardless of its location, the race consistently attracts over 150,000 participants representing more than twenty nationalities, as well as 30,000–40,000 supporters, trainers, members of the media, and general enthusiasts on-site. The competitors and fans spend the night in tents and caravans in the competition area, keeping close tabs on the race (and sleeping very little, I'd dare to guess from my Coast to Coast experience in New Zealand).

From my seat on the Hellsténs' couch, Jukola seemed like the rugged and more technical big brother of the Ragnar Relay Races in the United States. I'd encountered some Ragnar racers a few years earlier, distinguished by a stream of headlamp-clad runners on the shoulder of the road with decorated vans cruising and honking alongside them. Started in Utah in 2004, Ragnar is a booming overnight relay series with races in seventeen U.S. cities and counting. Every twelve-person team covers around 200 miles, divided into three legs per person and taking around 36 hours. Appropriately, the name Ragnar comes from a ninth-century Scandinavian king and hero, described as "a conqueror, a wild man, a leader, fearless and free-spirited."

Like Coast to Coast, nontraditional competitions such as Jukola and Ragnar occupy a growing place in the athletic world, and are excellent outlets for people seeking a change from the repetition and precision of traditional races. The relay format offers an added appeal by lessening the spotlight on each participant, one of the most common deterrents to racing that I hear.

But I'm still a purist at heart; and based on my orienteering debut, it would be a long road to Jukola if I ever decided to go for it. In the meantime, watching from a cozy couch, new friends on both sides, and a sauna heating up just a room away was a fine alternative to me.

"My dear American friends—before we get started with any introductions, I would like you to know a little bit about my background. My father was a shaman from Lapland and we used to have this tradition for Midsummer . . . a little ritual. So I would like all of you to participate."

He had just arrived, and the Badger was already in rare form, barefoot and wearing a yellow nautical-printed toga, a wicker basket clutched in one hand and a large wooden rattle in the other. It was Midsummer's Eve—a holiday in which Finns flock to countryside cottages for a weekend of grilling, eating, drinking, sauna-ing, swimming, making bonfires, and celebrating the never-setting sun. I'd wrangled up a small group for the occasion: Antti-Pekka (A-P) and Kari, two running friends from Turku; Joonas Harjamäki, the steeplechaser from Helsinki, with shaggy blond hair and a badger tattoo to match the nickname that he refused to explain; and Matt Ackels and Claire O'Connor, two of my closest friends, who were visiting from Texas. My Watson Fellowship was quickly coming to an end, and my swan song would be a holiday weekend spent in a one-room cottage with a mix of very old and very new friends.

After an eardrum-busting reunion in Helsinki, Matt, Claire, and I had hit the road to check out our weekend digs before our Finnish friends ("Frinns") arrived. We were headed to a sheep farm in Kangasala, a rural town two hours north of the capital; we'd rented a one-room cabin for the weekend, but were having a hard time finding it. After about four drive-bys, we finally stopped at a property with a tiny plaque on the mailbox that read "Pia & Bob Taylor," recognizing Pia's name from the original website posting.

We'd never heard of Bob, and we never did find a house number, but we were tired of driving, the cabin was vacant, so we figured we were at the right place. The property was a hilly plot of land with a huge, padlocked house; our tiny brick cabin with a tin roof and light blue door; an outhouse near the cabin, tastefully decorated with magazine clippings of animals and flowers; an area for picnicking and grilling; and acres of dense woods that eventually ended at a lake, where the owners kept two canoes. The cabin was a little tight for the three of us, much less our three guests; the 20×20-foot structure was stuffed with a bunk bed, cot, kitchenette, table, and, of course, a sizable sauna. But having camped in cold weather with Matt and Claire before, I knew that we could squeeze ourselves into a very compact space if we needed to (and we did).

Our Frinns arrived around 7 P.M., and the Badger took over from there. After gathering everyone around on the grass in a semicircle facing him, he kneeled down, reached into his basket, and revealed a large stuffed animal he introduced as "Crab, King of the Lake." Then he broke off into a long smattering of Finnish, occasionally bowing and shaking the rattle toward the King and to the sky. Next, after a quick demonstration, he went down the line, one by one, handing each person a Finnish beverage, waiting until it was empty, and then gesturing and grunting until everyone had crossed their arms and fallen onto their backs.

A few minutes later, Badger's voice shattered the silence: "Aw, come on, MAYNE! That was a load of Finnish bullshit. But *now* we are ready for Midsummer!" Ice broken, our celebration commenced. By no means pressed for time—the summer solstice meant the longest day of the year, and midnight looked more like dusk—the six of us tag-teamed an enormous dinner on the grill: chicken, eggplant, sweet potatoes, onions, peppers, peaches, baguettes, halloumi cheese, and the guys' favorite, "wieners-in-a-cup" (sausages so large they were best handled using a paper cup as a grip). Such a fine feast required fine drinks to go with it; not sure of our taste, the guys brought enough alcohol to host the entirety of Kangasala.

After dinner, we did as the Finns do: alternating steaming sauna stints with refreshing lake dips (or, for those less inclined to trudge through the woods, buckets of ice water dumped over our heads). It was an honor to teach my Texas friends the art of the branch whack, and they were quick learners and enthusiastic reciprocators. Between sauna sessions, we learned the Finnish version of the card game Uno (*yksi* or "ooksee"), jammed to Suomipop music, canoed below dive-bombing seagulls, and nibbled on the array of tar-flavored sweets our friends had brought. All the while, the Badger's trademark expression filled the room: "Aw, come on, MAYNE!" spoken like an American rapper with a peculiar Finnish twang.

We got off to a slow start the next morning, having extended the Midsummer celebration into the early morning hours. It may have been the day after a big holiday, but it was still a Saturday; in A-P, Kari, and the Badger's world, Saturday meant long run day. Once we were sufficiently caffeinated, the three Finns and I set off on a ninety-minute run through the Kangasala countryside, alternating long stretches of sleepy silence with animated recounts of the prior night's tomfoolery. The vacant dirt roads were forgiving on our tired bodies, and the gentle slopes finished the waking-up process our coffee had begun.

DISTANCE RUNNING IS A SPORT OF RHYTHM. Tempo runs and marathons reward a steady, controlled effort the whole way; interval workouts feature intermittent bursts of faster paces; and progressive runs and many championship races involve gradual crescendos to the finish. When Haile Gebrselassie broke the 5,000-meter world record in 1995, he credited the fast tempo of the song "Scatman (Ski-Ba-Bop-Ba-Dop-Bop)", stuck in his head during the race, with helping him maintain close to a four-minute-mile pace for 12.5 laps. The journey of every runner involves figuring out which style (or song) suits him best, and learning to use it to his advantage.

When you consider Scandinavia's distance running history, it's tempting to view the region as a has-been, an empire that crumbled around 1980 and has not yet resurfaced since then. But if instead you view it like a musical arrangement and consider the whole score, stretching back to the early twentieth century, a different story—one of undulation and persistence—emerges.

In Stockholm, with Brian Nielsen as my guide, I saw that the Swedish racing scene is alive and well (though I found no evidence of a modern-day Gunder Hägg or Arne Andersson). The Skärholmsloppet 5K, the DJ'd field relay, the kids' forest race, and the National Relay Championship indicate that today's runners want innovation and variety—and that race directors are delivering. Runday's after-work clientele, and the many adult race participants I saw, suggest that Sweden's recreational running community is on the rise, with health and socialization driving the movement.

The running climate I found in Finland continues to honor its legacy of world-leading runners. Individuals such as Paavo Nurmi and Lasse Virén are cultural icons who have been neither replaced nor forgotten. Remnants of the Flying Finns and their two twentieth-century dynasties are visible across Helsinki and Turku, with statues, museums, birthday parties, and races showing national pride and providing inspiration for younger Finns. Finland's golden age of track and field is still in the recent past, as Ari Paunonen and Henrik Sandstrom reminded me; those shining decades were propelled by the same small country with a relentless sisu spirit. If that spirit, still strong in events like Jukola, comes alive in track and field as it once did, I may live to see a third crop of Flying Finns.

I didn't know it then, but that Midsummer run in Finland would be the last run of my trip. I'd planned to keep running until I got home, taking advantage of the ever-changing scenery before returning to the Texas heat. But toward the end of that run, I sensed that it was time for a break. For the first time in my life, I neither waited for instructions from my coach to begin the layoff, nor for a signal from my body that I'd taken it too far. I decided to begin my annual two-week break the next day—which would coincide nicely with Matt and Claire's last few days in Finland and my reunion with my parents in France the next week—and then resume normal training in the United States. The emptiness I expected to feel was eclipsed by a tangle of positive emotions: exhaustion after a successful Midsummer celebration (not to mention an action-packed year), and elated anticipation for reuniting with loved ones. I knew the rest was essential so that once I got home, I could begin incorporating my new discoveries into a purposeful training plan, and hopefully, a long and successful running career.

Appreciating the rhythm of Scandinavian running got me thinking about the rhythm I'd developed as a traveler. Before leaving the United States, I sought comfort in predictability and preparation, always having a plan and controlling every variable I could. But my decision to travel for a year meant abandoning that way of living: Each country on my map ticked at a different pace, and every person who took me in provided a unique perspective. Finding my way in some places, like the United Kingdom and Australia, took little adjustment, while others—Ethiopia and Japan, in particular—required a couple of weeks. By the time I reached Scandinavia, the last major destination of my trip, I'd adapted to dozens of time zones, tempos, and schedules, and was approaching my seventy-second bed of the year. Along the way, unpredictability and spur-of-the-moment decisions shaped my new rhythm, and taught me to better navigate the unexpected twists and turns I encountered during my global running adventures. But after a full year of traveling, I felt ready to return home—anxious to blend my former approach to living and running with the open, spontaneous one I'd discovered on the roads, tracks, forests, and fields abroad.

The Finnish forests hosted the final runs of my trip, before my annual two-week break from running and my return to the United States.

Scandinavian Pancakes (Helena Hellstén, Finland)

In stark contrast with their American counterparts, these thin, delicate pancakes that Helena Hellstén made for me are tasty incentives to log a good run—especially when topped with fresh strawberries and a dollop of whipped cream.

3 eggs
2½ cups milk (optional: replace some of milk with cream)
1 cup wheat flour
1 tablespoon granulated sugar (optional: use vanilla
    sugar)
1 teaspoon salt
Butter, for frying
Optional toppings: powdered sugar, jam, whipped cream,
    berries, ice cream

1. Whisk eggs slightly in bowl.
2. Add all other ingredients to eggs, and let rest about 30 minutes. Batter should be thin but not watery, so add a little more flour if needed.
3. Heat a large pan to medium heat, add a pat of butter, and fry batter into thin and even pancakes (using about ¼ cup of batter for each one).
4. Serve pancakes warm with toppings as desired.

CONCLUSION

December 8, 2013

3:00 A.M.: A chronically poor sleeper and well-acquainted with jet lag, I know this hour well. I normally lie in bed awhile longer, trying to fall back to sleep, but not this morning. I'm in Sacramento to make my marathon debut at the California International Marathon (CIM), and I'm filled with conflicting emotions.

Confidence, derived from my training. After averaging 70 miles of running per week during my year of traveling, my marathon buildup included 9 weeks of 100 miles or more, peaking at 117, with long runs of up to 25 miles and dozens of quality workouts. Other than a couple of hiccups, including a tight quad that healed after two days of biking, my training has been consistent and well-rounded.

Nervousness, because I've heard all the marathon horror stories—about debuts in particular—and I'm not about to pretend that I'm immune from cramping, blistering, straining, or bonking just because my training has gone well. I have a great amount of respect for the distance before I even toe the line for the first time.

Gratitude, for being healthy going into the race. I know that getting to the starting line is half the battle in a marathon, and fortunately, I don't have any physical distractions this morning.

I'm also thankful that I still feel mentally fresh after such a long, grinding buildup. I've been back in the United States for five months, and I'm still riding the high from my trip around the world.

Relief, because my debut is finally here. I've been intrigued by the marathon since I cheered on my dad at the Dallas White Rock Marathon as a child and later my sister Rachel at both the Dallas and Austin marathons. I've wanted to attempt one myself since my freshman year at Rice, when Coach Bevan told me I had a good one in me. I've dreamed about becoming *a marathoner* since I watched the Olympic Marathon from the sidelines in London a year and a half ago.

Trust, in my coaches. I'm in my seventh year of running for Coach Bevan, who guided my transformation from a mediocre 300-meter hurdler in high school into an All-American and Olympic Trials qualifier at Rice. And Coach Vigil, who oversees my training from afar, is a skilled motivator and a proven coach, having built a cross-country dynasty at Adams State and coached Deena Kastor to bronze in the 2004 Athens Olympic Marathon.

Most of all, I'm overwhelmed by excitement. My mix of nerves and anticipation reminds me of how I felt on the morning of July 25, 2012, my last day in the United States before my yearlong trip.

3:15 A.M.: I turn on the bedside lamp. I know I have a long morning ahead of me and the less thinking I do, the better. I flip open Viktor Frankl's *Man's Search for Meaning* for at least the fourth time—I trust it to put me in a good frame of mind.

3:45 A.M.: After reading for half an hour, I get up and turn on the coffeemaker. Although I haven't tasted it since last December, I think of the thick, sugary coffee I enjoyed with the Yaya Girls, and I wonder if someday I'll run into one of them at a big race like this one. While the coffee brews, I prepare a pre-race breakfast that I've been eating since my first races at Rice: a sliced bagel with peanut butter on both sides, banana slices on top, and a drizzle of honey for an extra shot of sugar.

4:00 A.M.: As I eat, I study the course profile one more time. Coach Bevan took me on a driving tour yesterday, but I find it helpful to mentally break down the map into manageable chunks. When I finish, I flip through eight index cards, each one containing a word or phrase I chose for affirmation in my marathon buildup. Some come from runners I admire—like Billy Mills's "Believe. Believe. Believe."—and others are from my trip: *aizoh* (Amharic word meaning "chin up, keep going"), *sisu* (Finnish word for "guts, bravery, or resilience"), and *makenki* (Japanese word for "competitive spirit").

4:15 A.M.: Weather reports on TV confirm my expectations: temperatures in the mid-20s at race start, rising to 32 degrees by the finish. The Houston climate hasn't prepared me for this—it was 80 degrees during my final workout—but I've survived four NCAA National Cross-Country Championships in Indiana in November, and I know that I'll be warm once I get moving. As I organize my cold weather gear, I remember Juha Hellstén's remark: "there's no bad weather, just bad clothing decisions"—classically Finnish—and take his advice to heart. Today's uniform is a hodgepodge of shorts, compression socks, racing flats, arm sleeves, gloves, ear warmers, and a singlet from the Houston Harriers, a local running club. I crumple up my bib number before pinning it to my chest—a ritual I carry on from Coach

Bevan's triple-jumping days—put a few layers of sweats on top, and pull my hair back into a tight ponytail.

4:45 A.M.: I head down to the hotel lobby, full of yawning athletes receiving last-minute pep talks from their coaches. I immediately join Coach Bevan at our Christmas tree meeting spot. He's always treated race day like Christmas or a birthday, encouraging his runners to get amped up as if it were a holiday, so we took it as a good sign when Santa Claus himself greeted us by this tree last night. With one last hug and a reminder to "get tough!"—a phrase borrowed from Coach Vigil and the only advice he'll give me this morning—Coach Bevan sees me onto the elite athlete bus and heads back inside.

5:30 A.M.: As the bus winds through Sacramento toward the starting line, I listen to my pre-race playlist, which has been evolving since high school. Teddy Afro's "Minilik" comes on and I close my eyes, placing myself in one of Addis Ababa's blue minibuses and remembering the joy I felt upon reaching Mount Entoto to begin a run. I cling to that feeling as my nerves start to kick in.

6:30 A.M.: It feels odd to stray from my standard pre-race routine, but the marathon is not my standard race. Instead of my usual jog and swift 100-meter strides, with about 10 minutes of drills in between, I run my prescribed mile as easily as possible and loosen up with a few Ethiopian-style exercises: hunching my shoulders while my arms swing side to side, and twisting my torso, clasping one hip with both hands every other step. I skip the strides. I'll need all the energy I can muster in the race, and the first few miles will serve as the real warm-up.

6:45 A.M.: The race director corrals the elite runners toward the starting area, but I wait until the last minute to discard my sweats. Without their bulk, I feel free, and very cold. I have a "full" sensation in my legs, which Jon Warren, another Rice coach and a great runner in his day, had warned me about. I didn't understand what that meant until earlier this week, when I felt like I should use a pin to prick my legs, which are puffy and restless from the reduced mileage. Jon may also have been referring to the energy I've been accumulating these last couple of weeks; my running load has decreased significantly, but my appetite and food consumption have not.

6:50 A.M.: I take a big swig of sports drink—the same formula filling my seven bottles along the course—and head to the start. I position myself in the pack of runners behind the line, and do a little jogging in place to stay warm. At this point, I'm eager to get going, relieved that there is nothing left to focus on but the race itself. Coach Bevan and my dad have been reminding me all week that "the hay is in the barn," and now, it *really* is.

6:59 A.M.: It's still dark outside, so I listen for the starting instructions rather than watch for the official's arm movements. I've stood on hundreds of starting lines before, and these final moments feel as long as all the others. We get the one-minute warning, I say a quick prayer, and finally, the gun sounds.

MILE 1: I'm cold but invigorated by the darkness and crisp air. I fight my instincts when two women, Kenyan Sarah Kiptoo and American Lindsey Scherf, go out hard and quickly gap the other women. Instead of going with them, I revert to my plan to "fall asleep," borrowed from my friend and former Rice training partner Lennie Waite, and let the others pull me along.

MILE 3: I approach the first of seven elite fluid tables. A few men are in between me and the table, and before I can work my way through them, my bottle is behind me. I've been drilled on the importance of mid-race hydration, but I don't let it rattle me. It's still early, I haven't sweat a drop, and I have six more bottles spread across the course.

MILE 4: I pass my support crew—Coach Bevan; his wife, Vicki; and my parents—for the first time. I'm thrilled to see them, flashing a thumbs-up and a smile to show them that so far, I feel great. A few blocks later, I recognize the exuberant cheers of Claire Shorall, a loyal friend and Rice teammate, who is following the race on a bike, just as Juha Hellstén and Hayden Shearman did during my races in Finland and New Zealand.

MILE 6: I synchronize strides with fellow American Kristen Fryburg-Zaitz and her male partner, and feel comfortable in our small pack. I ran every workout in this buildup either alone or with my friend Ted Artz, a former runner at the U.S. Air Force Academy, pacing me while Coach Bevan biked alongside. I trust in the metronomic sense of pacing I've developed over many miles.

MILE 7: The second water station goes better than the first. I have to jostle a few people to reach the table, but I spot my bottle out of dozens (thanks to my mom's neon duct-tape job), grab it with both hands (gloves don't offer much grip), and take a few big gulps.

Tossing the bottle to the side, I nearly peg a spectator—typical of my many athletic attempts outside of running. Although I never stood out on my childhood teams—I was always commended for "hustling"—each was important in my development as an athlete and as a person. Thoughts of the thousands of coaches, teammates, and supporters I've had, both here and abroad, inspire me and give me strength.

MILE 10: *Be cool,* I tell myself, still feeling great and repeating the words I know my coach wants me to focus on for the first half. It's also the advice that Leo Manzano gave me back in London; though he was describing the first lap of a mile, it's appropriate for the early stages of a marathon, too.

MILE 11: As I charge up the steepest hill of the race, I draw confidence from my weekly hill workouts in Houston, as well as memories of Colorado mountain runs with Laura Haefeli and the long hill tempo with Livia Burri and Astrid Leutert in Switzerland. Looking upward and quickening my steps, I appreciate how the hills break up the monotony and allow me to use my muscles differently than on the flat.

MILE 13: *Halfway home.* I'm transported back to the midway point of the 22-mile Waiatarua Circuit, my longest run ever at that point, and I feel a similar jolt of euphoria. Kristen and I cross the timing mat at 1:14.28, the first actual split I've seen. In a nod to my Ethiopian friends, I chose to leave my GPS watch at the hotel and run by feel without the constraints of a clock. My split projects a 2:29 finish, a little faster than my goal. But the first half of the course had slightly more downs than ups, and I know the second half won't be quite so merciful. From here forward, I'll rely on Coach Bevan's trick of counting *down* the miles, knowing that I've already covered more ground than what lies ahead.

My debut marathon at the 2013 California International Marathon, five months after returning to the United States.

MILE 15: "Good job, Becky Wade! You're the second female—one dropped out, you're two minutes behind the other and gaining. You look GREAT!" He's done this hundreds of times before—thousands, really, if you count every lap of my races on the track—so my dad knows exactly what kind of information to feed me. His steady, baritone voice, next to my mom's buoyant "Go B!" puts me at ease.

MILE 16: *Here we go.* I'm now running alone, having recently left my two companions behind. Without their company, I have to make a concerted effort to keep pressing. I know from solo treks up Mount Entoto that I can push myself in tough circumstances, and that I might find new partners ahead. Before the race, my brother described a picture he'd seen of Sammy Wanjiru—the late Kenyan marathoner and Olympic gold medalist—and every so often, I try to relax my hands as he did, making my fingers into an upside down "A-okay" symbol, to remind myself that I'm fine, and that this is fun.

MILE 17: I'm now 2 for 5 on water bottle grabs. I carry this one with me longer than usual, and almost drink it dry.

MILE 18: Rounding a bend, I see Coach Bevan on the sidewalk opposite a rowdy crew of spectators, whose enthusiasm and coffee cups remind me of the Melbourne University Athletics Club.

"Can I move a little?" I ask, chomping at the bit.

"Be cool, Beck! Eight miles left—just keep rolling."

As I round the next corner, his words—"You look incredible!"—ring in my ears.

When I pass Claire again, she tells me that the female leader is slowing, and her confidence comes through in her cheers. "YOU GOT THIS!" I believe her.

MILE 20: *Moment of truth*—the infamous "wall" looms. I still feel okay, but I know the demon might strike at any minute. I remember Derartu and the Devil—Banchi's explanation for Derartu's sickness and failed workout—and I have to wonder: Is the Devil extra cruel at mile 20?

MILE 21: Fearing the wall, I cross the road to reach the sixth elite fluid station. It may have cost a few seconds, but it's worth it if it keeps the Devil at bay. I catch a half-dozen guys who provide a nice pace to match and urge me forward. I assume they're pulling for the American in this race, an event typically dominated by East Africans like the current leader, Sarah Kiptoo. Of course, they don't know that I owe a huge part of my preparation for today's race to my friends from Kenya and Ethiopia. I think of Vivian Cheruiyot and my flatmates in Teddington, as well as the Yaya Girls in Srulta, and I imagine their cries of "Aizosh, Becky! Ambasa!" (*Good job, keep going, Becky! You're so strong!*)

MILE 22: My feet are so tender, I actually look down to check that my racing flats are intact. I'm reminded of Zewdenesh in Ethiopia and the rocks she had to sweep out of her tattered shoes. My lower legs are also starting to feel numb, but I know that focusing on my discomfort is counterproductive. I try a Paula Radcliffe strategy, one I've read the English world record holder uses when she starts to suffer. *1, 2, 3, 4, 5* . . . in unison with every other foot strike, I count from 1 to 100, trying to think of nothing besides the number I'm on. I repeat the process a few more times, and in between cycles, I recall Coach Vigil's advice from last night: "Be confident and run tough, young lady!"

MILE 23: The final fluid station is another flop, but at least I'm close to the end. About three miles to go now—just one loop of the Rice campus. I know that I'm within striking distance of the leader, but it's becoming harder and harder to ignore the sensations of my feet slapping pavement, my legs wobbling like a toddler's, and my lower back tightening. I only told a handful of people that I'm racing—my family, my boyfriend Will, my roommates, and a few former teammates—and I think of them all. I want to do well for them as badly as I want the win for myself.

MILE 24: I see my support crew for the last time, and their spirit is electric. I instantly feel lighter. "You can catch her!" Coach Bevan yells. "She's fading hard, about twenty seconds up. When you come up on her, make a big move. Time to put the hammer down!" And as I move down the road, I hear his last bit of advice in this race. "Quick steps, and focus on your arms. YES, Becky! YESSSSS!"

The Finn Valley war cry.

MILE 25: I approach the lead female for the first time in the race, and she speeds up as I get closer. Heeding Coach Bevan's instructions, when I'm within about ten seconds of her, I attack the stretch of road between us, building as much momentum as I can so she won't be able to latch on to me. I reach her, and for a few strides, it seems like she's going to rally. I continue pressing, silently praying that she hasn't been stockpiling energy these last ten miles, but soon, she's behind me, her footsteps slowing and softening as I pull away. I know she's struggling but I'm not safe yet, so I drive forward down the straight road, wondering how it seemed so deceivingly short from the car yesterday.

MILE 26: I make the last turn onto the oak-lined avenue, full of cheering spectators and with the CIM banner and the California state capitol in sight. As I strain toward the finish line, consciously driving my knees and pumping my arms, I hear my mom's enthusiastic cheers, and a few seconds later, it's over.

After my marathon win, I was thrilled to begin working with agent Ray Flynn and to sign a contract with Asics, beginning my dream of running professionally.

I'M NOW TWO YEARS FURTHER in my life-long running journey. My winning time of 2:30.48 at CIM jump-started my career as a marathoner with a qualifying time for the Olympic Trials and a sponsorship from Asics, and eventually the Houston Marathon Foundation, Clif Bar, and 44 Farms. In the many miles that lie ahead, my mission remains the same: to represent my country and compete on the world stage for years to come. But equally important to me, and paramount to that goal, is embracing detours along the way, perpetuating the spirit of my Watson Fellowship, and staying open to diverse training methods and attitudes.

And each time I toe the line at another race, I'll think about the extraordinary people I met on my global running tour and say a quick prayer that today we will be very, very strong, and that the Devil will leave us alone.

Though I believe my potential ultimately lies in the marathon, I will continue racing a range of distances on the roads and on the track.

ACKNOWLEDGMENTS

Like my running, this book has been an enormous team effort. I'm deeply grateful to the countless people who contributed to my trip and to this project.

The Watson family and the Thomas J. Watson Fellowship staff: Thank you for the opportunity to chase my passion around the world for a year, which profoundly changed my approach to living and running. Dr. Caroline Quenemoen, Sandy Wallis, and Dr. Bridget Gorman: Your encouragement and support fueled my journey from the start.

Allison Devereux (Dev): You're more of a friend and a Renaissance woman than an agent, and these pages are a result of your ambitious vision. From Ursuline cross-country to this book, I love that we've been part of the same team for so many years. Trish Daly, my trusty editor: As a runner and a traveler, you brought the perfect perspective to this project. I appreciate your invaluable input and challenges to up my game with every draft. And Cara Bedick, my second editor: Your arrival was serendipitous and your experience priceless; thank you for wholeheartedly adopting this book.

My family has been, and continues to be, everything: Mom, my third editor, my go-to person, and me, on my best day, just a couple of decades ahead. Dad, my first running partner, my favorite White Rock Lake companion, and a reminder to slow down and make time for the crows and the squirrels. Rachel, my girl, my very best friend, and my lifelong yardstick for what's cool (thank goodness paper clip retainers are out). Matt, my traveling partner and life adviser, who inspires me to "give 'em the money hammer" and whose faith in me is always a step ahead of my own. Luke, my wombmate, my opposite, and the only person who could make me laugh with a "Becka the Wrecka" text moments after I crashed my car. Aunt Debbie, who's been with me from the beginning and whom I can always count on for fashion advice, packing tips, and coffee dates. And Alex, my soon-to-be brother-in-law and a very welcome addition to our family.

The Wade siblings in Dallas, shortly after my return to the United States: Rachel and Matt (twins), and me and Luke (twins).

Jim Bevan, my coach of nine years and the mastermind behind my running: You have the best instincts, the most creative mind, and the greatest passion for teaching and coaching of anyone I know. You've taught me to dig deep, to embrace the challenges that come, and, no matter what, to find the joy in every mile. Coach Vigil, my mentor and the ultimate ambassador for our sport: Your guidance on my trip and in my training has been priceless, and your belief in me is a wonderful gift. Maureen Shinnick, my high school coach and running mentor: You led by example (often behind a baby jogger), and made me a better athlete and a better person. The countless other coaches I've had the pleasure to run for since the age of ten—especially Amy Renyer, Larry, Jason, and Jonathan Jackson, Don Hardy, Anthony Mann, Charles "Squeaky" Hinton, Bill "MacDaddy" McEvoy, David Wildman, and Dennis Brett: Thank you for sharing your wisdom with me and for fostering my development as I chased success in the sprints, fell in love with the hurdles, and finally found a home in the long distances.

Jim Bevan and Joe Vigil, my coaches and mentors.

My Rice University, Ursuline Academy, and St. Rita Catholic School teammates: Thank you for inspiring me, for suffering and celebrating with me, and for giving me something to look forward to every day we spent together on the track and on the roads. My love for track and field is inseparable from my love for each one of you.

Will: The more of the world I see, the surer I am that I belong with you. I appreciate your sweet and patient support throughout this crazy writing process, and I hope this is the last adventure of mine you learn about from a book. I love you.

Leslie: Having been a friend for over twenty years and a roommate for three, you've stuck with me (and kept me laughing) through it all. Thank you for your precious friendship, and I'm sorry for the stress my trust in strangers has caused you.

My friends and extended family, the Rice, Ursuline, and St. Rita communities, and my *team* (Asics and Tony Herr; Flynn Sports Management and Ray Flynn; the Houston Marathon Foundation and Ally Walker, Wade Morehead, Erin McGowan, and Steven Karpas; Clif Bar and Ricardo Balazs; 44 Farms and Bob McClaren; the Houston Area Road Runners Association; the Road Runners Club of America; Dr. Lance McClintock; Dr. John Ball; Boone Ebel; Dr. Roberta Anding; Dr. Thomas Clanton; Dr. Marc Philippon; Dale Smith; Laurie Johnson; Katie Gwyn; Pieter Kroon; Michelle Mather; Mary Davies; Bob Schlanger; Vicki Bevan; the Firth family; the Devlin family; my Rice professors; and the Rice coaching and training staffs): Thank you for supporting my lofty dreams and for going the distance with me. Any success I've had is a composite of your investment in me.

Most of all, the many individuals, families, and teams that were so welcoming to me during my yearlong journey: Duncan Gaskell, Daren and Gráinne O'Dea, Chris O'Hare and family,

Richard Franzese, the Mickeys, the Haugh family, Kieran Carlin, Patsy McGonagle, Finn Valley Athletics Club, James Gill, Bianca Walker, Beat Ammann and Julia Stokar, LAC TV Unterstrass, Lisa Gubler, Ueli Bieler, TV Oerlikon, Livia Burri and family, Astrid Leutert, Sara Cavicchioli and family, Alessio Punzi, Joseph Kibur and everyone at Yaya Village, Dan Price, Xavi Curtis, Julia Bleasdale, Brigette Vallance, Hamish Beaumont, Melbourne University Athletics Club, Neil and Mel Sampson, Dave Paroissien, Simon Bucknell and family, Kyle Barnes, Scott Brown, Erin Feldman, Grieg Logan, Hayden and Charlotte Shearman, Barry Magee, Dr. Peter and Miki Snell, June Kendall, Paul and Callie Thomas, Bob Poulson, Namban Rengo, Bonnie Waycott, Mary and Peter Eckstein, Susan, Tim, and Heidi Griffen, the Hattori family, Zoe Papathanisou and Abbey Rexing, the Nielsen family, Lisa Naucler, the Hellstén family, Antti-Pekka Niinistö, Joonas Harjamäki, Pablo Vigil, Henrik Sandstrom, and the Paunonen family. Thank you for sharing your lives, your workouts, and your recipes with a curious stranger from Texas. Seventy-two beds, eleven pairs of running shoes, and 3,504 training miles later, my yearlong exploration of running cultures came to an end—but you remain with me in every step I run. Thank you, from the bottom of my heart, for affirming that I belong to the kindest and most inclusive community in the world.

PRE-RACE PLAYLIST

1. "Menelik"—Teddy Afro
2. "Holdin On"—Flume
3. "Falling Star r3k Remix"—Kid Cudi & Florence + the Machine
4. "Flashback"—Fat Freddy's Drop
5. "One Day/Reckoning Song (Wankelmut Remix)"—Asaf Avidan & the Mojos
6. "Taro"—Alt-J
7. "Overnight Celebrity (Remix)"—Twista featuring Kanye West
8. "Africaye"—Teddy Afro
9. "Crystalised"—The xx
10. "Let's Get Married"—Jagged Edge
11. "Hearts on Fire"—Cut Copy
12. "Dance Dance"—Jah Lude
13. "Beggin"—Madcon
14. "Love Me Again"—John Newman
15. "Only to Be"—Six60

BIBLIOGRAPHY

Alm, David. "Walk On." *Runner's World*. March 25, 2013.

Andersen, Jens Jakob. "Research: Marathon Performance Across Nations." *RunRepeat,* 2015.

Berg, Aimee. "A Small Runner with the Capacity for Big Things." *New York Times,* September 24, 2010.

"Cambridge and the Olympics." Cambridge University Sports Department, 2003.

Chase, Adam W. "Finding Sisu." *Runner's World,* February 19, 2013.

"Club History." Auckland Joggers Club.

Curtis, Xavier, and Eliza Richman. "Ethiopia's Food Culture." *AddisEats,* April 22, 2015.

"DandyRunner." *DandyRunner: Trail Running & Ultras,* 2012.

Dikos, Jackie. "The Simple Staple." *Runner's World,* June 28, 2012.

Dudney, Gary. "Coping with Altitude." *Ultrarunning,* May 7, 2014.

England, Dan. "Obstacle Course Racing Goes Big Time!" *Competitor,* May 24, 2014.

"Introduction to Ethics." BBC News. 2014.

Finn, Adharanand. "What I Learned When I Met the Monk Who Ran 1,000 Marathons." *Guardian,* March 31, 2015.

Fox, Kit. "Big in Japan." *Runner's World,* November 2015.

"General Information: Jukola Orienteering Relay Race." *Jukola,* 2011.

Gilmour, Garth. *Run for Your Life: Jogging with Arthur Lydiard.* Auckland: Minerva, 1965.

Gittings, Paul, and Natasha Maguder. "Haile Gebrselassie: I Will Run until I Die." *CNN,* June 13, 2013.

Goucher, Kara. "Are You a Track Fan?" *Competitor,* June 17, 2011.

Hill, Marika. "Big Crowd for Round the Bays." *Auckland Now,* March 10, 2013.

"Historic Sporting Highlights." Oxford University Sport, 2016.

"History of Coffee." National Coffee Association USA.

"History of Ekiden." Mizuno Ekiden, 2015.

"Ragnar Company History." Ragnar Relay Series, 2016.

"History, Tokyo." World Marathon Majors. Abbott.

IAAF World Cross Country Championships: Guiyang 2015, Facts & Figures, 2015.

Jetelina, Margaret. "Technotrail Blazer Joseph Kibur." Ethiomedia, January 7, 2006.

Johnson, Len. "Tan Time Trial Puts All Comers to the Test." *Age,* January 28, 2005.

Larkin, Duncan. "3 Secrets to Success from the Legendary Emil Zatopek." *Competitor,* October 13, 2015.

———. "Bekele Speaks about Rupp's Silver Medal." *Competitor,* August 7, 2012.

"Largest Races, 2013." Running USA, 2016.

Larner, Brett. "Acupuncture: Reversing the Stressful Effects of Running." *Runner's World,* July 22, 2010.

———. "Handing Off the Tasuki." *Runner's World,* July 1, 2010.

"Lasse Virén Wins the Distance Double Double—Montreal 1976 Olympic Games." Olympic.org, June 18, 2012.

Litsky, Frank. "Emil Zatopek, 78, Ungainly Running Star, Dies." *New York Times,* November 23, 2000.

———. "Gunder Hägg, Last Holder of 4-Minute-Plus Mile Record, Dies at 85." *New York Times,* December 2, 2004.

Makihara, Kumiko. "Go, Speed Racer, Go!" *Runner's World* (South Africa), November 2015.

McNulty, Chris. "Highest Donegal Honour for Patsy McGonagle." *Donegal News,* June 14, 2013.

McQuade, Drew. "Penn Relays: Race Walkers Are More than Hip." Philly.com, April 20, 2010.

Meyer, John. "Joe Vigil to Receive Legend Coach Award from USA Track & Field." *Denver Post,* May 30, 2015.

Mirhashem, Molly. "Why the Boston Marathon Is the Best in the World." *Boston Magazine,* April 14, 2013.

Molden, Simon. "The Inter-Varsity Cross-Country Race." Cambridge University Hare and Hounds, April 27, 2014.

Moller, Lorraine. "Essential Lydiard." *Runner's World,* November 16, 2009.

Nakamura, Ken. "Number of Sub-2:0X Marathons." *Track & Field News,* April 22, 2013.

Noakes, Timothy. *Lore of Running.* 4th ed. Champaign, IL: Human Kinetics, 2002.

"Oxford at the Olympics." University of Oxford, 2016.

"Oxford versus Cambridge." Oxford University Cross-Country Club Old Members, December 1, 2012.

Plymire, Darcy. "Running." *Sports in America from Colonial Times to the Twenty-first Century: An Encyclopedia.* Ed. Steven A. Riess. New York: Routledge, 2011.

Priestly, Lauren. "Round the Bays Started Small." *Auckland City Harbour News,* February 19, 2013.

Quarrell, Rachel. "Boat Race 2015: A Brief History of the Oxford-Cambridge Varsity Event." *Telegraph,* March 13, 2015.

"Race Profile." Coast to Coast, 2015.

Reilly, Brendan. "Where the Marathon Matters." *Runner's World,* February 2, 2008.

Robinson, Roger. "A Brief History of Barefoot Running." *Runner's World,* April 8, 2011.

"Rock-Hewn Churches, Lalibela." UNESCO, 1992.

Schatzle, Joe, Jr. "Finding Fartlek." *Runner's World,* November 1, 2002.

Sears, Edward S. *Running through the Ages.* Jefferson, NC: McFarland, 2001.

Smith, Daniel P. "Sub-Four Magic." *Runner's World,* May 6, 2014.

Stevens, John. *The Marathon Monks of Mount Hiei.* Boulder, CO: Shambhala, 1988.

"Stockholm Stadium—A Classic Arena." ASICS Stockholm Marathon website.

"Tsukiji Fish Market." *World Heritage Encyclopedia,* 2014.

Wei, Stephanie. "U.S. Universities Won More 2012 Olympic Medals than Some Countries." NerdWallet, August 13, 2012.

Wilber, Randall L. *Altitude Training and Athletic Performance.* Champaign, IL: Human Kinetics, 2004.

Williams, Pat, and Jim Denney. *Extreme Focus: Harnessing the Life-Changing Power to Achieve Your Dreams.* Deerfield Beach, FL: Health Communications, 2011.

Will-Weber, Mark, ed. *The Quotable Runner: Great Moments of Wisdom, Inspiration, Wrongheadedness, and Humor.* Halcottsville, NY: Breakaway, 1995.

"The World's Fastest Mile." IAAF, *Spikes,* April 4, 2014.

"World Fastest Times 2014." Association of International Marathons and Distance Races, December 31, 2014.

"World Record Holders." Oxford University Athletics Club, 2012.